Sandy –
Don't want to forget ♡
is the whole story. Hope everything well
with you & yrs.

Regards. Best wishes.

David

Cowboy Ace

The Life Adventures
of
David Wilhelm

Proudly Published in the USA by
Thornton Publishing, Inc
17011 Lincoln Ave. #408
Parker, CO 80134

Phone: **(303)-794-8888**
Fax: **(720)-863-2013**

BooksToBelieveIn. com
publisher@bookstobelievein. com

ISBN: 0-9844838-5-3

ACKNOWLEDGEMENTS & DEDICATION

**To the Patient One,
My wife, Jean**

Much of the material and my experiences are taken directly from diaries that I faithfully kept during my military flying. They reflect my feelings at the time.

Table of Contents

1

HOW IT ALL STARTED

This is a rather monstrous effort- writing these memoirs. To begin with I am no storywriter, author, raconteur- just a guy that learned Basic English composition from Matthew Flinders, a very demanding precise teacher at the Arizona Desert School in 1934. This story does scan quite a few years, so it does represent how I lived and adjusted to the changes from 1919 to 2010 - 91 years!

I am writing this story mainly for my heirs. There may be some incidents that shed light on my development and choices that I made during my life that may be of interest to more than my family.

I have learned much of my lineage from information I received from a second cousin of mine, Michael Cudahy of Milwaukee, Wisconsin. He was assisted in his research of the origins of the Cudahy family by Joseph Kennedy of Callan, Ireland, another more distant relative. They searched records they could locate including church and county records to resurrect the history of the family. Others than my family might be interested in the story of some poor dirt families who emigrated from that a devastated

Ireland in the nineteenth century to became a leading American industrialist in the United States.

During my ninety-one years, I have experienced an ever-changing remarkable period of American life. These years saw innovations and changes that went from horse and buggy to Model T Fords to NASA, from primitive crystal set radios to television, crank up telephones to I Phones, hand cranked calculating machines to computers, home remedy medicines to antibiotics, from personal birth control to the PILL, from Puritan life standards to permissiveness, from a farm rural to urban America life-all this with a background of World War I , World War II, Korean War, Vietnam War, the Cuban missile crises, the Cold War, Desert Storm, 9/11 attack of the World Trade Center, Iraq war, to Al Qaeda and Taliban terrorist attacks. These developments have taken place in the last one hundred years. The twentieth Century was monumental with changes comparable to historical events such as the Fall of Rome, the Crusades, the Renaissance, and the French Revolution. Only in reflection do I realize the changes that have taken place in my life.

It's possible these years should be called the War Years. World War I lasted three years, after 12 more years was World War II, the Korean War just seven year later, and then Viet Nam some seven years later. The United States was engaged in war between 1916 to 1968 for about 40% of the time! Being an island continent that was insolated by the Pacific and Atlantic oceans, the United States suffered no military action on our soil. We did not suffer the calamity and destruction of our cities or death to our citizens that Europe did.

The transformation of the way of life of the American citizen was accelerated by World War II, when the demand for military arms, equipment tanks, aircraft, ships and food for the Allied troops moved men and women into the factories and cities of America.

Most notable was the employment of women in jobs formerly held by men with the realization that women could operate away from their homes and children. Women were no longer "stay at home Moms" but factory and company workers. That move was the emancipation of women in the United States.

It is interesting to see how my generation has adjusted to all these new developments. I am amazed as I look back on the last years of my life that so much has changed with only minor complaints from Americans. We are not aware of this revolution unless we stop to reflect. I wonder if, when any of my children or grandchildren reach 90 years old in the year 2100 whether they will experience a similar evolution. I worry and hope that civilization will find means to avoid the wars. Let's hope that mankind will have made some progress towards peaceful methods of handling international conflicts. Some of my successors who might read this memoir will be able to answer this conjecture.

I was born in 1919 and lived with my family in a comfortable and modest home located in the North Side of Chicago on 1126 Wentworth Avenue. The area was a comfortable upper class all white Wasp part of the near north side. Our house was a Classic red brick modestly comfortable home. My recollection was that the house was not grand or large. Pictures of a Chubby smiling David in his baby buggy in his warm fur coat with a proud mother are seen in some old picture albums. My feeling was that everyone was nice to me and life was just a bowl of cherries. I played happily with sister Jean and brother Edward and don't recall any fights, arguments, or grudges with either of them. As the youngster of the family, I did not feel anyone picked on me and did not feel "left out". So I started life blissfully happy. I had no scars that I would carry into life.

Our next-door neighbor shook up that old conservative neighborhood. My recollections of the facts of this event may not be exactly accurate, but the gist of this murder is essentially accurate. I do remember the interest and excitement that I had. Leopold Loeb and brother, our neighbors up the block from us, became nationally known because the boys tried to commit the perfect crime by kidnapping and killing a young boy. They accomplished killing the boy, but their plot was transparent so they were soon apprehended, convicted of manslaughter and sentenced to life imprisonment at the Joliet State prison. (One was killed in prison; the other was such an exemplary person, that he was released from prison to organize anti-crime work in Chicago). Since we lived next door to the Loebs, this whole event was all consuming for the period of the crime till their capture. That's the only time in my life that I have lived next door (that I know) to a murderer!

Mother and Father were a close married couple with mutual respect and love. In their thirties they were handsome, lithe, and almost dashing. Father worked long hours in the meat packing industry, which began early in the day and lasted till late each evening. I remember his taking us on Sunday auto trips, swimming afternoons, and enjoying the laughs of the radio programs of Jack Benny and Fred Allen. Sundays were the days I remember seeing father. Mother enjoyed the company of their children, and she spent her life having fun with them. Every evening we all dined together after we had washed our hands and combed our hair. She was an active bridge player and weekly golfer. As was the custom she always had help around the house. She was a companion of mine all my life starting at my earliest days. Our life long companionship lasted for as long as she lived. So I was raised by a hard working father, a loving mother, and with a brother and sister who were close companions. In this comfortable and loving manner, I entered my life in the Twentieth Century.

I was very impressed that father worked longer hours than his peers. He would take a 7 A. M. train from the country to Chicago and not return till 6:15. His fellow workers would often return at 3:30 in time for a golf game. I remember being proud of him for working so hard. I believe I inherited that work habit by the example of my father.

As Father' work effort rubbed off on me, I seem to arrive the earliest in the morning and departed the latest in the day. I am sure some of that extra time was spent inefficiently. To put it another way I am sure I wasted time and effort. Both Mother and Father were goers and were always applying themselves diligently. It was just natural "not to sleep in".

2

THE CUDAHY AND
NEW WILHELM FAMILIES

I was never close to Grandmother Cudahy. When I last remember her at her home at 22 Banks street in Chicago, she was losing her eye sight and widowed. Under those adversities, I think that it is difficult for me now to evaluate her. Mother used to take me to visit her at her dark house at 22 Banks Street which had the shades drawn and temperature in the living room at 80 degrees. The only sound was the grandfather clock slowly ticking the time away. Mother always had to douse her cigarette and remove her lipstick for her mother's approval. These visits were tough duty for me. So, my relationship with her was zero.

Mother's brother Edward was affable, good looking and socially relaxed and an un-brilliant man. He acted confidently if not conceded and, as if he had rightfully earned the leadership of the Cudahy Packing Co. After Grandfather died, he ran the Company with little imagination. He and my father were not close friends even though they were compatible. He married a wealthy steel company heiress until she died of an excess of alcohol. His second wife, Eleanor Cochran, was an attractive person and close friend of my mother.

A friend of the family, Pat Crowe coaxed young Edward from a street car to his carriage and hustled him out to a shack by the stockyards in Omaha, where he then chained him within the shack for a couple of days. The kidnapper then demanded $50,000.00 from Grandfather. While the family huddled in anxiety and great despair (according to my mother), Andrew Grey, the family carriage coachman, hitched up the team to the two wheeled carriage (as told to me by Andrew; the carriage was in their barn in Mackinac Island) and took the money and placed it an agreed spot under a bridge. Uncle Ed was returned the following day unharmed. The kidnapping created National publicity since there was no law against the crime. Pat Crow, an acquaintance of Uncle Ed, was apprehended soon thereafter but was given no prison term. This event was instrumental in bringing about the Federal Kidnapping law.

Mother's first sister was Helen Niblack. She was a beauty with great charisma, hunted to hounds on a sidesaddle, a keen bridge player, and rabid fan of the Chicago Cubs. She was warm, friendly and a real charmer. She was responsible for organizing a children "drag hunt", of which I was the Master of Hounds. We jumped obstacles as I led the young chargers around an area with panel jumps in an area west of the Onwentsia Club. Her husband, Austin, was a hard drinking wealthy bon vivant. He rode hard, and played hard in business and social life. He caused considerable rift within the family when he allegedly had an affair with his sister-in-law (Peg Cudahy). That Act did not make for great approval among the siblings. Supposedly Grandfather Cudahy answered margin calls on the market in 1929 to prevent him from total financial ruin.

The third sister, my Aunt Florence Spalding (my mother was the first sister) was a warm loving mother of my close cousins (Chuck and Vaughan). She was lots of fun, always had her house open for the young and particularly me. Her husband, Vaughan Sr. , rushed to the martinis pitcher as quickly as he arrived home from his office early each day. He talked bigger than he was, but was warm and pleasant, if he had not gotten into the sauce. Most often by dinner time he became alcoholically noisy and offensive. I know he made Flossie's life unpleasant and unhappy. She stuck it out because divorces were not acceptable to the Church or friends. She created a warm home for her three great sons and seemed to overcome the miseries she had with husband.

The fourth and youngest of my mother's sisters lived in Long Island. She was first married to Leander McCormick, a philanderer, who philandered too often which brought about a divorce. She subsequently married Jack Stearns, a stockbroker, who reminded me of Mr. McGoo. Right of the right wing of the GOP but a very likeable fellow. He was a comfortable "slipper by the fire" kind of a guy. I saw them with mother at their Breaker's Hotel cottage in Palm Beach when I would fly over from Sarasota where I was an instructor in P-51 Mustangs.

Mother and I had numerous frequent quiet and pleasant dinners with them.

All in all Grandmother Cudahy arranged to have her daughters marry wealthy and socially accepted men. She was instrumental in influencing the moving the Cudahy Packing Co. headquarters from Omaha to Chicago so she could find more "acceptable husbands" for her daughters. She spared nothing to advance her daughter's (and her own) prestige. The exception was my father who was by her standards a poor boy. He however was the best of them. The three girls were all fine wives, attractive, energetic, good mothers, and always close to their siblings.

THE WILHELM FAMILY

Charles M. Wilhelm and Eugenia Wilhelm, my Grand Father and Grand Mother on my father's side moved from New York to Omaha by way of Rockford, Illinois where my father was born. Grandfather established the largest furniture and decorating store between Chicago and Los Angeles. He was a chipper, dapper, Rotarian, city leader, and everyone's friend. He was the typical local small town favorite. He wore a toupee that with his vigorous walk and personality made him appear younger than his age. Everyone knew Charlie Wilhelm. He was a prominent citizen with a profitable local business. The last time I saw him was when he was widowed and returning from St. Petersburg, Florida from a winter vacation. As his train stopped for twenty minutes in Sarasota, we had a friendly visit. He was very "easy" adventuresome and enjoyable man.

My Grandmother Wilhelm was a dignified diminutive lady who was learned, well informed, and well read. She would deplore my conduct when she would come to Chicago to take care of us children. She worked to improve my reading habits, but it seemed my first choice was to play baseball with the other little squirts in Lincoln Park. I am sure her intellectual zeal rubbed off on my father, but unfortunately did not rub off on me. She was however pleasant, cheery, strong and articulate person who took charge of the house with authority and respect. I enjoyed her very much.

I remember how comforting she was at the time I shot a mail order 22-caliber blank cartridge pistol (Johnson and Smith mail order, which I had ordered surreptitiously) off onto my third finger of my left hand. After an antitetenus shot to appease my discomfort that I was administered by Dr. Coleman, our family doctor, I broke out in a desperate swelling hives-she was completely competent, relaxed and comforting to my miseries-for which I still feel grateful.

The Senior Wilhelms had two children, my father and Esther Cooper who lived in Omaha. Dean Cooper took over Orchard and Wilhelm Company on Grandfather's death. Esther inherited the femininity and attractiveness of her mother.

DEAN AND ESTHER COOPER

Dean Cooper was a sound business man who held many civic pro bona jobs. He was not charismatic, but able and the most welcoming man you could imagine. He saved Anne and me from miserable housing in leasing an elegant apartment for us, the Knickerbocker, when we were floundering trying to find a decent place to live. He was President of Orchard and Wilhelm.

The Coopers had two adopted children, both of whom were mainly absent when Anne and I lived in Omaha in the early fifties. The daughter Rose was a wild one and Sam was a hard working prosecuting attorney. I had the feeling they were not close to their parents, and that we might have filled a void in their life.

3

FATHER

My mother and father were married in Omaha and moved to Chicago when the Cudahy Packing Co. moved their headquarters to the Windy City (about 1910). Family finances were dependent upon the success of the Cudahy Packing Co. and the salaries of my father and the dividends to my mother. As executive Vice President, father was the second in command after his brother-in-law, Edward, who was the CEO and the major owner of the company. He controlled the policies and philosophies of the company. I do not know what authority Father had in the management of the company. He did not discuss that with his children. I was too young to have interest in his work at the age of ten or twelve, so I did not have an understanding of his responsibility or authority. But I do know that he felt that Uncle Ed did and acted as he saw fit whereas Father felt he was an employee without the authority that he wished. My mother certainly had that feeling and was always unhappy of that treatment. In retrospect and to be fair, I understand that it would be difficult for one that "owned" the company to relinquish management to one's brother-in-law. He was destined to be subservient. The "brother-in-law syndrome" made for a lifetime of unpleasantness in father's work.

Father agreed to move in 1926 to Los Angeles to try to rectify the financial plight of the Cudahy Packing Co. plant. The plant was losing money and needed correction or sale. That was a huge challenge for him since the area was doomed with failure because of lack of supply of live cattle, poor retail markets, and high feed costs. I heard from employees in Denver that father had made significant improvements in operations and proposed significant changes through out the company. However the economic facts dictated the closing of the Los Angeles operation.

**My mother and father
home from Hawaii**

Father was a person with great intellectual interests. Father loved the quiet of his voluminous library in Chicago at 2430 Lake View Ave. The room was a beautiful French paneled room with comfortable chairs and seating with a handsome French marble mantle with candelabra lights over the fireplace making it a charming room. I can still see him pouring over Balzac or other weighty philosophers. He enjoyed his quiet time in the library. He also was very alert to all the current national and world events. He would contend with his learned son-in-law, Daggett Harvey, in quizzes such as "Information Please" or Time magazine contests. He did not object to mother being absent Saturday afternoons either with me or with some ladies playing bridge. When the family would move into Chicago from Lake Bluff, father was always elated that his social life would be curtailed, the commuting would be eliminated and he could spend more home time.

Father was a handsome young man of 5'10" 166 # in his younger days in Omaha. He was trim with sharp manly features, erect and with alluring twinkle in his expression and appearance. He expanded that weight till at his death at the age of 60 years he must have weighed 180. He was overweight. He frequently was on diets to reduce. The weight loss was only temporary so there was too often dieting and then splurging. He walked over to Clark Street to take the street car to the Cudahy office on Wacker Drive. He did not take our limousine. When in Lake Bluff, he would walk to the Northwestern railroad station for his train trip to and from work in Chicago. That was his weekly exercise. In the summer he would play golf maybe twice a month with his pals Hampy Winston and Beaver Baum. His golf was recreational and he did not engage in intense work on the practice tee. In the fall he often went to Useppa Island off the west coast of Florida for Tarpon fishing. He also was a member of a duck shooting club in southern Illinois which he attended spasmodically. In his squiring days in Omaha he is seen in old photos swimming and playing left handed tennis-trim and handsome. His big workload limited his participation in recreational sports.

He and I attended the Northwestern University Football games in addition to the Army-Navy game at Soldiers Field, and to the Chicago Bears and Cubs games at Wrigley Field. I remember these trips with the fondest memories. We both yelled and screamed for our Hack Wilson or Bronco Nagurski. This entertainment was something that father and I enjoyed and those activities brought us close together.

Father was well informed and acquainted with Washington and World affairs, crossword puzzles, and Culbertson Bridge. He competed joyfully with his son-in-law, Daggett, in the quiz shows of radio and Time magazine such as "What's My LINE" and "INFORMATION PLEASE".

My relationship with father was marred by my being away from home from the age of thirteen till his death in 1945. (I went away to Tucson to school when I was thirteen year old (1932), to Andover when I was sixteen, Yale when I was nineteen, and then to the Air Force when I was twenty three till 1945. During those years I did spend the summers and Christmas vacations at home, but those vacations, it seemed, I spent much of my time with all my contempories. Father worked hard and I was involved in many things, so it seemed we did little together. I am sure he did not wish to interfere with my activities so we just did not see each other to a great amount. I am sure I was at fault for at my young age I did not recognize the value of a close relationship with a father.

I played with my pals who were back from school or college at the vacation dinners or parties. Since in the summer father left the house around 6:30 and returned around 5:30 in the evening, my times just did not jibe with his. During the day I would be on the golf or tennis court or polo field. As a result we had little time together. In reflection, it should have been for me to make the necessary adjustments. Lake Forest was a place with too many temptations.

Father had a serious drinking problem. I am sure he was an alcoholic. Who knows what was the cause of his excess drinking? Too much social life? Frustration at the Cudahy Packing Co. ? The wrong genes that predisposition him to alcohol? I am sure father would go for months without a drink, but all of a sudden, the world would fall in and his bouts of drinking would end him up in a hospital. The drinking caused continual concern of my mother not knowing when he might go on a binge, but she was always caring and ready to help.

After one of his drinking bouts , I was told that" father is not well" and he would spend the day in their dark sitting room up stairs by their bedroom.. That was always mysterious to me. That was mother's protective way. I did not know his sickness was attributable to drinking. (That bedroom had gloomy memories for me because that was where I was parked when I had the measles- no light and darkness all day). Naively I just thought it to be some kind of a cold. When Mother and I were staying at the Arizona Biltmore in Phoenix during my spring break from the Arizona Desert School, Father phoned mother from a business trip. Mother recognized that he was in bad shape, and she warned him in no uncertain terms "you had better straighten up right now or you can stay away for good". She was ticked! I don't think she truly meant it but it sure sounded as if she did. The admonition probably slowed father down for a while, but certainly did not redirect him permanently. I think that was the only time I remember ever hearing an angry voice between mother and father. They always seemed compatible and respectful of each other. So the drinking was a problem, but it certainly did not interfere with a close loving relationship that they had.

Jean, mother, father and I sailed on the Queen of Bermuda to that lovely island in the spring of 1937 for a spring vacation. I remember eating breakfast with the family, but then Jean and I were out on the tennis courts or with a bunch of the other young preppies to the beaches of Bermuda. This conduct was rather typical. Just not much joint family togetherness. Mother and Father enjoyed the fact that we were having fun with our age group. During spring vacations from school and college, also I was absent from the family since I usually traveled with classmates to Nassau or Bermuda.

Father was very proud of my going to Andover and Yale (his class was 1905). He was very supportive and active in helping and encouraging my polo organization and playing in Lake Forest and otherwise and followed my Andover and Yale records very closely. Mother seemed to have little input regarding the schooling, but father was attentive. When my marks during my Lower Middle year at Andover put me on PRO, father was quite explicit, "keep your marks up, or you go to work"! I was duly convinced that he was not kidding. The result of his admonitions was I got off PRO and attained a B average thereafter.

He was very proud of my war experience. In fact, he collected, saved, and had bound every letter I wrote home from my flying days. (They are quite boring mainly because they were censored and we could say nothing of what we were doing or where we were). I know how worried and involved with my survival he was. When HE RECEIVED WORD THAT I HAD FINISHED COMBAT FLYING AND WAS ON MY WAY HOME, HE SUFFERED A HEART ATTACK AND DIED BEFORE HE EVEN GOT TO A HOSPITAL! Mother told me the exhilaration of that announcement of my safety and return was too much for his heart to handle. He had a heart attack and died. I did not learn of his death until I had landed in New York from Italy when I went jubilantly to a pay phone to call home. The joy of returning was shocked by the word of his death from my mother. He had died apparently while I was crossing the Atlantic in a large slow convoy of ships. That was a devastating blow for me that felt like a bullet passing through me when I heard this. I was so jubilant, thankful, and ecstatic on returning home and looking forward to seeing both mother and father only to hear "father died two days ago". Shock overtook me, but what could I do but just go on and so I went back to the reassignment officer, told him of the death, and was given leave to return home to await further orders. As could be expected there was no sympathy at the base, and it was only pack my bags, get a train and go home. That return was a joyous / sad return.

I had been looking forward to seeing and getting closer to my father after these many years absence, but that never came about. As a result I never had a grown up mature relationship with him. I had no male counsel or no one to explain what this whole life and business world was about. I was on my own. All my life's decision was for me to figure out. It was the beginning of a life where I felt it was up to me to make decision without fatherly advice or consul.

I have always regretted losing his love and affection for me that I know he had. I regret that my relationship with him had grown apart because our lives were so different. Maybe if I had been more thoughtful and mature, I might have not only received some of his kind, quiet, and intelligent attributes, but I might have helped him over some of his problems. Unfortunately, my last remembrance of him was at Dale Mabry Field in Jacksonville, Florida in 1943 (where I was sent for overseas assignment) when he and mother came to that post to say goodbye to me.

4

MOTHER

Mother and I were great pals from the very early days to her final blind days. She had many ups and downs in her life, but sailed on with valiant courage to the end. I think she was somewhat typical of her age in that she rather felt she was destined to be in command, she expected to act as an exemplary woman who was an example for those less fortunate than she, and expected others to accept her station. It was always said when Queen Victoria desired to sit down, she just sat down and there always was a chair that she settled into. She expected the chair and got it. Mother felt the same way.

Mother and Anne with Jeannie & David

She was a disciplined person who followed certain procedures her entire life. Up early in the morning, breakfast in bed with hot water and lemon to drink, check scales so her weight never varied a pound, one drink before dinner, exercise every day, and, after giving the cook her orders, she made telephone calls to her friends. She loved golf, played well enough to win a Western Amateur Tourney one time, played tennis with strokes like Susan Lenglon, and swam sidestroke with her head out of the water like a turtle. She loved bridge with her lady friends or in the evenings with father and other couples. She was not great at art museums or operas, although she did attend weekly Friday concerts at the Chicago symphony after a ladies lunch at the Casino Club. She played the piano from earlier training but did not continue playing with great enthusiasm. She was always on time for any appointment. She was personable and was respected by her peers and by the help at her house. She ran the house with absolute authority, clarity and fairness and as a result Gunnar and Herriot Swalgren worked for her for over 25 years. She would call in the cook as she would lie in her bed with her breakfast on her tray and give the menus for the day and even tell her how to cook and make some of the dishes she would order, even though she didn't know how to boil water. ("The Crème Brulee crust should be crisp, but not hard, and golden brown").

The Catholic Church was important to mother. She said her prayers and did not eat meat on Fridays. She was a staunch Republican. Father was liberal in his thinking, but he was jaded by the harassment of the

Justice Department re the Sherman Act and usually fighting with the United Packing House Workers who were continually threatening a strike. These two harassments were enough to persuade father to become a Republican. Father did not go to church even though he was a Presbyterian. At my tender age I thought the Democrats were more carrying for the poor, so I was sympathetic with them.

In the 1970s, when mother became blind and in bad health, she had unpleasant relations with some questionable nursing care help. The help often were without imagination, lazy, and dull. They sort of said "I'm not taking any more orders from that person" and out the door they would go. Most of these recruits from help agencies were enough to make one blow one's top. There is no question that as she became old, she became more demanding, less patient, and less understanding.

I am sure this is why we had a swinging door with nurses exiting as fast as they came in. However, as luck might have it, a Ms. Applebee appeared on the scene to be companion and helper. She was a gem. She was smart, and mature enough to understand mother's quirks. She found mother to be fun, enjoyable and understandable. She was 45 years old, attractive, smart, and alert. She respected mother's imperial nature, personality, and strong character. She stayed with mother for about six months before moving to Maine to be the General Manager of the Elizabeth Arden spa. Mother and I (who was mainly in charge from Denver in recruiting help) regretted her departure.

Edward, my brother and five years older than I, was playing in the backyard of the 2430 Lake View Avenue apartment in about 1937 when he ran a rusty nail into his leg. The wound was treated with merchrocome, which was obviously not effective upon the infection that set in. The wound developed into ostio mellitus that ravaged him for many years thereafter. From the age of 11 years old he endured yearly operations to clean the infection from the bones of his legs. I remember his thighs and legs with great caverns in them where the operations had healed and left nasty deep scars 4 to 8 inch long- a far cry from the delicate and small incisions of today. Antibiotics had not been discovered at that time so the only remedy was an operation at the infection location where they physically removed the infection. Antibiotics would have cleared the infection.

I am sure he would have lived a great life had medicine been more advanced. He was in and out of hospitals as long as I remember. During this time you can imagine the attention and love that mother and father gave to him. Even though he was popular with his friends, he had a difficult time staying connected with friends or with the contemporary life because he was in a hospital recovering so much of the time. He was out of the loop. When he was fifteen years old, he was sent (I think rather than choosing) to Phillps Academy Andover for his last three years of high school. Andover was a large independent school attended by capable mature young men.

Coming from the small Arizona school, The Evans School, I believe the jump to Massachusetts was a real challenge. But he adjusted well with the change according to Bill Embree, a classmate of his and good friend. (Bill became a close friend of Anne's and mine after we both had moved to Denver after WW II). He did not go to college for reasons unknown to me but after graduating, he went to work for the Cudahy Packing Co. and moved to Omaha. I know he had a serious love affair there that blew up. I imagine that going to Omaha knowing no one and working at the grim old slaughter house had to be lonely and difficult for a lad of nineteen years. His sickness had finally been defeated, so that was an improvement for him.

In 1935 he came to Chicago for Christmas. Jean and I were absorbed in our own life and we gallivanted around with invitations to balls and dinner dances with friends. We knew "everybody" and he knew few. Because of his sickness and absence from the Chicago scene, he was left out of many of the activities. It seems to me that he had to be lonely and left out. In reflection I feel guilty that Jean and I were not sympathetic to his possible problem and did so little to assists him. We could have made a big effort to include him in some of our fun.

I was home when Edward committed suicide by shooting himself in the head. The pain suffered by mother and father had to be unbearable. I being sixteen I don't recall that week after his death, I was so shocked. Mother and father and maybe Jean went to his funeral and burial whereas I was left at home. I think rather than having me exposed to the sadness, it was thought I would be better off not to expose me to that event. I think that decision amazes me now.

After his death I never once heard mother or father mention Edward's name or refer to him in any way. Their approach was to keep it to themselves and go on in life. I don't know what kind of a scar it left upon either my mother or father. I have no recollection of any mourning or recollection of anniversaries or even birthdays and certainly no words with me.

Considering the hours of nursing and caring for Edward, it must have been a devastating blow. What did we do wrong? Should he have gone to Omaha to work? Was Andover too large and competitive for a sick lad? On and on. There must have been many WHAT IFS. But I never saw a sign of grief or pain from Mother or Father. The ship just sailed on.

Mother and I had fun together. She hired livery stable horses from a Clark Street stable (1930-31) and we would mount up on our steeds at a spot on Lincoln Park West Drive, walk our horses through the Inner Drive (we had the right of way, of course, and don't think that mother didn't expect all traffic to stop for us) over to the bridle path along the Outer drive. We would then go cantering up and down the lakefront from Belmont Harbor down to the Oak Street beach. (That is now all part of the six lane Outer drive). We played golf together in events at Shore Acres in Lake Forest and the Everglades in Palm Beach. We went to Sunday afternoon events at Orchestra Hall and the Field Museum in Chicago. She visited me at the Arizona Desert School at our spring break. She and father took Jean and me on excursions with them to Bermuda, French Lick Springs and other spots.

When I was ten years old, I remember my mother taking me to Mt. Carmel Catholic church for my Catholic Confirmation, and my going to confession telling the good father behind that mysterious sliding panel door all my sins of the past week. Of course, I did not see that I had been such a sinner. I thought it a very peculiar thing going to confession for I could not understand why 20 "Hail Mary's" expunged those sins that I never believed I committed in the first place. I would fess up things such as "I did not say my prayers before I went to bed at night". Then the kindly Irish voice would hand out my sentence. "20 Hail Mary's and 20 Lord's Prayers".

I concluded the easy route was getting the father's sentence and not to say my prayers-the penalty was easier than kneeling down every night. (The prayers were only said when my mother might be watching). It did little to increase my knowledge of the Bible and less to interest me in Catholicism. In fact, I think my mind crystallize that church going was a duty that I must accept at that time and as soon as I could escape from that ritual, I would distance myself from this weekly burden.

Either my good mother was not an inspiring religious teacher or I was an immature student who preferred baseball to praying. I think it's possible that my present doubts about formal religion were established in those compulsory church going years. To this date I am very suspicious of formal religion and the formal scriptures said in prayer books in the Episcopal or Catholic services. Did those early Hail Mary's really do it?

After father died as I was sailing home from Italy in WWII, I returned to Lake Forest briefly before being reassigned as an instructor in P-51s in Florida.

Since I was in Sarasota in 1946, I could get a training plane from our base in Sarasota and fly over for the weekends to see mother in Palm Beach. It was a 45 minute hop under the auspices of the US Air Force. So I saw mother many weekends that winter. Mother's health was still good enough that she was playing golf and bridge and enjoying her friends. I do know however she was lonely living alone, but during this time in 1945 she was participating in life and seeing all her old friends.

After a year I was furloughed from the Air Force and returned home to Lake Bluff in 1945. Mother was grateful for my return to her empty home. In the fall she chose to move from Lake Bluff after the leaves had fallen in the fall time and her friends had forsaken the country to the Drake Apartments for two months prior to heading south. It was good transition from Lake Bluff to Florida. I felt that she was not completely happy with her solitary living. She had no serious romances. I think she just thought a marriage was not for her. She had one brief bow, but she brushed him off quickly. As result she lived her remaining life alone and ever more dependent upon me.

Towards Christmas she would make the move south and spend the rest of the winter in Palm Beach. Her life may have been like many other widows-slowly going down hill. Her health began to slip, her smoking contributing to her bad health. Bit by bit her life seemed to be less rewarding. After a dinner at the Everglades Club in Palm Beach, she awoke the next morning BLIND. She called her sister, Florence Spalding, to tell her she could not see who immediately attended and consoled her. Subsequently, she became more removed from her friends, less patient (she had trouble listening to Books on Tape "From Whom the Bells Toll" when Anne and I flew to Palm Beach to try to get her interested in listening to Tapes). The difficulties of blindness meant that being a participant in group conversations of more than four people became difficult to follow and be a part of the conversations. Finally after some seven years of deteriorating health from arterial sclerosis, she finally died in Palm Beach in 1969. She was 82. I was 50 years old. She had smoked cigarettes in moderation all her life. Her funeral was in Lake Forest and her body put to rest next to Father in the Lake Bluff cemetery (Just to the left of the main entrance).

That was a sad week for me because my sister Jean died of colon cancer in the Passavant Hospital in Chicago two days later; so I had lost two very close love ones in the same week. I seemed to bare up even though I had a terrible hollow feeling. I arranged for mother's burial and then attended mother and Jean's funeral on successive days. What a blow.

It was hard getting back to Denver, but I did have my Anne, Jeannie, David, Andy, and Peter, which was a real salvation for me. But this was the end of my own blood family. No grandparents, mother, father, brother, or sister- all gone. I was 50 years old, Jean 53 old, and mother 82. So I had to say it's a new road ahead and get on with it, but be grateful to have been part of the lives of such great people. Tears come to my eyes when I write this. They were all people I loved dearly. It is a loss I will always feel. End of story.

**Sister and brother-in-law
Jean and Daggett Harvey**

5

THE CUDAHY PACKING COMPANY

The Cudahy Packing Co. was a national company , a member of the big four meat packers in the United States. Swift, Armour, Cudahy, and Wilsons supplied the majority of the beef, lamb and pork in the country. They were labeled "The Beef Trust" for good or bad.

My Grandfather's older brother, Michael ran the company from 1890 until his death in 1910, when my Grandfather, Edward assumed the Presidency until his death in 1940 when his son, Edward Jr. assumed the Presidency until his son liquidated the archaic company in 1962.

Much of the value of the company was apportioned to Grandfathers five children unequally. Since Uncle Ed was the CEO, he obtained the largest share. In addition, the Company paid dividends regularly except for five years from 1890 to 1970. My father was Executive Vice President and the number two officer in the Company. He was a small owner of the Company.

Joseph Cudahy Kennedy of Callan, County Kilkenny, Ireland, and Michael Cudahy, a second cousin of mine from Milwaukee, Wisconsin, together published a book entitled "The Cudahys-an Irish

American Story" (Inland Press, 1995). Joseph researched church and county records along with collaboration with Michael Cudahy of Milwaukee to produce an informative history of the Cudahy family. In addition a Catholic priest by the name of Father Kane wrote a history of Edward A. Cudahy (Grandfather).

Messrs Armour and Cudahy contributed their Omaha and Chicago plants to the Armour/Cudahy Company in 1890. Not shortly thereafter Michael Cudahy and Philip Armour decided to terminate their partnership with Armour assuming ownership of the Chicago packinghouse and Michael taking over the Omaha operation. Thus the Cudahy Packing Company was incorporated in Delaware, and was listed on the New York Stock exchange. Grandfather went to work for the company as assistant to his brother. The rest is history. The Cudahy Packing Company became one of the "Big Four" (Armour, Cudahy, Wilson, and Swift) that dominated the meat packing business for a half a century.

The "Big Four" failed to modernize their practices and their physical plants so that new management, slaughtering facilities and modern operations supplanted the old which became worthless and basically were scraped. This was a rather sad end for four companies that failed to modernize.

Edward Cudahy, my Grandfather was the son of Patrick, my Great Grand father arrived in America in 1860. By 1880, he became the general superintendent of Plankington meat packing compnay in Milwaukee, a consideral feat for a young unschooled immigrant. In

1890 working with his brother, Michael, they bought the old Thomas Lipton plant and converted it into a meat packing plant.

Michael Cudahy and Grandfather increased their operation by building and buying seven packinghouses (Omaha, Sioux City, Kansas City, Wichita, Denver, Salt Lake City, and Los Angeles) in addition to establishing "branch houses" in many parts of the United States. (Originally sides of beef, hogs, and lambs were railed from the packing houses to branch houses, which then sold the product to jobbers who sold the product to retailers). One did see throughout the country, green Cudahy "Puritan" delivery trucks delivering meat from their branch houses, "Old Dutch Cleanser", Rex Lard, and other products. The dream of a successful business had been realized in some 45 years since arriving in the United States!

In 1910 Michael died and Grandfather assumed the job as CEO. In 1938 Grandfather died and my Uncle Ed took over control and my father became Executive Vice President. Uncle Ed and father ran the company till father died in 1946. After that Edward with the help of Edward, the third, took command until liquidation of the company in 1970.

It is my opinion the relationship between brother-in-laws (father and Uncle Ed) was never comfortable. Uncle Ed was a fun loving nice and attractive guy without much imagination or realization of the state of the company or the industry. Father was the innovator trying newer marketing and structural changes that were thwarted by Uncle Ed. Since Uncle Ed held controlling interest and did overrule father's plans, it made for an awkward relationship that did not help the company or the individuals involved.

New techniques of slaughtering and distribution of the business changed. The plants became specialized either in beef, hogs, or sheep- no longer slaughterers of all species. Direct distribution to retailer instead of through branch houses, change in modern operational methods and end of railroad distribution in favor of truck transportation. Price controls instituted a mandatory government grading system that spelled the end of brand names of the companies carcass beef, such as Puritan, Armour Star or such. Cudahy now sold a commodity rather than a company product. All beef was government graded so Cudahy and all packers sold essentially the same product. New competitors arose and profitability depended upon volume, modernization, and innovation. Cudahy along with the others were left at the switch and so they went into a steep decline and into eventual liquidation. Uncle Ed's son, Edward, liquidated what was left in 1970.

Meat plants moved to where the feed was grown, where the cattle were fed and where the weather was more conducive to efficient production of live fed cattle. With trucks delivering the beef carcasses directly to the retailers, there was no longer use of the railroad, the stockyards, or branch houses. The industry built new meat packing plants such as IBP, Montfort, and others and the old companies were liquidated.

6

CALIFORNIA

It was the opinion of my Father and Uncle Ed that something had to be concluded regarding the future of the Cudahy plant in Los Angeles. The large packing house was losing money and needed help to determine the future of the operation. Father volunteered to move to Los Angeles to make that evaluation. That was a big challenger, but he was up to it.

So our life changed from living near the cold shores of Lake Michigan to the land of opportunity and sun- California was a big decision. Mother was a garrulous, adjustable person who had confidence that she would find friends and adjust to the new challenge. Being in good health and at the age of forty five, she was up to the adjustment. Her three children, Edward(13), Jean(10) and me(7) were semi independent and therefore companions of mother. Of course, I had no love for Chicago so a new adventure sounded AOK. Father would be totally involved with his difficult challenge so I am sure he had no concerns about friends, social life, or activities.

So we sold the house on Wellington Avenue and struck out for Pasadena via the Atchison, Topeka and Santa FE Railroad. It was going to be a long trip-two nights and three days, which excited me. It was like going around the world to me. (For different reasons it must have been arduous for mother and father). We five travelled in a Pullman (first class) with a Drawing Room (with upper and lower berths, an attached couch and enclosed bathroom)connected to a Compartment (upper and lower berths with a chair that covered the toilet). It was most ample in space for the five of us since I was exploring a good part of the time. I was relegated to the couch which was comfortable enough except it had no window for me to view the country side during the night. I was forced to wait till mother woke up and then I could creep into her bed and view the great West. The direction of the couch was the same as the train's so, if the track was straight I had no trouble staying in bed as we rolled along, but when we hit sharp curves the Rockies, I had to hold tight so I would not roll onto the floor. We did not complain for those state rooms were the most commodious possible.

We three had plenty of exploring to do for those three days. Each car was different. The Section Pullman births with curtained uppers and lowers on either side of the corridor down the middle with a bath room at either end, the dining car, the coach car, club car, and then the observation car. The dining car was elegantly staffed by well trained black waiters serving the well appointed Fred Harvey tables appointed with the Harvey china ware. The food was delicious and prepared by one of their often trained French chefs. Meals were a real ritual as we sat next to the big windows and watched the world go by. We all five loved that. The Club car had a shower room, and a barbershop. Of course, I had to take a shower and even get a hair cut. Don't miss a trick! The observation car held the big attraction, for there was a little platform/porch on the back of car with about four chairs to sit upon. Since the Chief was pulled by a steam engine, a shower of cinders from the coal fired engine continued to drift in the air from the locomotive into our hair and head. We would be covered with cinders and soot as Jean and I played a game of counting skulls of dead cows along the right of way. The ever dry lands of northern Arizona provided the terrain for those drought stricken animals. These days were the beginning of drought and Dust Bowl days, so we had plenty of skulls to count. The train and sights made an exciting voyage for me.

The route of the Santa Fe took us through the heart of Navaho and Hopi Indian reservations. We stopped at Albuquerque, Gallup, Holbrook and Winslow both to rewater the locomotive and to see the Indians. The train made stops to take on water for the locomotives and to give passengers a chance to see the Indians from the various Nations. They would put on Indian dances and display their pots, plates blankets, Indian clothes, belts, moccasins, baskets and other items in use at their homes on the Reservations. In 1926, there were few tourists, the Indians were authentic, few automobiles or roads so each stop was an exciting and unique experience. In retrospect this was almost a visit just to see and understand many different tribes rarely visited by most of Americans.

As a side trip we left the Chief at Williams and took another two hour train ride to the Grand Canon. We stayed at the El Tovar, one of the grand Harvey hotels of the West. Mary Coulter, the longtime architect and designer of many of the Fred Harvey hotels and buildings at the Grand Canon including the Bright Angel Lodge, El Tovar and the La Placada at Winslow. Still operated in splendor.

After returning from the Grand Canon to Williams, we loaded onto the Chief for our final leg of our safari.

We went to the dining car once where Jean displayed her gentility as we sat at our white tabled dining car table when all of sudden she exclaimed "I hate spinach" as she despoiled the table cloth. The accommodating waiters seemingly happily replaced the table cloth.

Happily for my parents the trip was over and so we promptly went to the Huntington Hotel where we would stay until father purchased a home. I was entranced with the hotel with its swimming pools, ball rooms, orchestral stages and other amenities. The hotel offered untold mysterious adventures. One unfortunate prank that Paul Day Pattinson (a friend) and I perpetrated was when we dumped a barrel of roofing tar and then lit it on fire. After the fire department put out the roof fire, all was quiet. I don't recall the discipline, so it could not have been too severe.

After a short while Father bought a house on 1126 Hillcrest Ave. The house was of Spanish architectural design, separated from the house next door with a portico over the driveway. We had a long driveway where I spent too many hours driving our Model T Ford back and forth.

A large fish pond with a huge Neptune statue sprayed water over the whole was located at the top of a long sloping backyard. Another usual prank of young boys **was to "run away" from home.** I "ran away" with a pal of mine by retreating down that hill to a large sewer line where we hid. After a day of searching, mother, not too happy, rescued us. It wasn't much fun, so we did not repeat that kind of an episode.

Father presented mother with a huge black Packard car. I am not sure that's what mother wanted, but it was used on family excursions. One such was a Sunday outing on a drive up Mt. Wilson to see the observatories and have a picnic. Since the car boiled over as it objected to the climb up that mountain on any hot day, we ended up mostly coasting home and having our picnic next to the garage at home. Father was rather disgruntled with that result.

Sand Box David

In the summer father rented a house in Santa Barbara on Mission Drive just north of the Biltmore right on the ocean. (House burned down; Mission drive does not now exist). I had wonderful times on the beach (almost out our front door) playing in the sand, swimming, and particularly riding the surf with Edward. We had a 12 foot flat bottom canoe. Edward was in the stern basically steering the boat while I paddled up front helping keeping the boat in line with the wave as we whisked towards shore. We were dumped, dunked, overturned, but I became a real water rat feeling completely at home in the water. One time I paddled my 6 foot rubber mattress from the water in front our house around a breakwater that jutted out about two hundred yards, and then down into a bay where the Miramar Beach and Hotel was located about a quarter mile away. By the time my mother located me I was paddling along about three hundred yards from shore. I arrive at my destination with satisfaction only to be greeted by a distressed mother. " never again". But that ocean was great and was a great place for a young boy to become a water rat.

On return to Pasadena, I was entered at the Elementary Polytechnic School for boys. My learning was poor. I was caught trying to invade our class room as it was locked by climbing through a window and getting unceremoniously caught so I had to be extricated by a teacher. I was thence sent to a small classroom of six boys for my education. I only remember a large chart where the main effort was to get gold stars by your name.

Most early Sunday evenings, the entire family would congregate around our Atwater Kent radio to listen, as the static clicked away, to Jack Benny, Fred Allen, Amos and Andy and such. There were lots of laughs and enjoyment.

In the fall Mother would take me out to Gus Schulenberg riding stables. He had a stable, some jumpers, three Gated horses, and a big Thoroughbred ex racing stud. Mr. Schulenberg recognized my interest in riding, so he offered that I might "breeze" his big stallion. So, after a gallop around the quarter mile track, he said "Kid, just let him stretch out and go". So every time I went there I enjoyed breezing the old stud. I ended up going into a horseshow and winning the walk trot and canter class winning the Silver Cup and Blue Ribbon to the enjoyment of both my mother and father as witnesses.

Well California ended for me in 1928. I loved the water activities, but Father's work was finished, and the Cudahy operation closed down (see next chapter), and we all got on the Chief and rode back to the cold Windy City.

7

CHICAGO AND THE DEPRESSION

Even though father had improved the financial results of the Los Angeles plant, the California cattle feeders could not compete with the Colorado and Texas cattle feeders in producing finished ready-to-slaughter cattle. A slaughter house depended on a large volume of beef cattle to slaughter to operate profitably. The cost of feed (usually corn) to fatten the cattle was more expensive in California than in Texas, Kansas, Nebraska and Colorado, the main feeding states, thus making California fed cattle more expensive and non competitive. The meat packer was able to produce fattened cattle in the Plains states, slaughter the cattle locally, then ship the carcass beef at a cost lower than California produced beef. As a result since the California carcass cost was more expensive than the beef carcass raised in the East, "eastern beef carcasses" were shipped west and the meat packers in Los Angeles bought the carcass beef rather than slaughtering higher cost live cattle. As a result it became uneconomical to slaughter cattle on the west coast. With low volume the slaughter house was doomed. The dye was cast for the end of the Cudahy plant in Los Angeles.

With this happening, Father and the Wilhelm family moved back to Chicago.

That transfer to Chicago of our family was a happy move particularly for mother with all her family and friends in Chicago and Lake Forest. I think we children just accepted the move.

I left one good friend in Pasadena, Paul D. Pattinson, who became a fellow student both at Andover and Yale and the U. S Air Force. I tracked him down in Italy where he was a **B-24** bomber pilot in the Air Force at a neighboring airfield. Even later Anne and I visited him and his wife in Douglas, Arizona. We had a long acquaintance with him at unexpected locations and situations.

We took the Santa Fe on the Super Chief back to Chicago. Upon arriving in Chicago, since the apartment, that my family had just bought, was not decorated or finished, we moved into the Ambassador West Hotel to await the finishing of our new home. Staying in a big hotel was a kick. Eating in the big dining room was a lot more exciting than eating at home. A string ensemble playing Straus waltzes accompanied our dinner wasn't quite like eating in the kitchen at home... The leading lady of the musical "Good News" was a temporary resident and so my good mother introduced me to her, who then invited us backstage to see the show. I thought she was a real queen, and used to ogle at her when I saw her at the hotel. After two months the thrill of a big hotel had worn off and we were happy the apartment was finished and ready for occupancy.

My parents had acquired this new apartment in a new building overlooking Lincoln Park, Belmont Harbor, lagoons, and Lake Michigan. Wonderful view to the east. The address was 2430 Lake View Avenue. The ninth and tenth floor of our apartment was above the street traffic noise.

Three new twenty-story apartment buildings adorned the street with new Packard's and Lincolns with chauffeurs and doormen attending the building's stylish entrances. One block to the West was Clark Street, one of the roughest streets and neighborhoods in town lined with street cars, movie houses, bars, garages, and unattractive two story brick buildings. If we left our windows open in our bedrooms at night, by morning we would have an accumulation of black soot on the windscreens. We had little 10 inch angled vertical glass deflectors on the inside of the windows that would direct the dirty air upwards as it blew into the room, so that air did not blow on one directly. Lovely Chicago air!

The well-know St. Valentine's murder took place two blocks from our apartment, where members of the Capone gang dressed as police, rounded up seven members of the Bugs Moran gang, lined them up against a wall in a garage and blew them to pieces. A little further to the west I could see the location where John Dillinger was shot to death by the Chicago police as he exited a movie house with his moll. We were on the dividing line like much of Chicago- the affluent neighborhoods and the poor areas side by side.

The spacious apartment of some 6000 square feet accommodated the entire family in addition to maid's quarters for three. We children all had our own large bed room and bath, mother and father had a bedroom, two bathrooms and a sitting room, while the downstairs had all the rooms of any comfortable home. My favorite room was a wood paneled library downstairs. The panels had come from some villa in France that gave the room a warm comfortable feel. The fireplace warmed the rather cozy room so the books in their shelves and comfortable chairs made it a charming well-used room. Many pieces of the furniture are in our townhouse in Denver and many volumes of old leather bound classics were distributed to my children in 2007.

Jack Peacock, the brother-in-law of Henry Fonda, the actor, who was the head of the decorating department of Orchard and Wilhelm of Omaha, and was commissioned to decorate the new apartment. He was a dashing Douglas Fairbanks Jr. swarthy, swashbuckling man with plenty of charm and lots of BS. Originally he envisaged a flowing fountain in the dining room, with Grecian nymphs gracefully dancing around a freeze around the Doric columnar room. Jean's room had Marie Antoinette pink canopy beds, and there was an elegant marble-floored entrance hall with a great curving stairs to the upstairs. It was necessary for mother and father to rein in Jack, so much of the old Athenian touches were removed. It was elegant, handsome, and spacious to say the least.

The house was staffed with Gunnar and Harriet Swalgren, a cook, and another maid. Gunnar and Harriet worked for mother and father for at least twenty years. He was an ex Swedish navy prize fighter who was a great pal of mine even after he left our employ in the late forties and lived around the block from our house in Lake Bluff as the Chief of Police. He and I went to prizefights including the Joe Lewis-King Levinsky fight in Comiskey Park. We drove in from Lake Bluff, parked the car, were ushered to our seats, and in 46 seconds the Brown Bomber had knocked out his hapless opponent. Three hours for 46 seconds! In all I think we children were able to "make it" under these humble (?) surroundings.

We moved into this grand apartment in 1928- the year the great depression ravaged the United States. The stock market had crashed, fortunes were wiped out as window-jumping suicides proliferated (including some friends of my family), unemployment was over 32%, prohibition brought on gangsterism, and Herbert Hoover stumbled on as President. As factories closed, masses of unemployed turned to the streets, hovered under newspapers to keep warm and trash fires to keep out the lake winds of Chicago, while they sold apples and anything to get a few pennies to survive. Charity soup kitchens supplied some nourishment. I recall in astonishment seeing hundreds of men covered with newspapers trying to keep warm on the lower level of the Michigan Avenue Bridge as the winds of Lake Michigan whipped over them... The country was in chaos. There was no inspiration and hope from the White House and little Federal assistance. At the same time that Babe Ruth was told that he was making more money than the president to which he replied "I'm having a better year than him".

In this environment my family was building this elegant home. How Come? First I know they made the commitment prior to the Crash, so in a sense they "had to go through with it". The Cudahy Packing Co. was doing well and distributing considerable cash from my mother's stock ownership and father's salary, and so the ship sailed on comfortably for all of us. We all went to private Chicago Latin Schools; the staff stayed on, and lived pretty much oblivious to the state of the union. Father used to bring a big spreadsheet home showing us where all the money was coming from and going to and tell us we must stay within the budget. So things were comfortable for me in my little cocoon.

I was enrolled at the Chicago Latin School, which I attended from 1929 through the winter of 1932. That stint of schooling was not a very inspirational or contributive experience, for I seemed to spend a considerable amount of time before the headmaster, George Norton Northrop for conduct that was not appreciated. The time that I took a leak in the teacher's basket was decidedly a no-no. There were other incidents that did not endear me to the teachers. Maybe it was a time of life that pent up youth energy had to have an outlet. Anyway I am not proud of my conduct, and regret I studied little and learned less. I was totally uninspired.

Living in Chicago in the winter was difficult for a young lad. At 11 or 12 years of age I had a lot of steam to let off. We had no gym at the Latin School, so we had to find other ways to let go. There were the museums with mother and sometimes movies at the

Palace Theater (double features plus a short vaudeville!! including Sally Rand, Queen of the Fan dance), but those activities did not let off much energy.

The Racquet Club offered Saturday morning activity. Since the adult members did not use the facilities till after 10 or 11 in the morning, we had the run of the swimming pool, bowling alley, squash, racquet, and tennis courts. That activity was healthy, fun and beneficial to all.

Latin School football was a drag because I was not too large, didn't run with any speed, and I did not enjoy the cold and mud. So I turned to other nefarious and mischievous activities such as throwing rocks and bolts from the twenty second story roof of our apartment through the skylight of a large garage at the street level, pelting snow balls at delivery men from the 2430 backyard unto the delivery entrance to the neighboring building, or blocking the rear freight elevator so deliveries could not be made. What an attractive young lad.

The summer was better because I could play baseball in Lincoln Park or lie on my bed with baseball mitt in hand throwing the ball in the air and catching it at the same time as I listened to Hal Totten broadcast the Cub games from Wrigley Field. Father did take me to watch those mighty Cubs frequently.

In fact, father gave me a panama hat that I took to Wrigley field and proceeded to get signatures of most of the Cub players inside the hat. I would go down to the bullpen where the spare players would be sitting and they would say "hey kid, get me some popcorn", so

I would scamper up and get a bag and present it to them. I got about all the player's signatures in my panama hat until one player (unknown) caught the ink pen on a strand of my panama hat and a gush of ink obliterated all those collected signatures.

It was with great joy that my mother took me with her to Arizona to visit Brother Edward who was at the Evans school just east of Tucson. The intention of my mother was not to remove me from Chicago, but to visit Edward. During that visit I caught one of those horrendous head colds, so rather than taking me back to foul weather Chicago, she decided to leave me there after researching some other schools. She had heard of the Arizona Desert School, so she made the visit and enrolled me for the last three months of that year with the plan of going back to the Latin School in the fall. That's where she made a mistake—I stayed there for three years!

8

THE ARIZONA
DESERT SCHOOL

How lucky could I be? Instead of the ninth floor of smudgy old Chicago, I was given the opportunity to go to school out in the West where the air was pure, the vistas stretched for miles, and life existed astride horses and the outdoors. My mother decided to visit Edward at the Evans school, (who was recovering from many operations that were trying to cure his ostio melitus infections), located near the base of the Rincon Mountains just east of Tucson. Since mother wanted some company and since I was an unenthusiastic student at the Chicago Latin School, and since I had a big head cold, she decided to take me with her on that visit. While in Tucson mother took me up to the Arizona Desert School to explore and inquire about the school. That's all it took. The whole introduction entranced me. The entire idea of going to school in that environment had much greater appeal than Chicago. Mother relented to my pleading only if I stayed there for only the next two months and then returned to Chicago next year. With that loose understanding, I was enrolled for the next two months of March and April of 1933.

The small school was located six miles north of Tucson nestled in the hills of the Catalina Mountains. The school buildings consisted of Spanish Santa Fe style one-story buildings surrounding a patio where much of the activities took place. The classrooms and boy's bedrooms rooms that accommodated the forty five students surrounded this patio. A large Saltillo tiled floor living room served as the meeting room, library, assembly hall, bridge room, or what have you. Additional classes where study was conducted, was under a Palo Verde tree next to the Pima Canyon creek. The athletic facilities centered on horses. We had a skin dirt polo field complete with a slope from north to south; plenty of rocks, and dust, a sand tennis court and a chapel nestled in a natural amphitheater in the Catalina foothills about a ¼ mile from the school buildings. The corrals that housed some fifty horses and tack rooms completed the facilities. The school owned a small herd of beef cattle that grazed the local sparse rocky cactus area.

The area north of Tucson at the base of the Catalinas was open cow country with a girl's school, the Hacienda del Sol and the Flying V ranch headquarters the only sign of habitation for miles in every direction. The school was located at the mouth of Pima Canyon where often in the spring water rushed down by the school. Some seventy years later today that area is covered with homes with the desert barely noticeable. The only road to the school was a two wheel dirt track off of the dirt Ina Road. The Desert School was located on the bahada of the mountains overlooking the 30,000 population of Tucson.

The instructors were qualified talented men who drilled into our heads Latin, French, English grammar, basic Math, and current affairs. Matthew Flanders was an Australian that taught us basic grammar and sentence structure. He was a stickler for correct composition. French was taught by M. Thomas who schooled us in pronunciation and elementary grammar and idioms. I remember everyone in his class verbally contorting his mouth and throat to correctly produce the correct sound and difference between "eu, " "eux" and "eaux". He was very French and gentle. You could not have missed him as being French what with his mustache, hawk nose, tennis shoes, and beret. Matt Baird, the headmaster, taught current events and Latin. The polo coach, Lewis Brown, was a six goal polo player and that was his fort. Considering I was an average student, more interested in horses than studying, I went to Andover well prepared. That says a lot for their teaching

One of the many chores that Matt thought up was to build a trail up the Pima Wash and canyon. Laden with crow bars, picks and shovels we students would proceed to build a walking trail up to some cottonwoods about an hour and half walk where there usually was surface water. We little grunts worked along with Matt to clear rocks, cut brush and cactus and basically make a very walkable trail up into the mountains. In 2010, there now is a plaque commemorating a local politician for having the trail built! There was no recognition or admission that the boys of the Desert School really built the trail. There is no justice in this world!

Matt Baird conjured all types of work projects for us to do to fill in any spare moment. This effort was to build a Chapel. It was rather special-not because of its theological impact but because of the activities and labor that went into making this spot so serene and beautiful. We little ants hauled rocks to make an altar at our mountain chapel, a pulpit for the visiting preacher and seats for all us students. This was a mammoth effort that was built well enough so that it stands today, 70 years later buried in desert brush. We attended chapel every Sunday evening; hauled water to its birdbath daily; and on special religious holidays had candlelight processions and services. The year (2000) I clamored my way through the cacti and brush with Jean and John Donaldson to find the old remains that were very identifiable. (If anyone wants to locate it, go the Pima Canon trailhead marker and walk through the brush approximately 300 to 400 yards slightly west of north or about 345 degrees from the trailhead marker.)

Matt had it figured out. Keep the students busy, make them competitive and challenged. So he establshed the annual contest- the Championship Belt. For whoever earned the most points won the annual prize. Guess who won year after year? Me. If one worked extra hard, he received points for the time he put in- all of which were summarized onto a chart to contribute to winning the prize. Other chores that qualified for points were weeding and care of the front garden, care of saddles and tack, carrying water to the chapel birdbath, miles ridden on horse back, and maintaining the tennis court. Matt accomplished free care of the facilities and possibly contributed to the spirit of contribution among the students.

Matthew Baird, the inspiration and headmaster of the school came from Ardmore, Pennsylvania where he was married and divorced. He went to Princeton (maybe Class of 1924), Oxford, became Headmaster of the ADS in 1930(I would guess), was dismissed as Head Master in about 1940 for improprieties with a student. I don't know the facts about his relationship with student Van Vleck. He became a General in the Army and taught at the CIA after WWII, committed suicide while dying of cancer in the late sixties. He was a tall, handsome, former Oxford crewmember with a disarming manner with people. About 6'2" feet tall, trim, bronzed.

Matt chewed tobacco, Brown Mule, and had the ability to swallow his cud of tobacco if anyone of importance or parent of a student was seen approaching him. I am sure he did not learn that at Oxford! As a result of his interest in chewing, the "Brown Mule Club" was started. Qualification: Sit on the top rail of a fence and chew for twenty minutes. If you did not get sick, you became a member of this select group! I failed!

He made an announcement every evening before dinner and was continually involved with all the educational and sports activities of each day. He inspired Tucson citizens to come as audiences to our "Rodeos" and Polo Games. The polo field was circled with autos watching us little animals performing all kinds of horse events or contests. We clung to his words and encouragement and his enthusiasm for life.

He was the spark of the school; all we little creatures respected him so that he received complete support and cooperation from all of us. In spite of the fact that we continually did physical and menial jobs keeping care of the school (sort of slave labor) building trails, dams, and chapels, no one complained. We all followed his leadership. I have always felt grateful for his friendship and having known him. He was almost a substitute father.

Besides school once I drove from Arizona through St. Louis (to get his pipe tobacco) to Lake Forest in 1932 to visit my family and take me home. His personal respect (I believe) for me was recognized by others when I received a call (while at Andover) from John Donaldson's father asking me to come to New York to talk with Matt who was extremely despondent, depressed and suicidal. I believe that Mr. D. felt I could raise his spirits. I had dinner with him and stayed two days at the Lewison's (his wife's wealthy stylish Jewish family) just to talk and visit with him. I think I did raise his spirits at that time. Some years later he divorced Aubrey L. in Tucson and then went to work in the training and educational division of the CIA where he became a General. He was always an inspiration and a friend of mine. In the Sixties Anne and I visited him in Virginia a few years before his death when he appeared unhappy and lonely without the enthusiasm of old. He had cancer of what degree I do not know, and after its further progression committed suicide soon thereafter. Quite a guy.

Polo and horses dominated outdoor activities of the school and certainly dominated my interest and enjoyment. We played all the other schools in Polo and the University of Arizona J. V. John Donaldson played one, Henry Thompson played two, I was captain and played three, and a Bob Johnson played back. We beat all the other schools and I was rated by the United States Polo Association at one goal when I was 14 years old. (That was unusual for the age). Also I was privileged to play #2 on the faculty team, the "Wallagers"of Bill Choate, the cowboy #1, Lewis Brown #3, and Matt Baird #4. The "Wallagers" played other teams around the state so I got to play with the "big boys". We played at home on a rocky dirt field that had a slope from north to south, covered with stones, and not quite rectangular in shape. It was a little tough on our pony's' legs and the dust was a little tough on the players' lungs.

I owned a strawberry roan gelding who was a good kid's polo pony-handy, quick, and easy to ride.

Wimpy & Me
Polo 1934

Poor fellow however had been fore footed when he was young and fell on his front teeth thereby knocking them all out except one lonely incisor on the upper left of his jaw. He maintained his health in good shape while being fed loose hay in the corral, but alas when we were away from loose hay on the range, all poor " Wimpy" could do was gum flowers. In a dry season that made it pretty tough on old Wimpy. Luckily he spent 99% of his time in the corral.

The other horse that I owned was "Blue", a mouse colored mare who I inherited from my brother from his days at the Evans school. She had ears like a mule and looked liked a mule. She was blue grey in color. She played polo with great reluctance, some fear, great trepidation and lots of cunning. Whenever another horse would come charging into her to "ride her off"- that is bump her- she would cower, cringe, and slow to such a slow pace that the ball was gone and I was out of the play. With adequate spurring and, if I got the ball alone with no horses close so she was not threatened, she would run like Man of War in fear of being overtaken. When our evening time arrived and our outdoor day was over, she served as my taxi from the corrals to my room at the school. I would canter her Indian style-no bridle or saddle up to my room, hop off and give her a loving slap on the

rump, and she would scamper back to the corral where Bill Choate would let her into the corral. She was probably the smartest horse I ever owned.

Blue & Vaquero

I believe the school gave an individual confidence and independence. We were Big fish in a very small pond. We were comforted by being able to do our job the best we could and we were content to succeed. For example, two or three of us were allowed to go off by ourselves on horseback camping ventures leading our packhorse loaded with a diamond hitched load of food, bedding and cooking equipment. We would trail up Pima Canyon, build a corral for our horses, and set up camp, explore, cook and bed down. There were no cell phones, so we were on our own. It seems that's pretty good training for 13 and 14 olds. We would stay out two days, organize, pack up, cook (bake bread in our Dutch oven, and prepare other gourmet foods such as beans). We had to do all the planning and arranging ourselves. We had a few problems that we did have to rectify. One time during the night our horses broke loose from our inadequate homemade ocotillo corral requiring us to walk home in our 2 ½" high healed cowboy boots to retrieve our horses, return to our camp sight, repack our equipment, and finally return home. We learned that walking in high heeled cowboy boots produced blistered feet so we best build a better corral the next trip.

We also took great camping trips in the school's Model Ford station wagons around Arizona and Sonora, Mexico. The most memorable was to the Kibbie Ranch, the Alamo, near Magdalena in Sonora. The big cattle ranch had been turned into a Dude ranch. We played polo with and against the Mexican army team who brought horses and polo players to play at the ranch and guest teams on a dirt skin field that was so dusty you almost had to wear goggles to keep the dirt out of your eyes. Sort of like a Moroccan dust storm. Averill Harriman, a decent polo player from his Long Island polo education, was one of the guests that played with us. Mr. Kibbey, the owner of the ranch, was killed directly in front of me in one game when his horse and another horse both running at a full gallop collided with each other at right angles pinning Mr. Kibbey under his horse. He was taken to a Nogales hospital where he died.

Besides playing polo, I would go off with a Mexican cowboy. He first would put a sack over the bronco's head, put on his saddle and hackamore, and then climb aboard. Since we started the day in a sand wash, the horse would make few bucks before he calmed down. We would then ride all day without uttering a word to each other. Neither of us could speak the other person's language. It was just riding the range and being a cowboy on my horse that I liked.

The Arizona Desert School Polo Team

We went to bed sleeping on cots on an open veranda within the walls of the Alamo as we were lulled to sleep by the guitar playing and singing of the enlisted men of the Mexican Army. With all the activity we did not hear the music too long.

While at the Kibbey ranch often we would load up the Ford Wagons and take excursions. A notable trip was via a dirt road trail over to the Gulf of California to Puerto Libertad, a fishing village of the Seri Indians. We would throw our bedrolls on the ground, put a fly sheet over the portable mess table, gather some firewood, and settle in. Our camp site was about 500 yards from the Seri Indian village. Early morning before the glaring hot May sun arose, we would take our fishing rods in a rowboat out in the sea and within one hour fill the boat with yellow tail, mackerel, and cabrilla so full that we would have to go ashore to unload. We would donate our catch to the Seris who would in turn sell the fish to truckers-sometimes for pesos and more often for liquor. Within hours after the fish had been sold, the Saris would get stinky drunk. One evening they burnt down their flimsy village even though those thatch shacks were not much that was all they had. They were so poor that they would sit around our campsite at our dinner time and eat any scraps that might be left over-including orange peels.

It's interesting to note that in 1996 the Alamo had turned into the fortress home of the biggest drug dealer in Mexico. Jean, Peter, and I drove down there about 1996 and its splendor had disappeared. Its walls were crumbling, the corrals were in disarray, but the memory of the Kibbey ranch had not faded. I still have two photos in my house in Tucson of the Alamo in its glory.

I remember only two mishaps during those years at the Desert School. Everyone had chores around the school, one of which was feeding some 50 horses in a large corral. One time walking through the horse corral, I walked too close to the rear end of a mare who let fly with her hind legs and hit me just above a very important personal organ. It cut my skin through my Levi's, but I was fortunate for that was the only damage. Think what might have happened to my future family if the horse had only lowered her sights three inches! The other incident I recall was throwing an empty canvass water bag over the horn of the saddle on the way back from the chapel as I was mounting, which spooked the horse so I never got my leg over and into the saddle. My left foot caught in the stirrup and the horse galloped towards home with me bouncing along the rocky trail with my foot caught in the stirrup. Again nothing broken, just a lot of raw spots.

The school year started in late September and ended the first of May. We had no vacation at Christmas, but would host orphans at the school. We would give them presents, have luncheon, ride horses and play games. Since we were allowed only one present from our parents on Christmas day, we spent little time personally celebrating the day.

Our only vacation break was in the spring usually going to Phoenix with all our horses where we played polo against local teams. My mother came out a couple of times for those vacations. We stayed either at the Ingleside Inn, sort of a barracks setup, or the Arizona Biltmore, which was no barracks.

In the fall before school opened, I usually went out to Arizona two weeks before school started to help wrangle the horses from down valley, or to help by working cattle on the Ruby Star Ranch. In the spring after school was finished I stayed for a camping trip or some other excursion. You can see I had no great desire to return to Chicago.

This was a better way to spend your 13, 14, and 15 years rather than at the Chicago Latin School. My mother and father wanted me to return to Chicago. They missed their son, but I put up such a storm that they relented and allowed me to stay west for three more years.

First, it made me independent of my family. Granted I enjoyed the life at the ADS, but being away from home I became self sufficient and independent. My only family contact except for Spring break was letters, since phones were not used for visiting then because of the high expense and unreliable long distance phone service. Living those years away from home made Andover, Yale, and the Air Force no great leap.

Second confidence was developed. I recognize that the Desert School was a very small pond. But the fact of excelling with your peers certainly increased one's self-confidence.

Third, the exposure to horses and cattle for those years laid the groundwork for the business I pursued all my business life. The sequel was just a progression from the thorny slopes of the Catalinas to offices of a pretty substantial cattle business.

Fourth, the Sonora desert, the cooing of the doves, the cackle of the quail, the occasional rushing water in the canon streams, the sunny days and heat—they are all in my blood and a place where I feel comfortable. I had years in Lake Forest but those years did little to make me want to return there. So I am thankful for those Desert years.

However, my long period of residency in Arizona probably robbed me of spending time with my father and the benefits that would have been gained from that companionship. But I am sure I did not consider that at that time of my life. I was never homesick. I looked forward to each new year with anticipation.

9

PHILLIPS ANDOVER ACADEMY

It was a long way from the Arizona desert to lush green or snowy New England. It also was a drastic change of a school of 40 gold spooned white boys to a school of 900 students of different ethnic and economic backgrounds. I went from the hot dry parched desert covered with saguaros and ocotillos to lush green lawns sprinkled with giant elms amidst snow or rain. Unlike the Desert School many of the students were benefited by a generous scholarship program thereby allowing boys of humble means to attend.

Sweeping lawns, huge elm trees, magnificent Georgian styled Classical buildings spread over 160 acres made the Andover campus a magnicent setting for a school. A large chapel that could seat 1000, an art gallery of Classical style, a library, dining halls (Commons) divided into three large dining rooms, a many columned administration building, a gym, hockey rinks, baseball "cage", classroom buildings, and many resident dormitories comprised a handsome campus.

From an Educational level the school had few peers in the United States. The academic requirements were exacting and challenging. The professors were teachers and not researchers, whose primary interest and effort was producing written papers or books. As a result Emory Basford (English), Porky Benton (Latin), Flop Fallensbee (Biology), were interesting and engaging instructors whose talents and efforts made learning the tough courses more easy to learn and retain. Contrast that faculty with the Yale Profs who were required to produce papers for the scholastic world which preempted their emphasis on classroom teaching. Certainly the professors at Andover left a greater impact on me than the teachers at Yale.

Scholastically, I was an average student. After a good start my first term, I slipped into poor marks and "PRO". My father promptly announced "you are going to work and not stay in school unless you improve your marks and get off pro". I knew it was not an idle threat- he meant what he said. I was a disaster in Geometry. Better in Biology. But I did heed my father, went to work and got my marks up to a B average. I finally maintained a B average till graduation. In retrospect, I regret I did not see the benefits of working harder and putting more in that head of mine. It seemed that my intention was to "get by", rather than take advantage of the rare intellectual opportunities that existed at Andover.

I socially adjusted to the size of a student body of 900 with no problems. Quite a difference from the forty students at the Arizona Desert School. I was not homesick. There was too much going on. I wanted to be part of the action. I had been away from home in Arizona for three plus years, so absence from home was nothing new to me. I was housed in an old Victorian wood framed house (Tucker House) with six other boys on two floors.

My roommate was Hunter Marston from a Long Island/Wall Street background. Our relationship was distant but not unfriendly, and certainly lacked any mutual enjoyment. We parted on a friendly basis after that first year.

Robert Spink Davis, who lived on the third floor of the wood framed 1895 Tucker House, and I became close fiends, subsequently roomed together for a total of six years at both Andover and Yale. That was sort of a record. Spink was a disciplined student who could never be distracted from his studies. I think, if a blond nude had walked by him as he studied, he would not have looked up from his desk. Spink played the right wing on the first line of the varsity ice hockey team, and good enough tennis player to make the varsity team, later the lead lawyer with Edwards and Angel in Providence, and a volunteer in many important charitable and business organizations. He was a member of innumerable Boards and was an all out energy guy. He fought a bad cancer scare and won that one for some ten years prior to his eventual death from that cancer. Chemo one day, sick the next, and back in the office the rest of the week. He sculled in his one-man skull each morning on Narragansett Bay each summer. He kindly invited me to Providence many Thanksgivings during our Andover years. After college Jean and I have visited Bebe and him at Poppasquash Point near Bristol, Rhode Island in addition to his visiting us in Tucson, and Rand. We have vacationed with them on great trips to Israel and China. We have often cruised with them in Narragansit Bay aboard his boat and with the Livingston's in the Bahamas. It's been a long and close relationship that I think we have both cherished. This relationship began at Andover. I lost a close pal and fine American when he died of cancer in 2005. I was a pall bearer at his funeral attended by many friends from Providence, Andover and Yale.

I went out for club football-a Roman-weighing 115#, and was not an able, good or enthusiastic football player. *I did not like* all those big guys pushing me around in the mud. I was slow and small. I needed a horse. Since I couldn't skate, and did not want to swim in the winter, my only athletic choice was wrestling. Even though I made the team, I did not enjoy the mat burns or groveling around in someone's armpit (I got impetigo from some Quincy High School adversary and spent a week in the infirmary getting pussy scabs out of my hair). That was the worst sport I have ever had the privilege to compete in. In the spring I went out for baseball, but, since I could only make the J. V. team, I went out for tennis, played #2 and #1 and was captain of the team my senior year. Harry Thompson, son of a Boston tennis pro, was an excellent player who played #1 and who helped make our doubles team good (we even beat Frank Parker, the #1 ranking player in the United States and his partner at Choate). I played #2 for two years and #1 after Harry graduated.

One of the most enjoyable remembrances I had was the camaraderie at the PAE house, a fraternity

(Abolished many years ago since it was judged to be discrimatory). It was generally conceded that PAE was the most desired fraternity, so I felt fortunate to be picked. Wonderful fellows like Hovey Seymour, Walt Rafferty, Spink Davis, Juney O'Brien, and Jack Leggett were all members and people I kept in touch with most of my life. Hovey was killed when his plane crashed from an aircraft carrier while training for the Navy at the beginning of the War. Walter died twelve years ago at his home in Greenwich. They were leaders in the school and fun friends. Our day trips to Boston on weekends often were frolicking at the Old Howard burlesque with Hovey jumping on the stage from the nearby box to interrupt some bawdy double entendre. We were also allowed weekends off campus, upon the school's acceptance of any invitations. If one was on PRO, he could not leave the campus, so that was a big incentive for me to get on the ball.

I did not smoke and narcautics was no problem at that time at Andover. A group of us Catholics banded together to "cover" for each other, so one person would sign in for the group and the others avoided churchgoing either at that service or at the school Chapel. That avoidance worked for three years with no discovery from school authorities.

I graduated with no scholastic honors, a B-average, commendable success and recognition in sports, "best dressed in class", and socially acceptable. There was little impetus among my classmates to "do good" in the community. That was not the big calling at that time. By the year 2000, helping and volunteerism was almost a requirement for admission to Andover. I did not attend graduation, because I chose to return to Lake Forest. In retrospect, I think I learned to concentrate, learned how to study without guidance, and made some great friends. I am indebted to Andover for their excellence with the hope that some good did rub off on me. I would say that my performance was average and certainly I studied not out of the zeal of learning, but out of interest to stay out of trouble and enjoy people and friends.

10

YALE UNIVERSITY

I think I was apprehensive starting a new adventure with new people, new surroundings, and new work. Yale was so well known, I was inquisitive and excited about that unknown road ahead. Of course, in 1938 most of us had not been toured to any prospective colleges and knew little of the East or other universities. I was just sent to Yale. My father had gone there so it seemed quite natural for me also to go there.

Spink Davis, Hovey Seymour and I obtained a two bedroom and living room apartment in ancient Vanderbilt Hall, so, since we had been pals at Andover, that familiarity was a joyful comforting assist in making the transition to college. Even though the white concrete prison looking Vanderbilt Hall building was a spooky, formidable and cold structure, I accepted it with gratitude. Even though the building was surrounded by a great iron fence, which increased its prison looking appearance, I had wonderful companions and a comfortable lodging.

In 1938 Andover contributed about a hundred students to the freshman class of one thousand so that I knew quite a few of the class thereby making the transition to college easy. In 1937 for my freshman year Les Wheeler and I drove straight through in my old Buick from Lake Forest to Yale which included a short sleep in the woods of Ohio. I remember a sleep in the car because we were miles from anything, and a noise during the night scared us enough so that we fired up the old bus and sped away from our unlikely attacker thoroughly frightened. My first year was not exemplary as to studying for the college activities attracted me away from the books.

My sophomore year I loaded up two polo ponies, Jolly W and Red Turkey, in my basic two-horse trailer, hitched it to the old 1936 Buick and drove from the Onwentsia stable to the armory stables next to the Yale Bowl in New Haven. In 1939 the highways were all two lane, no freeways, so we lurched and chugged along the 1000 mile bumpy roads slowly. I had no problem finding lodgings for the horses at the end of each day, since I was mostly driving through farm country where a friendly farmer would welcome us. Horses were common and so their arrival was no great novelty to them, even though polo ponies were quite different than their heavy draft horses. All the farm families were so welcoming that I enjoyed the acquaitenances and they were interested in some kid driving polo ponies to school. That was unusual. That informality and hospitality would be hard to find today. The 1000-mile trip ended with no problems, but with two horses very happy to conclude their 30 hours of bobbing and bouncing on those imperfect roadways.

One of my roommates was Hovey Seymour. He was a man of many virtues: a running back star on the football team, great sense of humor, excellent student, playful, brilliant mind, and modest. He came from a very modest family home in Greenwich. He was one of the most respected and popular persons in our class. The other roommate was my Andover roommate, Spink Davis of Providence, R. I. We three got along famously and were great friends. On our floor was Donald B. Lamont (a Successful oil Wildcatter, one of my closest friend all my life), Tim Carpenter (Stockbroker and author) and Frank Kemp (Sheep business) all great pals. Next entry to our building were Pat Westfeldt (Corporate Lawyer), Louis Laun Asst. Secretary of Commerce), and other friends. What an experience to meet and know well such great fellows. If friends are important to ones well-being, then certainly Yale made that contribution in my life in a grand manner.

After freshman year, Hovey, Spink, and I moved to Pierson College (Yale undergraduate school was divided into ten "Colleges" which accommodated us) where we lived in a three bedroom living room apartment. We furnished it with a $10.00 couch and $5.00 used chairs. Meals were served in the college dining room, which were acceptable if not inspiring. The accommodations were all one would want for studying, sleeping, and "bull sessions".

Yale also had many fraternities which were really eating and social clubs with no sleeping facilities. I was a member of DKE. Initiation, hazing, dances, pool tables were all a part of its life. The fraternities at Yale included a large percent of the class and were not a big part of anyone's life. I used DKE to eat breakfasts from time to time and often a pool game after supper at our college dining room. Fraternities were established after I graduated.

Senior Societies were completely different. There were six Societies of 15 male members each a total of 90 members in a class of 1000. There was little concern about them being discriminatory, because they were composed of such a small per cent of the class. I was a member of Scroll and Keys ("Keys"), one of the two most sought after societies. Skull and Bones is probably the best known whose membership was composed of the heads of different activities of the University, such as captain of the football team, head of the Yale News, and other accomplished positions. Their emphasis was not on personality or compatibility but on accomplishment. Keys on the other hand was composed of leaders with persuasive or winning personalities. Keys sought members that were potential leaders in America. Both Keys and Bones required contributions from their members such as participation in debates, serious and humorous prepared and extraneous speeches, singing, conversation and conviviality. There were no parties or drinking sessions.

These two Societies practiced secrecy so that one was expected "to leave the room" if their Society name was mentioned. I am not sure of the reason for this, except probably the Societies wished to maintain their privacy and retain their activities for themselves. (Three of us seeing the front door open in the Bones building one evening as we strolled by, invaded and took pictures. This was such an affront to them that I never heard a word about the intrusion. They were chagrined. Since the buildings of the different societies were super secret, this was monstrous feat, we thought). No one admitted being a member or mentioned the Societies while I attended Yale. On reflection Keys was one of the most contributive organizations and activities for me at Yale. It built confidence, creativity, companionship, and respect for your fellow man. We met every Thursday night of our senior year for a glass of sherry (only), dinner and songs around the large round table served comfortably by Simon and then activities till about ten each night. The activities were a challenge as one was judged by the other members of one's abilities in extraneous speaking, debating or other activities. Being judged by your peers was challenging. All of our members enjoyed and had respect for each other's efforts and abilities. I believe, because of our active participation in the events, a bond was formed that has lasted our lifetime.

Today the Senior Societies have changed. The fifteen members of Keys are undergraduates of unbelievable abilities, achievements and scholastic excellence. The present group is made up of nine women and six men. Reading their biographies most are contributing additional time and abilities in entrepreneurial or charitable efforts. Almost all are receiving considerable financial aid. When I was in Keys in 1941, some members worked for their tuition, few had jobs outside of school, and the consist of our group was all Male Anglo. The current makeup of its members is bi-sexual with ethnic diversity and few

Anglos being members. Members now come from Public schools with few from the private schools of the East. I know our scholastic achievement was not on a par with the present members. During our times the future potential as an effective citizen was the highest qualification for acceptance into Keys. Even with this change in the makeup of each class, the appreciation by its members appears to be as great as when we were members.

I played tennis my freshman year and was captain of the team. My sophomore year I started to play tennis on the Varsity team but someway the trips and the continual "challenge matches" made tennis a burden rather than fun, so I opted to switch to polo. I played Indoor Polo all four years and outdoor for three years. Indoor first year with Alan Corey (eventually 7 goal rating and Bill Chisholm; later years with Jack Daniels and Bob Johnson Indoors. The later three years our outdoor team consisted of George Mead (killed in Guadalcanal), Bob Johnson, John Daniels and myself won almost everything including the Intercollegiates. We all carried four goal ratings except John (3 goals) which made our team a 15 goals team- a formidable force for a college team. I was Captain of the teams and earned my Major Y. since we won the Intercollegiate. We played Indoors in Brooklyn and New York Armories, Harvard, West Point, Pennsylvania, and some other locations. We vanned our horses to the New York area or played the host team's horses on other occasions. Jolly W, Brite Urbana, Red Turkey, and Ronrico were my various horses in descending abilities.

I spent many leisure times with Bobby Johnson not only in the big Apple after games, but also at his family's home in Peapack, New Jersey. There were four Johnson brothers (Frank-Harvard, Cotty-Yale, Benny-Princeton, and Bobby-Yale). Along with their father and mother they all sang cheerful songs after we ate happy dinners with them. The Yale polo games were on weekends and often away from New Haven, so that gave us a reason to frolic in the big city. Bob and I enjoyed eating at the bar of the Twenty-One Club because it was cheap and good. One evening Vivien Leigh, the star of "Gone with the Wind", was in our presence which made my day. It's still a great restaurant, but it 'taint cheap now.

My senior thesis was titled "The Progressive Attack on the Meat Packing Industry". This was an *indictment* of the meat packer's ("Beef Trust"} unsanitary slaughter of cattle and the handling of meat products. Upton Sinclair, the principle "Muckraker", brought charges in his book "The Jungle" against the Big Four (Swift, Armour, Cudahy, and Wilson)even though he did not identify specifically any company. The book was a sensation, and the packers became subject to Federal Inspection at all killing plants and distribution outlets. Even though resisted by the packers, the reform was overdue. They had been dumping the waste products from the kill into the Mississippi, Missouri and Chicago Rivers, meat was spoiling because of the infancy and poor refrigeration and cleanliness within the slaughter houses was poor. The packers needed to be reformed. They were reformed only by the stiff hand of Federal Meat Inspection Act under the supervision of The Packers and Stockyards act supervised by the Department of Agriculture. Without doubt the work of Upton Sinclair was a benefit for all the citizens of the U. S.

The professor who reviewed my thesis knew little of the subject so he seemed to enjoy learning about the particular subject. After the completion of the 120 page document and its acceptance, I qualified for my Bachelor of Arts degree from Yale in May 1942.

In 1942 the black clouds of War were approaching. Hitler's Axis Germany showed its intentions with its actions against Austria, Poland and Czechoslovakia. The arrogance and apparent strength of Germany, the weakness of America, (the 17th strongest armed forces in the world!) posed a real threat to France and England. Domination of Europe by Hitler was very real. When the Japanese air force bombed our massed fleet moored in Honolulu at Pearl Harbor on December 7, 1941, the world exploded and the USA was electrified. The following day President Franklin Roosevelt declared war on Japan, Germany, and Italy for that "dastardly act". Yale became a different place over night. Some classmates enlisted and were abruptly absent from their rooms or classes as they enlisted or made plans to join some branch of the fighting forces. Numbers dwindled. For me all of a sudden the ROTC program became a serious and important course. Since I had taken the Field Artillery course at Yale and been enrolled since my Junior year, upon graduation (June 1942), I was commissioned a Second Lieutenant in the Field Artillery of the Army of the United States. As a result of being a member of the ROTC, I was able to finish my senior year and graduate in the Class of 1942. Others in my class either volunteered or were drafted earlier in the year and left Yale before their graduation so that they had to return to Yale after the war to graduate and receive their diploma.

It's rather ironic that I joined the ROTC to play polo on their rather miserable horses, which turned out to be most fortunate. Being a member meant I was able to finish my senior year at Yale (and did not have to return to college to get my B. A. degree after the war). It also meant that our advancement in the armed forces was accelerated, since I did not need to spend three months in "Boot camp". (I had spent a month in Vermont at Fort Ethan after my Junior year.) In addition after I was able to transfer from the F. A. to the Army Air Corps and pursue pilot training as an "officer in grade" as a Second Lieutenant still in the Field Artillery. I became a member of the "Army Air Corps" only after I received my "Wings).

So those bright college years ended-now it was the road to <u>War.</u>

11

SUMMER TIME

735 Ravine Avenue in the small town of Lake Bluff, Illinois was originally our summer home and later our year around home. Father and mother bought the house in 1936. The house fronted to the east overlooking Lake Michigan and the Lake Bluff public park to the north. The one story wood sided house shaded by huge Elm trees was surrounded by a brick 10 foot high wall which enclosed a comfortable yard. The interior plan of the house was rather unique being like a spoke of a wheel with four wings in all four directions. The house had abundant doors opening from the bedrooms and living room giving one the feeling that one was almost living outdoors. Being close to the Lake, our temperatures were at least 8 degrees cooler than inland-just a few miles to the west. That was a boon to escape those humid hot spells that so often overcome Illinois. It was a modest home with large rooms and with a wonderful feeling of living close to the land.

The North Shore of Chicago was the home of the well to do. Lake Forest and Lake Bluff were located one hour north of the Chicago "Loop". Large estates frequented the area with Armours, Swifts, Mortons,

Glores, Thornes, and Schweppes to name a few. The town of Lake Forest had a lovely square, the stop for the Chicago and Northwestern railroad, the commuter train that carried the business men to Chicago on the 8:10 and returned them on the 5:10 in the evening. Lake Forest was also the home of Lake Forest College, the Lake Forest hospital, the Onwentsia and Shore Acre Country Clubs, Kraft's Drug store, the Deerpath Theater and Marshall Fields-what more could you want?

Few of the young took summer jobs, since their parents had the wherewithal to subsidize their children's activities. Our "group" consisted of high school to college age boys and girls who were enthusiastically involved in all kinds of activities. Tennis and golf were the main sports in addition to polo. Most applied themselves with diligence . Most parents were affluent enough that they did not need financial assistance from their children. Unemployment was still a major problem in the United States so jobs were scarce so summer jobs taken by these only deprived more needy from getting a job.. There were no couch potatoes in our group. (There was no such thing as television). We played competitive golf, tennis, and polo with vengeance. Our parents thought this way of life was more beneficial than seeking a menial job. The experience of competing- winning or losing- was a lesson in life. Granted this way was charmed, fortunate, healthy and enjoyable. Unfortunately, I don't think this experience is enjoyed by many today. Instead, it's get a paying job. I think it is unfortunate that a little "playing" is not part of life. There are benefits that one gains for one's entire life from competitive sports.

To be sure I used every minute of every day playing hard and working diligently to excel. I did not sit a moment. Few of my friends volunteered for charitable activity or part time jobs. In the 1930s, the country was emerging from the Depression and Franklin Roosevelt had initiated many work programs to provide jobs for those in need. Unemployment hovered above 15%.

During the roaring Twenties, polo was played with great enthusiasm, participation and attendance. There was both low goal and high goal polo played by officers of the Cavalry and the Field Artillery where horses were used extensible in the military, and by ranchers in the cattle country, and by amateurs. The Cavalry and Field Artillery played Polo at many bases throughout the United States and was a stimulator of interest in the game. Outdoor polo was actively played around the United States at Old Westbury, L. I. , Auburn, New York, Aiken, N. C. Lake Forest, Oak Brook, Santa Barbara, and many ranching Areas in Texas and California. Indoor Polo was played in many of the major cities of the East during the winter. Polo had been played in the twenties on the Onwentsia polo fields in Lake Forest, Illinois. However, the Depression of 1929 and the mechanization of the armed forces put a huge damper on the game. With the polo field and stables unused and available at the Onwentsia Club, we and I in particular canvassed some twenty young men to try the game. With a limit of $200.00 per horse, we coaxed an eager group to try to learn.

Les Armour and I helped the stable boy muck out the stalls, feed the horses and, if necessary, exercise them. We initiated in 1935 low goal polo at Onwentsia on a low budget basis among young high school, college men, horse dealers, gangsters and a few experienced ex players. We played three times a week and entered the Chicago Polo League.

Polo had everything- horsemanship, ball and eye coordination, physical contact, team work, physical endurance and aggressiveness, and danger-it's got everything that baseball, football, tennis, ice hockey, steeple chasing, and many other sports have all rolled into one sport. I enjoyed the game and also the training and developing green horses into good polo ponies. My most rewarding horse that I trained was an excitable thoroubred race horse who was a wild one. I spent many hours training and calming that Thoroughbred that I bought for $200.00 and who became a fine high class polo pony. Jolly W was a true joy.

I started playing at the Arizona Desert School when I was 12 years old.

We won most of our school games and were the champs of the boy's league of schools in Arizona. I earned a United States Polo Association rating of one goal, which was a feat for a 12 year old. In addition to the school team, I played with the Wallagers- a team made up of the Headmaster, Matt Baird at Back, Lewis Brown, the polo coach at Three, me at Two, and Bill Choate, the school cowboy at one. We played teams around the state, and I thought I was a stud playing with all those big fellows! But I loved it and with Brown pumping balls up to me, I had lots of chances to carry the ball forward to score goals.

I didn't play at Andover because only about five players participated and it was not an Andover accredited sport.

At Yale after my freshman year, (I was Captain of the Yale Freshman tennis team), I played both Indoor and Outdoor polo. We won the Ivy League indoors and outdoors my last two years. The opposition was Harvard, Princeton, Army, Pennsylvania Military Academy, and Cornel teams. Our Indoor polo consisted playing in our tiny arena at Yale, or at Squadron A (NYC), Squadron C (Brooklyn), or West Point. Our Outdoor team consisted of Jack Daniels (3 goals), myself (4 goals), George Mead (4 goals), and Bob Johnson (4 goals)-a 15 goal team that swamped our opposition.

Onwentsia

Back in Lake Forest we played low goal polo (5 to 10 goal teams) using the Onwentsia Club polo field (now the golf driving range) and the "backyard" of the Swift family (big enough for two fields). We stabled our horses in the old abandoned Club stables. We competed in the Chicago suburban league composed of Field Artillery Officers from Fort Sheridan, construction workers, horse traders, and gangsters. Our best team was composed of Armour, Bill Carney, Prentice Porter (a former good player), Bill Fergus (a hired gun) and me. It was a low goal team that fitted in with the locals.

A rather interesting opponent was the team headed by Len Bernard, an ex Capone associate. He was remembered best by his dismounting from his horse, flaying his mallet at the flag boy for what he thought was an incorrect call on a goal. It goes without saying that the elite Lake Foresters were slightly disapproving of his conduct.

No other Lake Foresters bestowed hospitality and friendship upon Len in the locker room after the games except for me. As a result of befriending him, he must have appreciated my attitude for he offered me Bright Urbana, a great indoor polo mare, to take back to New Haven on the condition that I return her when I was through with her. She was his best polo pony out of a sizable string of his horses. This was quite a grand gift, and in retrospect I marvel how this rough Italian gangster was so bountiful to me-he certainly was not trying to get in with the Lake Forest types. I just think it was those conversations and hospitality in the Onwentsia locker room that someway made him want to show his gratitude. (I alone would always go up to the locker room with him until he left). Bright Urbana made my string complete with Jolly W. Since war started for me as soon as I graduated from Yale in 1942, Bright Urbana was shipped back to Len with my great gratitude.

After the war Anne and I visited Len at his spread in 1948 at Arlington Heights, Illinois. His land provided two polo fields. He had made a bunch of money (how I don't know) and had a big lavish home with wild interior designs complete with live bimbos running around. Anne was duly impressed with my friends. Unfortunately, not long thereafter I learned that Len lost his life style and was sent to prison where he died! He was not a gentle person, but for some reason I liked him.

I did play polo in Long Island, Wyoming, Colorado, Mexico and New Haven for the span of ten years and then the War and working meant that was the end of my polo. Of all sports I have competed in, polo was the tops. It's a game for young men. I was sorry I could not carry on.

During those polo playing years, my greatest thrill was working, training, and playing Jolly-W, a 15'1" Hand chestnut bush race track gelding. He was an intensely high-strung bundle of uncontrolled energy when I bought him. After hours of training he became a high-class great polo pony. He was fast, handy, courageous, and tough. He steadied down from his horse racing days and became a calmer soul. He never stopped going all out, and never swayed from another horse's bump. No matter how hard he was bumped, he never went down. He was so excitable that before a game his sweat would pour off his belly in anticipation of the game ahead. I spent hours quieting him down on a lunge line in the Onwentsia indoor arena, or taking him swimming in Lake Michigan in front of our house in Lake Bluff. (I would ride him bareback into the water and then hang on to his mane as we swam- he loved it). Even though I liked the dances at Onwentsia, I often left the party at the Club in my Tux and went down to the stables to sit with him in his stall talking to him. At this point I think he was more important to me than girls, if one can believe that! He was a rather impersonal fellow, so I think he wondered who the creep was coming to disturb his sleep at midnight. Before going off to war, I gave Jolly W, now a quiet old gentleman, to Virginia Dennehy who taught her young son to ride on this now tranquil horse. He was a great Pal. (By chance my email now is "jollyw42@qwestoffice. net").

**Anne, Liza,
DC & Kate**

When I tried to play again in the seventies, I played Carl Grosses' and Jack Goodman's horses, but after having a couple bad falls (a horse fell on me on the boards giving me a concussion), getting completely exhausted, and playing poorly, I figured this was a young man's game and quit playing regretfully for good.

Now I have fond memories of great times playing polo and two crossed polo mallets on the wall of our screened porch at the house in Rand remind me of that exciting past.

Since I was involved with polo and horses, I met Olive Bennett, the riding instructor at the Onwentsia stables, and organizer of the rather large Lake Forest International horseshow. She was a Canadian who found a very rich architect (Edward Bennett- the chief architect and planner of the Chicago park system) and married him and his money so that she was able to give up instructing riding. It so happened that her daughter, Betty Mead, and I became riding and show jumping companions. They had a big brown gelding by the name of Sylvester, who I subsequently showed in jumping classes for them, but as things happened, the relationship between Betty and me developed into a two-year friendship. She was a comely, brown eyed, black haired, deep voiced, Grecian skinned lady, reserved, and a lithe as a feather dancer. During our relationship I saw her frequently, spent many hours with her, and thought of her fondly. I know I was not interested in a long term relationship with her and so she switched her attention to Harry Wheeler. I don't recall any sorrow in breaking up that relationship. Before long she did marry George Merck, called "Merck the Jerk" by locals, even though I think that was unfair moniker. Some fifty years later in 1993, I went to a U. S. Senior Golf tournament in Somerset, New Jersey and had two dates with her at evening dances at the Club. She had been widowed for some time. We had lots of fun dancing all evening and talking. She was the same good person as she had been 53 years before.

Not long after that flame burned out, I began to see Diana Hill who lived in Chicago. We started going together in 1939 and the romance lasted till the end of the War. She was attractive looking with a warm smile, large brown eyes, and a shapely body. She had a friendly demeanor, was feminine, gentle, unathletic, loving, able, compassionate, reserved and enthusiastic about life. She was most acceptable to my mother (which was comforting if not required), and would stay with us in Lake Bluff often. I really thought she was wonderful and I was truly in love with her. We corresponded all through the war, and my P-51 and Spitfires were all named "Diana-Goddess of the Chase". We both planned to marry after the war.

Upon my arrival home from overseas, our relationship was warm if not torrid. As I have said in another part of these memoirs, I arrived home from Italy, father had just died, and mother was widowed and living by herself and unsettled. I was confused and undecided so our marriage plans stalled. Instead of cancelling these plans, everything just disintegrated. After three weeks in Lake Forest, I was reassigned to Sarasota, Florida as an instructor in P-51s. I left Lake Bluff with a lonely mother and a dwindling love affair with Diana. It seemed that in those few days at home, Diana never reelectrified my feelings and off I went. It's highly possible her feelings also cooled. As it turned out, our romance drifted away. She was a wonderful girl, who eventually was unhappily married and divorced. Later in about 1975 after my mother died and I was selling mother's house in Lake Bluff, I hired Diana as our real estate agent to sell mother's house. Anne and I flew into Pal Waukee airport in my plane and Diana met us. She was so attractive and nice that both Anne and I enjoyed her company tremendously. I couldn't help having a beat in my heart for such a neat girl. She had such a gentle quite temperament. As nice of a person as she was, I am surprised and sorry she did not have a happier life. I did talk to Barbara Lee at Steven Conger's wedding party in Vail in 2004 summer and she reported that Diana had gotten remarried happily, so that's a good outcome. However, Diana died in 2007.

12

FIELD ARTILLERY
AND THE AIR CORPS

MILITARY SERVICE

I recently located three written documents that I thought could more clearly retell my story of my experiences as a World War II fighter pilot. First was a leather bound book named "The Chrysalis" which was a compilation of my letters about my pilot training written by me to my mother and father. In addition, I located two diaries that I wrote daily while I was in training and while I was flying in Combat.

By having those written records much that I have written in the following pages has refreshed my memory or corrected inaccurate recollections.

I was commissioned a Second Lieutenant in the Field Artillery upon graduation from Yale and then called to active duty on May 13, 1942 to report to Fort Sill, Oklahoma in the Field Artillery. I transferred later that year to the Army Air Corps. I trained thereafter in the Southeast training command of the United States. I was then shipped to Africa for additional flight training. I entered my combat duty

September 1, 1943 in Italy until I returned to the United States as a Captain in June 19, 1944. I then served as a P-51 instructor in Sarasota, Florida until I was furloughed from the Air Corps on July 26, 1945.

I began writing almost daily about my training in various training and fighter airplanes in the southeast of the United States and at airfields in Morocco and Algeria, North Africa. I continued to keep a daily log of all the details of my experiences while flight training and combat flying compiled, edited and presented by my father.

"The Chrysalis" and the two other logs kept by me reflect my thoughts and feelings AT THE TIME of engagement rather than RECOLLECTIONS after some 65 years. I found that there was a difference between my memory and what was written at the time. Often when I read about a specific incident, my recollections were inaccurate and or factually incorrect. In addition, I discovered details had been completely distorted, forgotten or omitted. As a result I have attempted in these chapters to give a picture of a twenty four year old lad's outlook as a pilot, both in training and in combat recorded at the same time as the events took place. I believe these documents gave me a great opportunity for me to recall the feelings of anticipation, excitement, fear, fatigue and even boredom.

The most dramatic event in my young life took place when the world erupted into World War II. Hitler had overcome the continent of Europe, was preparing to invade Great Britain, and the Japanese had destroyed a major portion of our naval fleet at

Pearl Harbor. President Roosevelt had declared war in his "Day of Infamy" speech (December 8, 1941) and Americans were in a frenzy to enlist and fight the threat of a socialist and communist dominated world.

Almost everyone wished to and did volunteer to enlist in the armed forces. A few were placed on "4F" because of physical disabilities, even though they desperately tried to become active participants. Many volunteered for active military duty but were not accepted because of health problems while many declined to serve because of religious or humanitarian objections to military action. Many of these volunteered for the Red Cross ambulance service or other dangerous service even though they did not become actual combat members of the armed forces.

Under these circumstances my life in Lake Forest and Yale was overturned, and I too was eager to get into the armed forces.. I had no idea of what was ahead. I made no analysis of the wisdom of the war or what was in store for me. Just like most all young men, I just wanted to join the fighting forces. In particular, I wanted to join the Air Force and be a fighter pilot. I had taken two years of military science at Yale and gone to a summer Field Artillery camp at Camp Fort Ethan Allen in Vermont in the summer of 1941; so in June I would graduate as a Second Lieutenant in the Field Artillery. At that time being a commissioned officer in the U. S. Army did not seem important or to be of any particular advantage. I did not understand that as a Second Lieutenant would hasten opportunities for advancement or assignment to the branch of the service I would choose. As I pondered my interests in the different services of the armed forces, I ruled out the Navy or the Coast Guard because I knew little about the high seas and, furthermore, I got seasick as soon as I looked at the ocean. I was not turned on by firing the French 75 or the 110 Howitzer, the logistics of ground war fare, or by other Field Artillery activities. The Cavalry had replaced horses (which, had they remained, would have attracted me) with tanks and trucks, both of which were of little inspiration for me. Happily Army regulations allowed one to transfer into other branches within the Army, if one was an officer ("Officer in Grade"), and, since the Air Corps was a division of the U. S. Army, that opportunity was possible for me. (With the advancing prestige of the flying arm of our armed forces, the Air Corps became "The Army Air Corps" and even later "the U. S. Air Force"). So with my interest in airplanes and with the exotic dream of flying, by choice and by elimination, I determined that I should transfer to the Army Air Corps and try to become a fighter pilot.

The choice of flying was the correct choice for me for many reasons. First, I was cocky enough to think I could take care of myself rather than someone else doing the caring. In a one-place fighter plane (not to be confused with a bomber) it was the responsibility of the pilot to be an effective combatant who depended upon his own skill, talent, and luck and good judgment to survive. Flying the single engine fighter plane the pilot was pilot, navigator, gunnery officer, and strategist. In combat, if you had an enemy aircraft on your tail ready to shoot you down, it was you or him.

No one else was there to be an observer or gunner to help you. You had no hand holder. It was up to you all by your own little lonesome.

A fighter plane did not have to fly in a restricted formation as if it were the infantry of the sky. Bombers were trained to stay in formation for mutual protection and to obtain accuracy of their bombs, so that when they released their bomb load, they were in the correct location considering wind, drift, and speed of the plane enabling their bombs hopefully to hit their targets. (These were the days before radar controlled bombs. The inaccurate Norden bomb sight was used). If a bomber was hit by flack from a ground antiaircraft gun or attacked by a German fighter and therefore forced to deviate from its course, the probability of hitting his target with his released bombs was poor. The bomber had to concentrate on maintaining his altitude and course to maintain an appropriate platform to launch his bomb load. A bomber could not take evasive action to avoid the enemy flak or fighters. Conversely, the fighter pilot and his flight of four could take evasive action by changing altitude or direction, thereby better evading flack and enemy fighters.

Also I chose the Air Corps simply because of the glamour and thrill of flying. The glamour of flying had far more allure than being a ground soldier. Having your own personal airplane, the thrill of soaring through clouds and blue skies, the thrill of power in that bird, and the challenge of individual combat against a personal enemy- all were unique in the job as a fighter pilot.

Of course the living facilities and food were without question more desirable and comfortable than being a "grunt" in the Infantry or Field Artillery. We almost always had shelter, whether a bombed out building or tent, rather than living in a muddy or wet fox hole.

Lastly, my interest in flying was born as a result of some early exposures to airplanes. My mother used to take me to Pal-Waukee airport on the north side of Chicago to watch air races. I don't know if that was for her interest or to give me an education. We would watch airplanes roaring around pylons at ground level racing for the finish line. It was thrilling. To expand on those thrills, Mother took me for an excursion ride, flying around the area in the noisy old Ford tri motor airplane. This was the first time I had been in the air; so that 1931 flight was a real kick. Later when I went east to school, I would prevail upon my family to let me fly by American Airlines to school at Andover. On those airline flights at that time (1936) the pilot would welcome me to the cockpit to watch all his procedures. There was no threat of hijacking or foul play on the flight deck then, so the pilots would let one watch the landings and explain what was going on. I also recall flying to New Orleans on an old Chicago and Southern Airlines flight and spending the entire time in the cockpit. The pilot seemed to have adequate time to explain the navigation aides and radio facilities to me. One spring vacation, I flew to Bermuda on that huge trans Atlantic Pan American Boeing Clipper ship. I remember that interminable, long, takeoff run in the Baltimore bay, as the water sprayed over the ship until it was finally air born. So my interest in flying had been smoldering for quite awhile before the year 1942 decision to enroll into the Armed Forces.

Upon graduation, I was immediately given orders to report for active duty in the Field Artillery. I had not received any transfer orders to transfer to the Air Corps so at that point I had no choice other than to report for duty. Abruptly I was thrown in with a mass of unknown new recruits at Fort Sill, Oklahoma. That huge camp had recently been expanded and was a sea of dust, wooden barracks, and steamy weather. Those first days were just a maze of orders and confusion. We were all equalized with the same clothes, same food, same lodging, same discipline etc. I am sure I was dazed as was everyone else, but slowly everyone searched for his own identity and where and how he could adjust. It certainly was an adjustment. But it was just the kind of a cauldron that a Yale preppy needed.

2nd Lieutenant, Field Artillery

The reason I had joined the ROTC was so that I could ride army horses to play polo. I had no plan to make the Army a lifetime occupation. I had no yen of becoming a Field Artillery officer. After a summer camp at Fort Ethan Allen in 1941 parading around in our woolen uniforms with wooden guns, perfecting our "close order drill" in 100-degree weather, occasionally firing French 75s, and attending classes on military history and tactics of war fare, I had unknowingly moved closer to becoming a second lieutenant in the Field Artillery. However, the wish to get into the most glamorous, the most sought after job in the armed forces lurked prominently in my mind; so even before I was called to duty, I put in motion, in an attempt to transfer to the Air Corps. But easier said than done.

The opposition to transfer was Colonel Dean Hudnutt, the head of the Yale ROTC unit, who had no use for the Air Corps and less use for some one who wanted to transfer from his branch of service. He figured he had trained his students to serve in the Field Artillery and he'd do his damndist to keep them in that service. There was an official regulation and procedure to allow for an officer to transfer from one service to another. But that haughty old Prima Donna Colonel who thought he was General McArthur , took my application, slipped it into his second drawer of his desk, and said "I've trained you in the Field Artillery so as far as I'm concerned your attempt to transfer is denied by me and your transfer papers will remain in my desk, period."

That really raised the hackles on my head so as soon as I could, I got in my trusty Buick and drove to the monstrous Pentagon building in Washington to the headquarters of the Air Corps. I knew no one nor had any introductions. Just blind determination. After many inquiries from various offices and parading around that monster building, I located the correct office and the officer who was in charge of processing transfers requests. I duly filled out the transfer application and submitted same for acceptance. In addition I learned that the regulations allowed one to request a transfer submitted at one's own "Area Corps Headquarters" (Illinois for me). So I went to the post office building in Chicago and put in a second application. Why not? Two is better than one. So I felt I had done all I could to circumvent that old Prima Donna bastard, Dean Hudnutt. (A few years earlier I was redressed by him for addressing him as "DEAN" instead of Colonel Hudnutt.) I thought he was Dean of the ROTC school at Yale, but that was also his first name. Could it be that he thought I was a smart ass calling him by his first name.

WAR DEPARTMENT
OFFICE OF THE UNDER SECRETARY
WASHINGTON, D. C.

April 23, 1942

Mr. David C. Wilhelm
1521 Pierson College
New Haven, Connecticut

Dear David:

Thank you for your letter of April 20th.
I am sure that after you have been in the Army for a
while you will understand why they do certain things
certain ways. It has always been that way and I am
sure it always will be.

I was very careful to go to a specific
officer in A-1 Procurement to obtain the information
which I forwarded to you in my letter of April 15th.
I think he knows his business thoroughly and you may
rely on that being the shortest route for you—the
only route. Please remember this, that in trying
this route no matter what happens you will at least
come out with your commission in Field Artillery.
What I am trying to say is that you will not lose
any time except a few weeks, perhaps. Further than
this, you will come out with what you want, a pilot's
commission in the Air Corps, in my opinion.

I am sure it is superfluous to ask you to
be patient. You probably will not be in any event.
All I will say is that you will be happier if you try
this.

My best regards, please, to your Mother and
Father when next you write.

Sincerely yours,

A. C. POTTER
Special Assistant to
Under Secretary of War

Impatience

Quite quickly just before graduation in early June of 1942, I was called to report to the FARTC (Field Artillery Replacement Training Center), at Fort Sill in lovely Lawton, Oklahoma. I was assigned to a two story barracks, with a top floor cot in a large room with many uneasy roommates. I had my footlocker and my sack; so at least, in this 30,000 soldier populated camp, I had a base. The temperature in July in Lawton hovers around 100 so the second floor barracks was even more toasty. My first assignment was to command a "Cooks and Bakers" battery. They were required to learn "close order drill" before they could be cooks or bakers. I believe they were all the mentally retarded that had been conscripted, and, since they did not know what to do with these fellows, the army decided to make them cooks. What wisdom of the THINKERS! That's why the food was so delicious! That first job was a challenge. I was in charge of these renegade dropouts. My first assignment was to train them in "close order drill". I found I had men going forward at the command "to the rear MARCH" and to the rear at the command "Forward, MARCH". In the intense Oklahoma heat, dressed in heavy woolen uniforms, living in the second floor of that barracks, the conditions and work was to say the least uninspiring. As June stretched to July and August, I was getting more entrenched in the F. A. , when in mid August I received an order to be transferred to the Field Artillery Advanced Artillery Officer's Training Course, which was one more step towards advancement and a permanent position in the Field Artillery. I had heard nothing regarding my transfer to the Air Corps-my heart hit a low point when I received the order for that transfer to the advanced Field Artillery School.

Recreation was non existent in Lawton, Oklahoma so I was fortunate to have a good friend from Andover days, Greer Hardwicke, living in Oklahoma City. He and his family were good enough to invite me on weekends to play golf and enjoy their hospitality. Besides playing golf with him (he was a scratch player), we would go to his Club for dinner. Being a DRY state everyone had their own bottle stored at the bar, which they did their best to finish it off prior to leaving for the night. Unfortunately, Greer eventually drank himself to death and died young. I was most grateful for their great hospitality they offered me. What a change from a crowded Fort Sill.

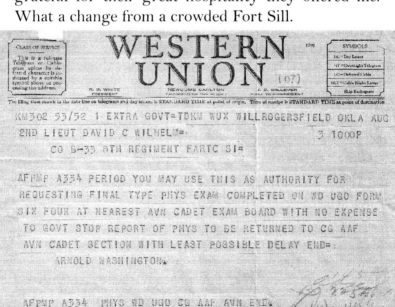

Finally the WORD

I suddenly and totally unexpected just the day before I was going to leave my beloved cooks and bakers battery and move to another assignment and location on the base to enroll in the advanced training school, I received a Western Union telegram saying "Your transfer to the Air Corps has been approved. Transfer immediately to Montgomery Field, Alabama for active duty in the United States Air Corps. Signed Arnold", the Commanding General of the Air Corps. I am sure that was not personal correspondence. What joy? I was ecstatic. I couldn't move fast enough. I had no friends that I had to say goodbye to, so in five minutes, I was packed up and off to Montgomery, Alabama. Goodbye Field Artillery and good-bye Fort Sill!

**Murray McLaughlin, Basin, WY,
DC, Howard Baetjer, Maryland,
Richard Faxon, NJ
New Officers Pilots**

ARMY AIR CORPS
MAXWELL FIELD
Montgomery Alabama

I packed up and drove east and registered for the Air Corps at Montgomery Field, Alabama. At the first orientation class for the Air Corps I noticed a fellow sitting in the front row of the class that looked so much like a friend who had visited John Coleman in Lake Forest, that I proceeded to walk to the front of the classroom and say "you look like a friend of mine called 'The Head' (Bruce Baetjer)."He responded "he's my brother". Howard Baetjer was accompanied by Dick Faxon, a classmate, and good friend of his at Princeton. I had a recent acquired friend named Murray McLaughlin, a fellow from the University of Wyoming whom I had just met. We quite quickly decided that all four of us should rent a house in Montgomery. The four of us found a pleasant little house in a quiet residential district, run by a proper formal elderly lady. She was motherly and wanted her little soldier boys to be completely comfortable. We respected her desires, wishes and dignity, so we got along very well.

Our life at Maxwell Field on the obstacle course, the class rooms, our eating together and ground school helped us four to form a close bond that lasted through the entire war. Since we were compatible, we decided we should see if we could not continue that compatibility and continue our training together. Time and again either because of random official orders, or intentional desires to assign us to different branches of the Air Corps (instructor me), bomber pilot (Murray), fighter pilot (Fax), so we had to fight to change orders so that we all went to the same squadron of a Fighter operation together. Others in the class did not seem to have the same motivation, so our attempts did not conflict with others. We accomplished this togetherness by Baetj and me pleading our case to stay together as a foursome before Generals and officers. Baej was very theatrical and put on forceful and convincing arguments stating why our happiness and good spirit would have a beneficial effect on the outcome of our being effective pilots. We stressed the importance on the happiness of pilots would have much to do with an effective air force. That was lots of Ivy League B. S.!

Thus began the unplanned association of the three of our four that lasted throughout the War. We studied, flew, anguished together in training and then flew combat together for a year.

The only lapses in our togetherness were when Howard Baetjer was shot down mistakenly over Yugoslavia by an American bomber gunner. At this point I took it upon myself to write Howard's widowed father that I had followed him down two or three thousand feet and witnessed his plane on fire. Having not seen him parachute, I assumed that he had been killed. I thought I was doing a favor for his father (who had already lost another son in the war). I obviously should not have speculated. My good intentions caused undue pain and sorrow to Mr. Baetjer. Howard did in fact "jump" and landed safely in the hands of Mihilovich's Chetniks over Yugoslavia. After a spectacular escape along with fellow allied captives, Howard returned to our squadron in good shape and eager to fly again. Unfortunately, we flew a difficult mission to Vienna and he was shot down by a Messersmidt 210 (which I witnessed) and this time after jumping, he was captured by the Nazi and sent to a Stalag Luffte prison camp for the rest of the war.

The other three of us avoided problems and stayed together. Howard's loss was a bitter blow to all of us. The four of us had formed a close warm relation. Besides flying in the same training and combat units, we played bridge, took trips to Naples, tried to pick up girls, discussed politics (we were all Republicans), and generally had great and good times together. What a plus this was for our wartime experiences.

Baetj was a nervous fellow and always seemed to have concern (rightfully) of getting washed out. He was tense at the controls and often seemed to have minor problems, such as scraping another plane with the wing of his plane while taxiing. He also was tense at the controls and just did not fly gracefully and in a relaxed fashion. I am afraid to say that I think he was not born to be a fighter pilot. In contrast Fax was a cool cat who was careless, but intrepid and relaxed in his aerial fights. His plane flowed as he had been as the left wing on the Princeton hockey team. In combat he would bate a Luftwaffe pilot and entice him into battle only to outwit him. I could hear him on the radio telephone as if he were playing with his opponent. He shot down 6 enemy fighters.

Murray, a University of Wyoming and Thermopolis, Wyoming engineer, was an excellent pilot, intelligent, calm, solid, careful, and effective. Not flashy but good.

He shot down seven enemy planes.

I was a good pilot and never a problem in my training. I was a calculating combat pilot, who attacked the enemy mainly when I thought I would have the odds with me. I did not attack a horde of enemy planes that I might come upon when the odds were badly against me. However, I would attack any group of enemy fighters if they were attacking one of our bombers. I was an effective fighter pilot who shot down either five or six enemy planes defended many American bombers from German fighters, and commanded the Squadron into battle often and the Group from time to time. (Official records say six, my count was five.) I was not shot down. I was hit by flack a couple of times-my plane not me. My crew chiefs Scotty and Richard Seick kept "The Goddess of Chase" in good shape so I had no engine problems. I am totally grateful for the caring of my planes for their good performance was a tribute to these men for neither my Spits nor Mustangs ever had engine problems or failures.

PRIMARY TRAINING
CARLSRTOM FIELD,
ARCADIA, FORIDA

Our pilot training started flying the Stearman bi-wing open cockpit plane, then to Basic Training at Bainbridge, Ga. Flying the Vultee ("Vibrator"), then to

Advanced Fling School at Marianna, Florida flying the AT-6, then to Fighter Training School at Pinellas Air Base at Clearwater Beach, Florida, flying the P-40, and finally at Advanced Fighter School at Eglin Field, Florida flying the P-40.

During that period my father compiled a booklet that reproduced the letters that I wrote to them while I was training. I have inserted certain excerpts from those letters with further details of the thoughts and what was observed at that time rather than my recollections after 66 years. This gives a different spin of those events. Sometimes facts unknowingly are distorted.

During our training we would "hanger fly" by the hours to hone up our knowledge for our ground school tests and discuss the different flying tricks that we might have learned. Our training was exciting and totally absorbing with learning how to fly and hoping not to get in any flying trouble that would get us "washed out". The numbers washed out in Primary School were a staggering 20%. Many more were eventually washed out or transferred to another branches of the Air Corps. Many, who wished to be fighter pilots, were transferred to other flying jobs, such as navigators, observation pilots, or instructors. The fighter pilot assignment was the top choice of all pilots.

Primary Flying School was at Arcadia, Florida about forty miles east of Tampa in the palmetto dry land cattle country. We flew the Stearman bi-wing plane, where the instructor's aim during the orienting first ride was to take us up and ring us out with loops, rolls, and any other maneuvers to try to terrify us and to see if we could take it, and secondly to make us deadly airsick to test our future resolve. We went through all our training as "Officers in Grade" (not Cadets). Since we already had our commissions, we wore our Field Artillery insignia and did not surrender them until we got our WINGS, when we would become Air Corps officers. This situation caused a degree of uneasiness because the cadets envied our privileges as officers and the instructor officers couldn't treat us like the cadets because we were in many cases the same rank as they. The Primary School had civilian instructor pilots besides Air Force pilots as instructors. Lo and behold one of the civilian pilots was Ken Fleming, the "Oaf", who was a good fiend of mine at Andover. He did not teach any of us, but he was a companion on our time off at Lido beach.

I quote a letter I wrote to my parents on September 28, 1942 that pretty much shows how obsessed we were on succeeding. If we washed out, we would also be assigned a boring job in the Air Corps. "My flying has been going pretty fair of late. I should solo by Friday".

"We enjoyed our weekends at the Lido in Clearwater Beach. We four bought an old 1936 Ford jalopy, put a 50 gal drum in the trunk compartment, filled it with Cudahy Packing Co. branch house (Tampa) gas, and let her roll. There was gas rationing in the United States, but our auxiliary gas tank gave us unlimited miles, even though we were carrying a lethal firebomb. Additionally our gas usage was totally illegal. I think that armed forces personnel took the attitude that one could do anything they wished provided their action did no harm to anyone else. We took huge and risky chances by taking massive violations of regulations by going AWOL for private excursions. We often would have someone else signing us in to obtain additional three day travel time. As a result we stretched three day permitted travel time to some ten days. I once went to Lake Forest when we were moving from one training base to another for about ten days. I had five days travel time, but was AWOL the rest of the time. One was not treated lightly for being AWOL, but we took the chance and none of got caught. "

BASIC FLYING SCHOOL
BAINBRIDGE- GEORGIA

Our next phase of training was flying the Vultee Vibrator at Bainbridge, Georgia. We flew a low wing dull airplane, the PT-13 (the "Vultee Fibrator"-Feb. Mar. 1943) as we slogged through terrible weather in the 1943 winter but advanced our training (aerobatics, navigation, instrument flying, aircraft maintenance). I came down with a terrible David Wilhelm cold, was grounded, and couldn't fly for two weeks. After I was cleared to fly again, my instructor was good enough to give me a cram course and catch me up with the others. He flew our training missions at 400 feet under the overhead of clouds to assist my congested head, so I did catch up with my buddies. That was a traumatic start, for two weeks it looked like my blocked ears and head suggested I would be dropped back to the next class.

November 11, 1942 a letter to my family: "Once more at another post but this time it is an army post in the true sense the housing and living conditions are poor, but the importance is in the air. One incident that caused a flare was Dick Faxon's fall out with his instructor. I think Fax had all he wanted of the fazing and told him to "shove it." He was forthwith told he would be washed out for insubordination and conduct unbecoming to an Air Corps pilot officer. Immediately Baetj and I went to the Commanding Officer and told him that Dick Faxon was a true gentleman and a credit to the Air Corps. After the CO consulted with his instructor, Fax was reassigned to a new instructor. So on we went – the four of us. "

We were glad to move on. The dreary weather, the cumbersome Vultee Vibrator, the uninspiring instructors and the anticipation of Advanced Flying School made our move a happy day.

ADVANCED FLYING SCHOOL
MARIANNA, FLORIDA

At the Advanced training school, we flew the North American AT- 6 (Marianna, F1a. Apr-May 1943), which was a big step up into a better and bigger plane. It was the first retractable gear plane that we flew, and it flew like a soaring bird, not like a wounded duck. At the Advanced training Field in Marianna, Fl. we studied and practiced on more of what we had been doing in addition to learning about aerial gunnery, dive bombing, and strafing. We by now had made pretty good progress with only about 100 days of flying. We received our Wings at its conclusion and became Air Corps Second Lieutenants. We were very proud of this because we had escaped being washed out. I certainly was far more proud of this diploma than mine at Yale.

Training became more intense with instructors expecting more and "riding" us very hard. The instructors had more flying experience and were often men of higher military rank.

November 30, 1943: "The instructors here are all flying officers but the relation between student and instructor is more military and formal

Now towards the end of this training I was getting more confident and cockier.

It is just about now that I feel I can fly this plane pretty well. We are awaiting the decision from above whether we four can be assigned to the same post after our next move. We hope to know the outcome in a few days." "We did find out because the orders were changed from different assignments and we four progressed to our next post after we had pleaded to the officer in charge of the assignment of we four together".

TRAINING SCHOOL PINELLIS AIRBASE CLEARWATER BEACH, FLORIDA

We were next transferred to Pinellas Army Air Base, Clearwater Beach, Florida for our introduction to "FIGHTERS". That base was used to check out pilots in flying fighters. Pinellas was equipped with P-40s, the Curtis WARHAWK. We had earlier thought we were going to be assigned to the P-47-the

"THUNDERBOLT" which was a tank of a plane that excelled as a ground support plane besides being an adept aerial fighter. The P-40 was scheduled to be discontinued and replaced by the North American P-51-the "MUSTANG". This plane was our dream that we unknowingly would fly within a year.

Checking out for the first time in a fighter with no instructor to hold your hand was a challenge and one of the most nervous moments I had in my flying career. All fighters used for trainers then were manned only by the pilot. You soloed alone with no instructor by your side. We spent many hours on the ground having blind fold tests, so we could put our hands blindfolded on all the instrument dials (air speed, oil temp, carb heat, wheels etc) so that when flying we could immediately and automatically focus on the desired instrument.

The Curtis P-40 was a liquid cooled lumbering old fighter that had been a valuable fighter but was getting outdated by the summer of 1943. Checking out for the first time was rather like diving off a very high diving board. It was scary. I did not know what to expect. The 1400 horse power engine made a terrible noise, stretched upwards for 8 feet in front of the cockpit window so you could not see forward while taxiing. You had to "S" the plane to see the runway as you taxied forward. The plane was unlike other planes we had ever flown, had huge torque on take off that wanted to pull you off the runway on takeoff. It had a narrow landing gear making it hard to land, and the controls were heavy and not responsive. (Later the Air Corps equipped the P-40 with an instructor seat so that an instructor could help in case of a panic attack). (And even later the Air Force had actual simulators, so you could go through the entire checkout-SIMULATED). It was very challenging taking that bird up by yourself the first time.

My text continues "The field at Clearwater on check out date was sort of a rodeo with all kinds of accidents, terrible landings and prangs (mistakes that damage the plane). I was lucky for I did all right. "

During our stay at Pinellas Army Air Base in Clearwater, we four with Murray's wife, Mary, and daughter rented a summer shack on the beach and we had a ball. We swam, got oranges at the packing plant, and frolicked with some local girls at the Yacht Club. We would finish flying late in the day, return where we would help Mary with dinner, and then go out with our lady friends. The girls were 15 to 17 years old! Cradle robbers we were. My friend was Martha Payne,

Who was a pretty little 15 years old? Fax took out her older sister (17). Usually it took a short visit with their doubtful mother before they were released. Mrs. Payne thought we were dears? We went often to the Yacht Club for entertainment.

"I might repeat one event that was pretty scary in retrospect. Once as I took off from Clearwater Pinellas airbase on a practice flight by myself and flew north in Florida hoping to "jump" a simulated enemy that might be cruising around. (Another trainee from another air base). I did get into a scrap when I dove on the "enemy" plane, swooped up underneath him and pulled up from underneath over and behind him. The only problem was at about 350 mph I hit the trailing edge of his wing leaving a tear in his aileron and knocked the Pitot tube off my plane (that was a little tube that provided the airspeed to the pilot that stuck out 35 inches on the front leading edge of my wing). This damage was confirmed on the ground by the "enemy plane" having a gash on his aileron and my plane having lost its pitot tube. The significance is that was as close as one could get to a mid air collision. At that speed we both would have been dust had I been a foot closer to him. I think I had to change my underwear after that adventure."

ADVANCED FIGHTER TRAINING EGLIN FIELD, FLORIDA

The main effort here at this base was to hone in on strafing, dive bombing, and aerial gunnery. I did well in the strafing and dive bombing, but did have problems in the aerial gunnery. A tow plane pulled a fifteen foot sleeve and I would fly parallel but going in the opposite direction and then at the correctly timed moment do a wing over so I would then have a shot at the target. This involved timing and having your plane perfectly coordinated so your shots would follow the direction you had sighted. (The plane could not be in slip or yaw, since you fired between the propellers the direction that the plane pointed). This was difficult for me.

And so the time had come to ship overseas- we went first to the Distribution area of Tallahassee to be assigned to the staging area at Newport News on June 17, 1943 (one year after induction). Mother and Father came down to see their confident little son off to we knew not where. (That meeting was the last time I saw my father before his death.) I know I was full of flying talk for that's all we had been living for ten months. They probably were not infatuated with that, but I am sure they were proud of their little 130# boy.

13

TRAINING IN
MOROCCO

Now we were getting closer to getting into action. After a tortuously long stay at the staging area, we finally shipped out of Newport News on the Empress of Australia (an old pleasure ship). We officers were in charge of cramming some 4000 soldiers in every cranny of the ship and then we set off alone–not in a convoy. The idea was we could outrun any German sub attack. (Very questionable for that old tub). The fifth night, when I was on volunteer watch, I spotted an explosion on the eastern horizon, which I duly reported. Our ship turned south and jigged and zagged for twenty-four hours taking precaution that a torpedo might be heading our way. Then we proceed into Casablanca- a day late. An American baby flattop had intercepted the German sub, which was waiting in ambush for our ship to arrive and to destroy us. The flattop apparently sank the Sub. That flare on the horizon was that event that I reported.

A few days later I met on the streets of Casablanca by chance, Pleasure Bent, a Lake Forest good tennis-playing friend of mine and naval officer, who had been on that flattop ship that sunk the sub so the whole incident was substantiated by him. As far as I am concerned, he was at the right place at the right time. He invited us four for dinner on his ship for a welcomed Navy meal with milk and ice cream! Oh, that Navy eats well. So we arrived in Morocco in good shape and ready for further training and grateful that we had avoided the net of submarines waiting to greet us.

There was real excitement after our six day trip as the Queen of Australia moved quietly into Casablanca harbor. We had sailed that crossing with the ship totally blacked out from dusk to dawn. It was eerie. The beauty of the harbor surrounded by Moroccan white buildings was marred only by the prow of the "Jean Bart" sticking up through the still water. The French battleship had been scuttled upon the surrender of the French fleet by Admiral Darlan. The 4000 troops jammed into the crowded steamy hold of our ship were truly grateful to breathe the fresh air after their days of entrapment. We officers had it easy for we were upside, crowded into passenger cabins with the privilege of going out on deck when we wished. We even had an Aussie "cabin boy", "Icky", who tried to help us.

After disembarking in Casablanca we loaded into trucks for a one hour drive out to the desert near a town called Ber Recheed about twenty miles from Casablanca. The air force tent camp was in the sand with only a few Palm trees that did not protect us from the 100 degree plus tortuous hot wind. We were protected from the sun by our four man canvas tent that seemed to magnify the heat inside; so it was hard to see if one was better inside or outside. We had water and latrine facilities nearby and mosquito nettings over our cots so we were in good shape. The dry desert evenings cooled the weather as the sun retreated so sleeping was good.

The airfield was merely a big sand-dust field with no defined runway, but just a large area where we could land and take off in any direction depending upon the wind. The weather was dry and hot which encouraged dust from the Sahara desert to drift through the area. The takeoffs and landings of the many plane's propellers increased the dust in the air.

The field housed tired P-40s, Spitfire Mark Vs, a few P-38s and the ever present C-47s passenger/cargo plane. Many of these planes had seen service in combat so they had seen maximum use before shipping to this training base in a tired condition.

We had little contact with the native Arabs, who were prohibited by armed sentries from entering our camp. They had an inclination to steal anything they could carry away. At all times, however, the Arabs begged us to sell them our mattress covers, which made wonderful robes for them. The best-dressed Arab was one who wore a United States mattress cover!

There was a Caheed just off our field, who lived in a circular walled villa adorned with green lawns, Palm trees, and water fountains. We imagined he was served by lovely graceful Arab beauties waving palm frawns to cool him. We did our best to make aerial snoops of his Villa, but as far as I know, he never deigned to invite any of us to his spot or visit us. We tried our hardest to try to figure how to get an invitation into that palace but we came up blank.

We four had our own tent so we had our foursome together as we sweltered in the day time on our cots. At night when the mosquitoes seem to emerge, we were all encased on our cots with our nets tucked in to keep those little fellows from inoculating us with malaria. We gulped Atabrin, the successor to Quinine, to immunize us if we got bitten outside our safety nets.

Soon after arriving at Ber Reechid and, after settling into our quarters, we four were assigned to a training squadron equipped with the Curtiss P-40 War Hawk. The P-40 was a faithful old fighter having been the celebrated fighter used by General Claire Chennault's "Flying Tigers" in China. It was a durable fighter in Italy, Europe and the Western Pacific. In 1943 the airplane was outdated. Too slow, heavy on the controls, awkward, and unresponsive to the pilot's commands. The P-40s at our training post were beat-up-back-from-combat warriors. Their engines were so tired, if you missed your landing and you had to go around (for another attempt to land), since your wheels and flaps were down, the planes had so much drag that their tired old engines often did not have the poop to make it around for another try. One often was forced to land in the desert which was usually uncomfortable and sometimes disastrous. That was a big incentive to make a good landing on the first try. The P-40 was powered by a liquid cooled engine with inadequate ground cooling ability so that one had barely five minutes to start up the engine, taxi into takeoff position, and takeoff or the plane would overheat and the flight had to be aborted. The searing heat of the desert required that we fly in the cool air of the dawn or dusk to prevent the engine from overheating.

We were grateful to be able to augment our 50 hours of P-40 flying in Florida, but we did not look forward to flying that old bird in combat. Since there were Spitfire Vs on the field, we voted to see if we could transfer to them. The Spit V was the famous British fighter that defeated the Luftwaffe in the Battle of Britain and therefore prevented the Nazis from invading Great Britain. We chose Baetj to plead our case. So Howard took out his crying towel, got in his Jeep, and traveled two hundred miles to NATOUSA, the flight command center of the USAir Forces in Africa, and met a top dog General, and pleaded our case. He approached the Commanding Officer to plead our case that we stay together and should fly the Spit. "Our morale would be deflated, our spirit broken if we had to fly that old P-40 warrior. " He continued "that ever since we had started flying, we have dreamt of flying the Spit. " Howard's appeal was heard, the papers were cut, and we were transferred to a Spitfire Squadron.

We were proud of our new plane and enjoyed the connection with the Royal Air Force. For some haughty reason we felt superior to those American fellows in those P-40s flying with that American flying equipment. Something about the romance of the RAF crept into our minds. We thought we had now been equipped better with British flying gear-helmet, Mae West's, radio equipment, new oxygen masks and a Spitfire Mark V.

We checked out in this tricky little plane that was quite different from an American plane. At the top of the "stick" there was a 6" loop/handle where you controlled the rudders, ailerons and the brakes. On the stick were two squeeze holds that activated the right or left air brakes. The brakes were effective for a couple of squeezes until there was no more braking action.

This meant judicious use of your braking power. If you "overused" and expended all the air power on your first use of the brakes, you were S. O. L. if you needed more brake as you rolled down the runway. You had to carefully use the throttle and rudder to maneuver the plane's direction down the runway. On the American aircraft the hydraulic brakes were activated by depressing the rudder pedals. The landing gears of the Spit were close together, so there was less stability than with a wide gear of American planes, so ground loops were quite easy to accomplish. The Spit was light, quick, and responsive (just the opposite to the P-40). In the air it would climb quickly, turn on a dime, and cruise at about 180 MPH. The Spit was a great defensive plane, if not a star on the offense. If a German plane chose to stay around and fight, it was in deep trouble because the Spit was so maneuverable that it could evade the oncoming enemy with an abrupt turn. But if the Spit had to pursue a fleeing German, it was often too slow to catch him. It was primarily a defensive fighter.

Me in Spitfire V

We flew this graceful little bird around beautiful New Mexico-like Moroccan scenery which had clear skies, low mountains, and great visibility. We would do our flying at dawn or dusk as we skimmed around over the mountains and desert. We became familiar with the airplane. We had no particular training in tactics, gunnery, or formation flying. We were just trying to get so we could fly the Spit well and get to know all of its tricks.

One sunny day the entire squadron (12 planes) lined up "line abreast", as race horses in England line up before a race, ready for takeoff waiting for the order "take off", when everyone in the line gives their plane the throttle ("pushes the tit"), and hopefully proceeds straight ahead so as not to cross in front of either the plane on one's right or left. It behooved each pilot to keep even with the others so that he did not get engulfed with the dust from a plane in front of him. Unfortunately, one time I lost control of my plane as it veered sharply to the left. I luckily did not collide with another plane as I staggered into the air going in a different direction from my companions. I missed the planes to my left. I must have veered behind them. I could so easily have collided with another Spit in that swirl of dust. The error was mine. I was fortunate that I did have a collision and did not terminate my future with the Air Corps.

Most of our flying was unsupervised by instructors so we took liberties that I now know we should not have. I am not proud of the fact that on many of our "training flights" as we returned home towards evening and the Arabic camel trains were returning to their encampments, we would drop down on the "deck" and buzz the slow moving camel trains. A second target was the Berber tent that would barely survive the wind blast from our plane as we skimmed over the tops of the tents. We thought it fun to see the Arab rider jump off his camel probably in some terror. How to win friends? I am sure those antics engendered hatred towards the ugly American. I am ashamed that I was part of this.

The 31st Fighter the Group, equipped with the Spit, flew their first operational flight while covering the English landing and evacuation from France in the ill-fated Dieppe raid. The 31St scored the first kill of any American fighter plane in the European theater. Our Group continued to fly the Spit till 1944 when it was replaced by the P-51 MUSTANG. We four were assigned, upon landing in Italy, to the 309th Squadron of the 31st Fighter Group, the oldest and best-known fighter group of the United States Air Force. We were all ecstatic of our assignment for it eventually meant we would be equipped with the P-51 Mustang when the Spit became outmoded.

There was little recreation during the day time in this desert spot outside of Ber Resheed. We developed lots of great ideas and philosophic conversations, as we laid low from the heat of the day. After our evening flight we would often try to engineer a ride in a truck to Casablanca. Then our search was for someplace to eat and have a drink.

Our best find was the Chez Blanche restaurant. There we reveled in good couscous and marginal Moroccan wine. Even though we marveled at how good the lamb was, we were quite shocked as we exited through the dirt floor kitchen to see the carcass from which we had eaten was lying on the floor covered with flies. But tasty food was hard to come by so this vision did not dull our appreciation of the meal. It was still a treat compared to the Mess at our camp. (French toast cooked two hours before serving and cold and three hour cold fried eggs).

The invasion of Sicily took place on July 10, 1944. The Allied forces were under the command of General Eisenhower, with General Alexander the operational commander. The Allied forces had defeated the Germans in Sicily and were ready for the landing on Italian shores. Towards the end of the Sicilian battle, General flamboyant George Patton, the Seventh Army Commander, caused a real rumpus when he slapped a soldier because he accused him of being a coward. General Eisenhower promptly fired his friend Patton for his action and denied his command of ground forces in Italy. Patton and Eisenhower were old West Point friends and Patton was an able aggressive commander. The action by Eisenhower was courageous, correct and difficult. Patton eventually was granted command of the Armed Forces that landed in southern France and subsequently led the American Forces into the occupation of Berlin.

Our squadron received orders to move planes, tents, kitchens, armaments and everything able to be moved to a new location, namely Berteaux, Algeria. We were thus in position to move up to be nearer to the anticipated landing in Italy. The World War I "40- and 8"- (40 men and 8 horses) old French railroad cars were loaded for the week's long trip with pilots and other Air Corps personnel. The flat cars were guarded by troops riding on each car to protect the baggage from the thieving Arabs. The trip was no picnic. Not only was riding on the flat cars uncomfortable, but essentials such as food, water, bedding were at best marginal. As you can imagine this was no express ride, for the train crawled for about a week to make this 500 mile trip. Even with protection and caution against thievery, the train arrived stripped of much of what was originally loaded. Apparently the pilots who had first arrived at Ber Recheed were chosen to ferry the Spits and P-40s to the new airfield near Algiers, while all the newer pilots and ground personnel had the pleasure of riding the train. Luckily I was chosen to fly.

Each "ferry Pilot" flew independently, each responsible for finding his way across Africa. That does not seem so difficult today, but to a greenhorn pilot with no navigation aids, a questionable map and limited time in the Spit, it gave me some qualms. My first stop after a three hours flight was Oran. It had a busy airfield with planes from many countries and many languages.

After refueling, I taxied out to continue the safari and stood at the end of the runway ready for the tower's order to "take off". After a couple of minutes, I was cleared for takeoff. I pushed the throttle forward, started gaining speed, but not down the runway, but on a 30 degree bearing to the left through the parking area of tied down planes. I was not trying to dodge anything, just getting the wild animal off the ground before I collided with a parked plane. Luckily I escaped the collision, got airborne and, although considerably shaken, I proceeded on my way without problems.

I arrived after a refuel stop in Algiers and then on to our new camp and airfield. We continued our familiarization flying, as we waited for orders to move up. The weather was more friendly and cooler; so we tried to be patient as we waited.

While in Berteau we were given time off to have a little R & R. Four of us pilots (George Loving, Fax and Ed Lyman) rented a little apartment for a couple of days directly opposite the Aleddi Hotel in Algiers which was very colorful. The town was white and gleaming, surrounding a lovely harbor outlined by the blue Mediterranean in the background. The city was a great place to stroll, with troops all resplendent in their various military uniforms. The Aleddi Hotel had a great promenade of steps leading to an entrance that was adorned with many attractive looking young Algerian ladies who were selling their well endowed bodies to eager soldiers for small fees. I am not sure how many contracted any of the prevalent diseases, but I am sure many disregarded the risk. We drank with abundance the fresh Spumonte (the local Champagne), eventually got cramps and diarrhea, a huge hangover the next morning, only to recover, and then go at it again the next day with the same aggressiveness. That was R & R.

The Casual Pilot in his Spit

While meandering around the streets in Algiers one day, I ran into George Haines who was also just touring the city. He was a good friend from Yale, who was stationed on a hospital ship in the harbor. The next day apparently his ship was hit by a German bomb and sunk. Trying to save one of his companions swimming around in the water, George drowned. I did not hear about this until after the War. His widow, Audie, after the War married my close friend, Bobby Johnson with whom I played polo for four years.

After a couple of weeks of flying and taking our last tune-up before being called up, we anxiously awaited our call to join a fighting unit in Sicily or Italy. General Patton and Montgomery were chasing the Germans from Sicily, so we anticipated Italy would be our destination soon. During this waiting period, the CO at our airfield was very disturbed with us pilots because so many planes had been dinged or damaged. "We just can't tolerate losing more planes due to mistakes". He announced that the next time anyone made a bonehead mistake, he would be reassigned and sent back to the States. Sure enough Dick Faxon landed "wheels up" the next day, thereby creaming the whole belly of his Spit. Once again after the Commanding officer told Fax he was on his way, the following day we four approached and pleaded with him that Fax be spared. The Air Force most certainly would be losing an exceptionally good pilot. We won the argument and so the four of us continued on together and Fax was not sent home.

We loaded into a C-47(DC-3) along with a handful of other replacement pilots, on August 31 1943, which was just 12 months after we were first enlisted in the Air Corps. It seemed longer than that with the many experiences and new horizons we continually faced. We stopped at Palermo, Sicily to inquire whether the grass airstrip at Monte Corvino, Italy had been secured by the American ground forces that had just landed at Salerno. I for one got airsick as the old tub bounced around on its trip. You would have thought that with all the flying I had recently done that that would not happen.

The American and British had landed a large invasion force on Salerno Beach a week before we landed at our air field to begin the assault on "the soft underbelly" of the Nazis. The Germans anticipated the invasion at that location so the ensuing battle was a bloody affair. After the Allies had secured the beachhead, the Italian government surrendered, King Emanuel resigned, and Italy became a questionable ally of the Allies. With the grass airstrip secured, we landed at Monte Corvino and were soon billeted in a bombed out ruined building adjoining the landing strip. We slept on the hardest of any concrete floors in this building. The Germans were still in the hills east of us some ten miles away in the town of Battapaglia , so they kept us alert by dropping a few ineffective artillery shells on us. The field was littered with destroyed Italian planes and other signs of war. Training was finished. We were ready to fly against the German Luftwaffe. We were hyped up eager and ready to go.

14

COMBAT

Now in Italy we were ready for what we volunteered for and what we had been in training for the last twelve months. We had no trepidation about our forthcoming flying against the Germans. We were so eager we did not recognize our innocence of our future duties. We had flown the Spit enough in Africa so that we had confidence that we had the flying skill and we had the airplane that was up to the challenge of the main Germans fighters, the FW-190 or the ME-109. We were just sure we could handle the combat ahead.

Spitfire

Our Super Marine Spitfire was built by the British to intercept German bombers as they tried to bomb the British into submission in the "Battle of Britain". The plane was tailored for what it had to do. Climb quickly, turn sharply, avoid German attackers, shoot with either two canons or two 30 Caliber machine guns, and have adequate speed to penetrate the oncoming German bombers. Since it was flying above its own homeland, it carried a small amount of gas to conserve weight that allowed it to ascend quickly into the altitude that the Germans were flying for a quick skirmish and then descend to be refueled and ready for another sortie. In addition, the proximity to friendly land above which they were flying made parachuting and forced landings more desirable from the pilot's survival than over hostile country. The pilot could get a new plane and go back into action quickly. If the Allies attained air supremacy and controlled the skies, the invasion of Great Britain by the Germans would be thwarted. The preservation of Great Britain prohibited their home land from being overrun and occupied, and preserve the base for the staging of the Allies arsenal for their invasion of Europe.

The Royal Air Force did ultimately achieve that victory and as Winston Churchill said, "Never have we owed so much to so few"–the pilots of the RAF who beat off the Germans" in the so-called "Battle of Britain". The British air victory was possibly the turning point of World War II, because Hitler cancelled the Nazi's invasion of Great Britain because of the loss of air control to the British. As a result the American and Allied forces began building massive ground forces in Great Britain, and a large armada of fighter aircraft and heavy bombers to eventually confront the Axis on their home ground.

In 1944, the Allies were struggling fighting both the Japanese in the Pacific and Nazis on the mainland of Europe. The huge Russian army was grinding up the elite German divisions at the gates of Stalingrad, the Germans had tasted defeat in Africa and were losing the Italian warfare, and had lost the Battle of Britain, so they too were being pushed in all directions. Names of famous defeats for the Germans were being etched in history in this period: El Alemain; Salerno; Ploesti; Monte Cassino; Riva Ridge; Stalingrad; Berlin and others. It was apparent that the Nazi's power was being eroded and that the Allies, even though taxed, were gradually gaining the upper hand.

The German high command with Hitler, Goebbel, Goring, and others in attendance, held an emergency meeting to discuss what action should be taken now that they had lost their fight for air supremacy. Unbeknown to those attendees was a secret plot had been hatched, to blow up Der Fuehrer as he sat at the conference table. A bomb did go off, but Hitler only suffered minor wounds and the assassination attempt failed. Had Hitler been killed, the Germans might have sued for peace. The perpetrators had planned to sue for peace with the Allies. General Rommel, a trusted field officer of Der Fuehrer and former hero of the German Army in Africa, was one of those involved in the plot and Hitler shortly learned of his involvement and forced his subsequent suicide. That event ended any attempted peace overtures. Think of the consequences had the plot been successful. There was a good possibility a peace might have been concluded and much of the destruction of European cities and humanity spared.

The landing in Italy at the Salerno beach (September 1, 1943) on the southern boot of Italy was Winston Churchill's plan to pierce the "soft underbelly" of Germany, march north through Italy, and then hit Hitler's Germany in it's middle. Churchill was forced to use his best persuasive powers to convince Roosevelt and Marshall that this major use of Allied resources was the prudent thing to do. After strenuous discussions, Churchill won. The alternative landing in Italy did divert German ground forces from the Russian front. The mission of our 31st Fighter group was to protect our advancing ground forces of the 5th Army as they moved north in the Italian boot against the German Armies.

Back to us. We were flying the original Spit V when we arrived at our airstrip at Monte Corvino, a location south of Naples and a few minutes from the Salerno beachhead. Murray, Fax, Baetj and I were all there together. (My wife Jean and I flew over from Palermo, Sicily in 2001 to see again the airfield, but no one in that area knew about it-probably turned into a housing development). How quickly memories fade.

We were ready, excited, and wondering when our first combat flight would be, and how tough it might be. The pilots that we replaced were burnt out and anything but encouraging about our safety, survival, or our ability. They were bored, waiting for their reassignment to the States, and seemed to be more interested in poker than their flying duty. They were not good welcomers.

At this time there was controversy over the continuance of American pilots flying the Spit. We new pilots had great confidence in our Spit as reflected in my log. October 2, 1943–"One thought has occurred in my mind and that concerns the switch of Spits to P-51's. Apparently, prior to our arrival in Italy, General Arnold & decision makers favored Americans flying American equipment, and they did not appreciate us Americans praising to the heavens of the Spit and making an illustrious record. To them the U. S. was building the best of equipment so we should be flying such. A Major Hill, the group C.O. with the absolute backing of all his pilots refused to surrender the Spits for P-51s on three successive occasions and thus aroused the ire of the high command. Hill was replaced by Colonel McCorkle, a young, 32 year old, West Point graduate, who flew P-39s in Alaska and P-51s at an O.T.U. in Bartow, Fla." He too favored the Spits, so his superiors agreed to continue the Spits, but nonetheless the high command did accelerate the P-51 delivery to replace the Spit squadrons eventually.

The Allied troops met the Germans dug in at Solerno Bay with their "88s", a German effective artillery piece, as the Allied landing crafts approached the beach. The slaughter was brutal, even so the Brits and Americans were able to establish a beachhead, land additional troops, and thus establish a foothold in Italy. The Germans retreated from the beachhead to the mountains around the town of Battapaglia where their artillery fired on the beachhead and our airfield.

I strolled down from our airfield to examine the aftermath of the landing. There I met a British officer as he sat in his pup tent. He invited me to have a cup of tea, while I talked about him, his family, the landing, and the British regulations for their troops. Subsequently, I had tea with him three or four more times. He was modest, humble, polite, and war experienced. He was a veteran of many months of battle in the Desert War with Montgomery against Rommel in North Africa, and as he told me, "I will stay in the army as will all my soldiers until we die or the war is over". No furloughs or rotation or termination because of longevity of service. In contrast when American pilots got "battle fatigue", they were removed from action and given time off or reassigned to training units. The Air Corps established that before a pilot was relieved of flying, he would have to fly 25 missions as a bomber pilot and 50 as a fighter pilot. The Brits procedure was to send one home when the war was finished. In my opinion as soon as a pilot could visualize the end, he became more fatigued and exhausted. I believe that setting those limits caused psychological change of attitude, rather than real fatigue. If you thought you were going home after 50 missions, you became increasingly more exhausted the closer you got to the 50th mission. But those Brits had no set timetable for finishing their duty, and as a result they just carried on. No bragging, just continuing until they were reassigned or killed. We were coddled by comparison. I believe that many of our pilots became less effective towards the end of their combat duty when they saw the end ahead. The Brits may have tired out, but I think the quality of their work continued till they were terminated by injury or reassignment.

Our four next to captured Italian fighter at Monte Corvino, Italy 1943

Our airfield showed signs of war. Bombed buildings, burned airplanes and trucks lined the runway. The town was wrecked and in shambles with no shops, running water or people. We had been seeing and hearing about this, but "seeing believes". There were operative Italian and German fighter planes that had been abandoned along the side of the field. We were fascinated to see the planes we would fight right there in front of us. Of particular fascination was the Italian Macchi fighter whose propeller turned counterclockwise. As a result of this, the torque tended to pull one, when advancing power to the engine, to the right rather than to the left as in American planes. The result was that corrections by the pilot required opposite applications of controls than he had been trained. One of our pilots flew the Macchi without any problems having been cautioned of this difference.

Because of the Italian weather, it took almost a month until we flew our first orientation flight on a trip around the Naples area. The Italian skies continued to dump buckets of water on our field, so we just became ever more anxious and did not fly. We had dances with the nurses from the neighboring field hospitals that entailed everyone poring down Italian gin, vermouth, and cognac as we danced to a victrola in one small room. The men and gals started drinking, and the party started to swing, soon only 15 people remained inside. Where did they go? My date was a Margaret Mitchell of the 95th Evac. Hospital. I don't know about the girls, but I ended up with a hangover to beat all. During this period of inactivity we played bridge and attended questionable movies. October 7, 1943–"Tonight in the large hanger we had the presentation of "Star-Spangled Rhythm", a batch of shorts. The seats were oil barrels, boxes etc. on a flooded floor. The screen for the film was the shrapnel marked wall. The public address or announcer system was such that only about 2% of the people could hear. Of course, the projector & system was delayed an hour and a half to get it going, and after struggling thru the film hearing only bits of speech, the electricity went off and the film ended with about 1/3 to go. The operators tried hard to put on the show, but there were too many strikes against them.

I took a Jeep tour with Fax, Baetj, Murray, and Ed (Lyman), to Pompeii, Vesuvius, Batapaglio (completely leveled), and Eboli (center of town leveled). We saw the results of war's destruction on all these small Italian cities. To while away the days, Ed Lyman and I bought some Italian School dictionaries and spent hours trying to quiz each other on the vocabularies of these Italian texts. We did not learn much, but we were a mile ahead of our cohorts and we were able to make an attempt of conversation with local Italians.

I was amazed that we were so close to the front lines of the ground troops. We were possibly 10 miles from the Front. I always thought we would be at airfields considerably out of harm's way. We did receive scant hostile fire in spite of this proximity. One or two shells from their 88s were aimed at our airfield, but no damage resulted.

As the Allies (American, English, Polish, Italian, African, and other troops) moved north towards

Rome, the 31st Fighter group was stationed at airfields close to the "Front" so as to be able to provide help quickly upon demands from the ground forces. After a month we moved from Monte Corvina to Pomigliano only a few miles north of Naples. We flew our planes north to our new location in a drizzly, low overcast, 1/4 mile visibility day. The field was surrounded by barrage balloons (to protect the field from the German planes that flew into our traffic pattern); so we were forced to weave our way through the cables hanging from the balloons to land. Since the Germans had pock bombed the concrete runway, we were forced to land on an adjoining mud runway amidst puddles, holes, and other surprises. I do recall my plane careened and slithered on landing but I did not ground loop or crackup. It was a difficult flight for a green horn, since I was inexperienced in flying in such hairy conditions. I was happy getting back on the ground.

The Pomigliano Air Field runway was repaired in a couple of days and thus became the only paved runway in that sector of Italy, and so the field became an unbelievably busy place. Polish observation planes (P-38s), Spitfires, P-40s and P-38 fighter squadrons, British dive bombers (A-36), medium bombers (B-25 and B-26) squadrons all used the one small concrete strip. In addition, freight and supplies were constantly being flown in by dozens of C-47s. Everyone needed landing and takeoff slots. The planes were flown by pilots of different nationalities all speaking their own tongues or very poor English. This made for confusion and impossible radio communication. It was complete mayhem.

DC, Murray, Baetj, Fax
Pomigliano, Italy

When we were not flying we would be assigned to the "Control Tower" to direct the air traffic and try to maintain some degree of order and safety. Since we had very erratic and limited radio communication with many of the planes because of the language diversity and marginal radio equipment, we would control takeoff and landings by firing red and green flares from a Very gun. It looked like the fourth of July firing rockets into the sky. As you can imagine this was a rather inexact method of controlling the traffic. Around the field circling were C-47s waiting to land, hoping for a gap in the runway usage. Since the combat planes had priority in landing and takeoffs, the cargo planes often desperately low on gas would circle like a hawk looking for that field mouse, and then when the runway was free, all the cargo planes would dive with abandon for the runway. Many times the C-47s were so close to each other landing that there were eight airplanes landing on the runway right next to or behind each other at the same time. Add to this confusion MADDAY (M'Aidez) calls from planes shot up from enemy fire were coming in to land completely out of control. They would just burst into the field in desperation and land. I recall one B25 coming in out of control careening down the runway and crashing in flames about thirty feet from me, as I was the acting air traffic control officer. What do you think the present day air traffic control officers at our large airports would think of this type of rodeo?

Very occasionally we saw the top brass. "Thursday, October 21, 1943—At the airfield before a flight of our squadron, I noticed 4 Star General's car so I investigated. Found that Lt. General Mark Clark was waiting Ike Eisenhower's arrival of his Fortress for a meeting. Eventually I found Gen. Clark saying to me, "Lovely weather these days, Lieutenant, isn't it?" Being educated at Yale, I knew that was the cue, so up I walked. The General then said "My name's Clark. " After a short handshake with notable lack of interest from the multitude of photographers, I said "My name's Wilhelm". For a few minutes he asked with whom I flew, said what a good job we were doing, discussed the difficulty of fighting in the rainy and hilly land, and said we'd be to Rome by Christmas. He was a fine looking, six feet two, erect soldier who had a most genial and friendly way of talking. I then shot a candid camera shot of Ike and Mark as the former climbed from his private Fortress. "

ROAD TO ROME

As the realization that the Road to Rome had to be opened up by penetrating the blockage of the Liri valley by the Germans, warfare became more intense. Both the Allies and Germans became bogged down and concentrated in the Monte Cassino area 50 miles north of Naples. Our squadron moved once again to a more forward airfield, Castel Volturno, located near enough to the front lines so that we could hear and see the artillery firing. This "field" was located just south of the Volturno River. Our airfield exhibited the resourcefulness of the Air Force engineers as they created a landing field in the middle of the Pontine Marshes. They laid a chain strip down in the wet marshy ground for the landing strip to enable the relatively light Spitfire to be able to land and takeoff and be located near the action. It behooved the pilot not to run off the runway on takeoff or landing or he would find himself in deep doo-doo- probably upside down or worse. That sometimes was a challenge because of the narrow short strip in addition to strong cross winds from the Tyrrhenian Sea.

During this period the flying was slow because of the inclement weather. Up to this time we had little opposition so our "patrols" were boring and dull. On November 26, we were resupplied with new Spitfire IX. It had a big Rolls Royce engine which gave it greater abilities. It could climb far faster than the Spit V, turn on a dime, and fire its guns with greater authority. Its speed was increased some 60 m. p. h over its older sister. Its limitation was it was not a long range fighter because of lack of fuel capacity. Compared to the ME-109 or Focke-Wolffe 190, it was the better plane. With this new powerhouse we just wished we would find greater opposition. I had flown from September 2 to November 27 a total of only 30 operational hours, but now with our new plane and with the ground struggle intensity at Cassino and the mouth of the Liri Valley; we knew we were going to see action.

BATTLE AT
CASINO

In this environment and with the Italian winter drizzle, we flew escort for the 12th Air Force's medium bombers (B-25 and B-26) and missions protecting the Allied troops over central Italy. The main German divisions had retreated north to entrench themselves in defensive positions at the mouth of the Liri Valley guarded by the historic Abbey Cassino, the only feasible land route to Rome. To the east were rugged mountains and to the west the Tyrrhenian Sea. Because of the effectiveness of the German fortified positions dug in caves, the Germans stopped the Allied advance cold. An American attempt to pierce the German lines was an attempt to cross the Rapido River, which ended up with the slaughter of some 1000 Allied troops in one night. Later historians criticized Gen. Clark's decision to even attempt to try the crossing since the German's 88 canons were dug in expecting the American attempt. The Allies also tried to directly assault the Germans at the entrance to the valley, but were unsuccessful in penetrating their defense. The Germans also used the ancient sacred Abbey Cassino monastery as a sanctuary for its troops and storage of armaments. It had been a resolve of the Allied Armies to preserve the Abbey, but because of the Germans were using it as a military munitions depot, the U.S. Air Force, after a considerable amount of debate with all their resources including our 309th Squadron (fighters strafing, medium and heavy bombers) pulverized the ancient Abbey. (December 2-4, 1943). The size and intensity of the assault left a pall of smoke and dirt that concealed the construction below. It was a regrettable action, but it did clear the way for the advance of the Allied Armies.

On Pearl Harbor Day the Luftwaffe brought forth their fighters as the Cassino Battle raged and finally we mixed it up with them. "December 7, 1943 - Today was one the 309th biggest battles in our Spitfire flying days. Today a flight of six Spits jumped twelve ME-109s & tore all hell out of them. The Setting: In the present Allied push towards Cassino, one main artery of supply—a paved road—was crammed hub to hub with trucks & therefore, a logical target for Jerry. Thus, Hobnail Yellow was patrolling that immediate vicinity to keep Jerry away & allow the trucks to roll unmolested. Sure enough, about 3 o'clock Hobnail Yellow spotted some MEs at 9000 feet right after they dodged through some clouds circling before they dove to bomb and strafe. The show started with B-stock (Blumenstock) and Ainsley hitting two sections with

Ainsley getting two, B-stock one. Captain Jared then came roaring down, pulled up on one, starting shooting, when the plane ahead of the one he was shooting at blew up, & then he got the other fellow, as he started to flame & the plane went into the ground with a crash. Captain Jared then got hopped by another turned on him, fired (with 30s only), and didn't claim him. Harry Barr dropped down, chased another, & shot him down. The box score: 12 MEs attacked by 6 Spits: 6 MEs destroyed; 2 probables. Spits no losses; a real day, and everyone celebrated that evening with a big party. By this action we (the 309th) again went into the lead of planes Destroyed, Probables and Damaged in the Mediterranean theater, and this gave spirit and pride to all. This was a good way to celebrate Pearl Harbor Day. "

Even that massive assault did not break the German defenses. The Allied command realized another approach was necessary to break that defensive line.

THE ANZIO LANDING

That new plan was to flank that impenetrable fortified line of defense. The Allied command decided to make an amphibious landing at Anzio (some 50 miles northwest of the destroyed Monte Cassino) thereby flanking the German entrenched positions at Cassino thus causing their retreat north up the Lire Valley. The Allied Forces landed on the broad beaches of Anzio with no opposition from the Germans. The lack of opposition was a complete surprise. For over two days there was no response from the Germans. After their determined defense at Cassino, this lack of action stunned the Allies. Unbelievably General Clark decided to consolidate his position to prepare for a counter offense by the Germans. This decision was conservative but extremely controversial. It has been asserted in retrospect that the Allies could easily have proceeded north, captured the symbolic city of Rome and established a new defensive line north of the City. Since the Allies chose the defensive position at the beachhead, the Germans were given time to bring in large numbers of troops who then formed a cordon around the beachhead and kept the Allies contained for six months. They dug in artillery and tightened the noose on our beachhead. The decision not to take advantage of the lack of German opposition has been widely criticized. Instead the Allies were pinned down on the beachhead for some six months. General Clark was responsible for this faulty and costly decision.

With the German blockade of our troops, our air opposition increased dramatically as the Luftwaffe attacked the Allied troops within the beachhead and we patrolled the area to minimize their effectiveness. We had plenty of action. In the questionable vision of our Air Force, it was decided to base a squadron of Spits within the beachhead on a short landing strips so there could be immediate counter responses to enemy assaults. We drew straws to see which Squadron of our Group (31st Fighter group) would be the "lucky" one for that dubious privilege-the 309th was spared. The Germans had artillery in place in the surrounding hills with their guns leveled into the entire beachhead and particularly onto the airfield. After destroying many planes and pilots this bright idea was cancelled. Dick Faxon once flying a mission north of Anzio, when he ran low on gas he was forced to land on the little strip within the beachhead. He said as soon as he touched down, the artillery of the Germans looking down from the hills, started shelling him. He jumped frantically from his plane as it rolled to a stop and ran for cover as the shells finally hit their mark-but without Fax. The strip was soon abandoned because the Germans were just having a "duck shoot" and destroying pilots and Spits.

Fax in his Spit

I had a few particularly interesting flights. On one mission I was chasing a single FW-190 and closing in on him, when all of a sudden, he did a hammerhead stall in front of me. That maneuver required the pilot to chop the throttle, pull the plane up vertically until it stalled and then let the plane head down. By doing this he slowed down and then dropped down to a position to my rear into firing position. That fellow was obviously a very experienced pilot and, as I heard, was a member of the famed Hermann Goring squadron. I lost the initiative, but with some violent evasive action I escaped his shots.

During the occupation of the Anzio beachhead, we had considerable action. Many of the pilots of the 309th got their first confirmed kills, whereas, even though I got some "Damages", I did not get a "Confirmed". I had various skirmishes but I did not finish the job. However, I did have some experiences that were exciting.

"April 7, 1944 – This morning's initial flying en masse found situation completely mixed up in the formation [of P-51s], and the morning almost realized disaster for me. Something went wrong with my oxygen system. When I got to 25,000 feet, I noticed I was getting hazy, fooled with the O2, but couldn't fix it adequately and I passed out. We made one turn, I went out, but came back quite soon. After we fired our guns in, we made a turn, & as we flew out, I went again. I can faintly remember trying to find the formation with my wingman asking what in hell I was doing. It is the most pitiful feeling, for I'd try to do something, but just couldn't get myself to figure out how to do it. I came down, tried to land at 10,000 (instead of 1,000 ft.), finally landed almost without realizing a thing. After I'd stopped & parked, I was still punchy, fatigued, & in a helpless quandary. Well, I figured I was lucky for it takes only twenty some seconds without oxygen at 30,000 to kill you, & fortunately enough oxygen was getting to me from time to time to revive me. "

After four (Jan. 22 - May 31, 1944) months the Allies hammered a hole in the German encirclement and broke out of Anzio (May 31, 1944). As the German defense at Anzio collapsed, the German troops at Monte Cassino now found themselves flanked and immediately withdrew north through the Liri Valley; and pall mall all the Germans from the two positions fled north to establish a defensive position north of Rome. The allies forthwith captured the symbolic prize, Rome.

After the capture of Rome, the Allies withdrew a considerable number of their troops and air power and prepared them for the Invasion of Europe. The diverted 3rd Division was assigned to the invasion of southern France (at the time of the Normandy invasion) under the command of General Patton who would drive his army to Berlin. So the Italian front now was mired down north of Rome with fewer Allied and German troops. At this point our squadron transferred from the 12th Air Force to the 15th Air Force and replaced our Spits for the Mustangs.. "

REFLECTIONS BEFORE
A NEW PHASE

The Air Force Command decided that the 52nd and 31st Fighter groups were no longer needed in northern Italy but were needed in the 15th Air Force to support the heavy bomber assault on the German homeland. Consequently the 31st fighter group would be reequipped with long range fighters (the P-51-

Mustang) and transferred to the 15th Air Force that could aid in the air assault by our heavy bombers on targets in southern France, northern Italy, Hungary, Rumania, Austria, and Poland.

I had flown 117 missions in the Spitfire V and Spitfire IX and a few in the P-51 in support of the Allied Forces from Salerno to the fall of Rome. The weather was rainy enough to curtail much of our flying. The opposition was spasmodic. There were many times when we saw no enemy opposition and times when we encountered moderate opposition. The Spitfire was a wonderful way to get broken into combat. We were grateful to the Spit for its honesty and abilities, but we were excited and ready to move on.

I knew that in the oncoming flying P-15s over important industrial cities in Europe and the Balkans that the Luftwaffe would protect them with their maximum effort. As a somewhat seasoned pilot, I realized that knowing your fellow pilots and particularly your wingman was of great importance. One's wing man was your fellow pilot that flew closely to the rear and behind your plane. He in a sense was your "eyes" to your rear, while you as pilot was scanning all the skies and particular the skies in front, below, above you and on either side.

With these responsibilities one should know one's wingman. There were the conservative (stay on tail of leader and leave your leader only on approval), the tentative(wants to become engaged, but is uncertain of his move), the fearful (wishes to avoid battle), and the bold and venturous(who is more interested and more likely to attack). They are influenced by innate caution, desire of safety, competitiveness, self assurance, and quest for notoriety.

Examples of the bold, venturous, and fearless and fearful is illustrated below. One was Sam Browne who flew in our squadron in downing over 15 planes. If there were a bunch of German planes flying in formation and he was by himself, he would charge headlong into the group and achieve victories and escape unharmed. Then there was the opposite (as taken from my diary)"A Grubstake Pilot:Hello HobNail, this is Grubsteak, there are 30+ in dog 5(certain area); A Hobnail Flyer: "Hello Hobnail red leader this is_____. My engine is rough, I 'am going home". His element leader:" At a time like this, you sad bastard". I had the same experience with a transfer, Major in Rank, who just as we were about to engage the enemy over the Udine in Italy that asked me to take him home because of engine problems (that quickly disappeared) after we had landed in Elba on the way home. Then lastly I was the wingman that "hung in there" no matter what his leader did. I had a wingman (McCubbin), (who was not a close friend, but he was a reliable fighter with me. One my first combat flight in a Spitfire in Italy, I was flying the wing of the Flight leader, when we were "jumped" by two ME-109s. My flight leader abandoned me and I, as green as a gourd, was left to battle for myself (successfully). The Flight Leader was soon given a Medical discharge.

It's obvious that one should became aware of the different types of pilots with whom one flew.

15

P-51 MUSTANGS OVER EUROPE AND MID EAST

The Best Fighter of World War II

The 15th Air Force was composed of some 700 B-17s (The Flying Fortress) and B-24s (The Liberator) and was the offensive arm of the Strategic Air Force whose purpose was to penetrate the industrial factories, the railroad marshalling yards, oil refinery facilities, submarine bases, bridges and viaducts and other strategic targets with the idea of destroying or at least incapacitating them. Our bombers were based on the east side of Italy not far from Foggia. Their missions were primarily flown over Southern, Eastern Europe and the Middle East. When a mission began all these bombers would take off from their fields and form up in a massive tight formation and then fly to the Initial Point where they would then redirect/turn and make the run for the target. The purpose of the Initial Point and a turn from that point was to try to confuse the Germans about where the exact location of the target. It was hoped that this would confuse the German fighter defense. One can imagine the length of the column of bombers headed for the target probably running some 25 miles long and being attacked by German fighters and anti aircraft fire. Since the bombers carried belly, waist, and tail gunners by tucking in close to each other, the guns offered crossfire protection from the attacks of the German Messerschmitt 109s, 210s and Focke Wolfe 190s. As much as they tried to beat off the fighters, they were at best only partially successful. With the greater speed of the German fighters and attacks from all directions, the gunners were not able to fully protect their plane.

To get geared up to protect the bombers, we rid ourselves of the faithful Spitfire. Some twenty of us formed up at Caste Volturno in a large V Formation and slapped a big buzz job on the tower at Pomigliano. This was met with great disfavor by the control officers at the field. I said goodbye to Goddess II, which had taken me through 117 some not too difficult missions with never a moment of bad performance.

Thanks to Scotty and Richard Seick, my crew chiefs, there was never a problem with the flying capability of the plane. I owe so much to them.

From my log: "On March 23, 1944–It was announced that we were going to Africa to pick up about twenty-five P-51s at Algiers & Casablanca. That meant we were off operations so that evening about thirty of us got into a wild celebration for the break from flying. Rather similar to the let down used to be after exams at college, so was this announcement. The party took place in Harmeyer, Stub, Leicht, & McCubbin's tent. The next day with heads of iron we piled into the C-47, had a dull & rough ride to Maison Blanche in Algiers, & then ten of us (Baetj, Brown, Mick Ainley, Ray Harmeyer, Harry Reich, Ed Lyman, Geo Loving, Ralph Adams, Woody, & myself) then proceeded to town & saved rooms at the Touring Atlantic Hotel.

Howard & I had one on floor 7, and the sight of the city & harbor was that of a very white city. For that evening & half of the next day, we lushed in the luxury of bath tubs, good food, ice cream, beer, soft sheeted beds, street cars, Red Cross dances, and everything unlike Italy. From the stay there, I reflected that the military in Algiers in the Army were living mighty soft with menus of choices for good food and lodging with many running about in either brand new jeeps or staff cars (as compared to our wrecks), with every soldier sporting Colonel's, Captain's or Major's insignia (as opposed to our outfit with two Majors, a couple of Captains, & the rest 1$^{st.}$), with large & elaborate clubs (nightly dances, coca cola, good liquor & music), and girls. From all this, I thought that the boys risking their life & limbs should be getting more of this, and the "back line" jockeys a little less. Maybe their life is dull, but there is no hazard & the fellows at or near the combat zone deserve all they can be given for their chance with death. The town is colorful with bountiful movies, electricity, troops of French, American, and English armies & navies, forty dollar whores that line the Aleddi barroom from 4-6, and the air of night sports, no black out, lots of cars, European clothing for civilians & all types of uniforms of soldiers & sailors. All this makes Algiers seem like a spa a long, long way from the battle front. "

"Today, the twenty-sixth, we jumped out to Maison Blanche, preflighted our planes, got our scope on the weather, made the clearance, & set off at 11 A. M. to the Fighter Training Center for lunch, where we saw Sil Weiner, Nels, & Penke Yollman (the last two couldn't take the flying and were headed home), had some chicken & then set off again for Castel Volturno at 2PM and arrived at 5 P. M.. At 250 to 280 MPH a thousand mile trip doesn't take long, & it makes it quite easy to have fried eggs, tomato juice, and coffee in Algiers, chicken necks at Berteaux (Tunisia), & hamburgers at Castel Volturno (Italy). We had clouds with a base at 3,000 feet so we dodged mountains a good part of time."

The arrival of the P-51 for combat with the 15th Air Force was well timed because the original plan of American strategists was to send their bombers to their designated targets without fighter plane protection, but when the 8th Air Force mission to Schweinfort lost 60 bombers on one mission, it showed United States high command that bombers needed fighter protection or their losses would be unsustainable. Their thought that the heavies could protect themselves against the German fighters was proven incorrect. With the arrival of the P-51, there now was enough long range ability for a fighter to cover the bombers all the way in and out from their bombing missions. Before the arrival of the P-51 the American and British fighters did not have adequate range. Our 309th Squadron would either fly Escort or Ram Rod missions. When we flew escort missions because of our far greater speed than the bombers, we were forced to decrease our airspeed as much as possible and at the same time fly a crisscross pattern over the bombers so we not did overrun them. This type of mission was more appropriate for the slower P-38s fighters. On the Ram Rod missions we would fly directly to the target area after having dropped our external belly tanks, and be ready to defend the bombers as they made their bomb run. The bombers would fly to the Initial Point and then turn and go directly to release their bombs over their target.

We transitioned for a couple of weeks as we checked out the new plane and all marveled at its performance. It could cruise at 360 MPH, climb like an eagle, turn with our opposition, and fly missions that took 6 hours. It was a marvel. We simulated dogfights with the Spit IX to prove which plane was the better. All things considered the Mustangs won hands down. We were all thrilled with its performance. As a result the enthusiasm of the squadron was buoyed. We felt that we had bettered our chances against the Germans.

During that practice period we had a few laughs. Howard Baetjer's brother, Bruce, was a Piper Cub Field Artillery forward observer attached to the 5th Army. He arrived for a visit with his brother with a bandage over the top of his head. After a joyous reunion, we asked, "What's with the bandage?" "I was flying a forward observation mission in a Piper Cub for General Crane who was seated behind me in that tiny plane, when all of sudden four ME-109s came screaming down shooting at us. We were flying about 75 feet above the ground so it took only a couple of minutes to plop down into an olive tree. The MEs did not come back after us, but we did make a hard bouncy landing. No accidents except for a few scratches. " Two weeks later Bruce had to go back to the hospital because he had an infection on the top of his head. "What happened?" "Well, General Crane was smoking a cigar when I crashed and apparently part of his cigar went into my scalp and the medics unknowingly sewed up part of it in my head. End of story. " We all laughed. I don't think he got a Purple Heart!

One of the more experienced pilots thought it would be fun to fly his new Mustang over erupting Vesuvious and take a look. He proceeded to inspect the interior of the crater and marvel at all the smoke and ash it was expelling. When he returned home and looked at his plane, he noticed that the skin of the plane was shredded and pock marked. In fact, the plane's performance was ruined. The plane was junked and the pilot was reassigned.

So after the transition we moved from the Spit to the Mustang and from our tent city at Castel Volturno to San Severo, on the eastern side of the boot of Italy. We boarded the Adriatic and were within a few miles of the many fighter and bomber airfields all close to Foggia. We were quartered in rooms surrounding a square patio some fifteen minutes from our airfield. The facilities were warm, convenient, and adequate.

The flying in the 15th Air Force was going to be different. We would be flying missions as long as 6 hours, which made for greater demands on the pilot. Since the P-51 was a single seat plane, we promptly prepared for those long trips for deep penetration into enemy territory; it meant that I should look forward to far greater numbers of enemy opposition, greater navigational challenges, since we would be flying over unfamiliar lands with no radio aids, greater instrument flying in bad weather again without any type of homing radio help, and greater flying skill trying to keep formations together particularly in bad weather. All of this would be conducted over enemy territory, so the thought of parachuting or crash landing and being taken prisoner was decidedly less inviting than flying over one's own lands. All of these thoughts entered our minds as we prepared for our new flights.

We started flying (April 16, 1943) "Ram Rod" missions (cover bombers as they dropped their bombs on the target), "escort missions" herding bombers to and from target such as the Udine Valley (Italy), Veiner Neustad (Austria), Ploesti (Rumania), Poland, Southern France, Germany and other targets within our 700-mile range. The missions were long and very exhausting. Since we piloted, navigated, fought, so at the end of these missions I would roll out of the cockpit wondering if I could make it-utterly spent and exhausted. Such exhaustion seems amazing for a young, good condition 25 year old lad! The two shots of whiskey awaiting us helped revive the tired body and mind. On most missions we met enemy fighters in varying degrees of their combativeness. The Germans flew the Messerschmitt-109 and Focke Wolfe-190, both good fighters, with good experienced pilots.

Ground Flying at San Severo

The routine of most flights was pretty much similar to the following:

3:15 A.M. - Roll out of bed and get some breakfast

4:00 A.M. - Briefing: In dark tent with big blackboard with briefing officer, pointer in hand, great map in front of him, and then he spoke of:

- Type of Mission (Ramrod; cover; escort etc)
- Composition of our Planes and Commands
- Length of mission
- Destination
- Navigation explanation
- Weather conditions AM and PM
- Gas Management
- Expected Enemy fighters and expected tactics
- Location of Flack
- The Initial Point
- Number of Allied Bombers
- History of target area

We pilots sat long faced, quiet and anxious on our wooden benches. Really tough targets always brought a groan of reality and anxious anticipation from us. The easy targets brought smiles. The atmosphere at those briefings was solemn and tense in anticipation of the danger ahead. Huddled in a command car, we then would then drive ten minutes in the dark and in silence to the airfield to start the mission. There was no jollity or wise cracks. Just anticipation.

5:30 A.M. - Preflight your plane as for gas, guns armed, controls free, tires etc.

6:00 A.M. - Start up and taxi into position for squadron takeoff.

6:10 A.M. - (Adrenalin growing) Takeoff 36 planes plus spares.

6:15 A.M. - 3 Squadrons form up into formation of the 31st Fighter Group as we circled the field.

6:30 A.M. - Start off headed for target area. Radio silence.

8:30 A.M. - Arrive at target area; search skies for enemy, spot enemy fighters who have been alerted of our arrival; drop emergency belly fuel tanks (hopefully before they jumped us); push throttle to the fire wall for full speed and prepare for battle; Engage enemy

9:15 A.M. -Start for home. Usually short of fuel, pretty well exhausted as we idled down the engine to low RPMs to conserve gas, undo your shoulder and seat belts, sit back, and head for home; Eat Hershey bar. (Often this relaxation was disastrous, as the Germans would follow us from the target area, and then attack.)

11:15 A.M. -Land at San Severo

12:30 P.M. -Debriefing hours.

1:00 P.M. - AT Ease

TOTAL: 4 ½ to 6 ½ hours of flying

At the time the bombers approached their target, we would arrive at the same time. During the period we would try to get altitude (25,000 feet) to be at advantage to the attacking German fighters. As soon as we spotted the Krauts attacking our bombers, we would go after them. Often the Germans would attack us first, and that would end our formation and order. As a result the pilots would have to fight as a pair or by oneself. Usually your plan of fighting as a team disintegrated and everyone broke up into separate scraps. After a half hour of this, with gas supplies now getting sufficient only for a trip home, we would head home.

One amusing incident happened over Ploesti when one of our pilots took a leak in his pilot relief tube, got jumped immediately after relieving himself, and during the ensuing chase by the Kraut, the urine from the tube backed up because of inverted flight and spilled all over the windshield. All of a sudden over the radio, "I've been hit and I have a glycol leak (radiator fluid). Going to have to bail out". The flight leader told the harried pilot to stay with it. The true reason for the yellow liquid on the windscreen was realized! He returned home humiliated.

The first 7 days after we began flying the Mustang (April 16, 1944) in combat, out of 25 pilots, we lost 12 to enemy action, almost 50% of the pilots of our Squadron. The somber looks of us pilots became more somber as the week progressed. It was incumbent that as flight, squadron, or group leaders we had to keep a "stiff upper lip", to keep the spirit and confidence at as high a level as possible. The impending danger was being felt by all of us. I don't think anyone shirked his duty, but things were pretty serious now. Every evening on the return from a mission, those of us who had not flown that day took a count of those missing as we awaited the flight's return. When Weinner Neustad was announced, we knew we would meet the best enemy fighters in the greatest numbers. Other targets brought varying reactions of relief or anxiety.

"May 5, 1944 Target: Ploesti Marshaling Yards and Oil Fields
Type: Ram Rod

"Back again we went to the 309[th's] hunting ground. We were area cover, so anticipated we'd run into about what we'd encountered the first day we made the trip. As we arrived at target, I was leading Yellow flight and we turned off into a group of B-24s just emerging from their break away thru heavy flak. On the way to help these fellows I lost the other section, so Husty Carey, my perennial hawk eyed wingman, found out about five I.A.R. & ME-109s were attacking or about to attack the bombers. One "Twenty Four" had just been hit by flak & was a solid sheet of flames (with only one chute), the formation very loose so we were just in time. We went down made a couple passes at these I.A.R. chased them off, & then I took after an M.E. Since I jumped him, I had no trouble catching him, so I closed to a hundred and fifty yards as he dove down, gave him a short squirt, with instantaneous flashes & fires from probably the gas tank. He did a roll which followed him through firing & just before I broke away his glycol went streaming, so he was a plume of black smoke from gas fire around cockpit & white smoke as his engine was about to burn up. The day was successful, for we got more victories (Murray-2, Mick-7, Ray-5) & no losses for the group. It was a rewarding day, & Mick's piling into the ground sounded good. We also shot at some I.A.R. , but I as others missed. They are slow, radial engine klunkers that possibly carry rockets, but they are so slow that it's nigh to impossible to keep from ramming one. "

Pilots differed in their abilities, their aggressiveness, their tactics, their abandonment, and their caution in performing their duties. Sam Brown was our leading Ace in the theater who flew in the 309th squadron. He would just dive headlong into a swarm of enemy fighters and usually come out unscathed with kills to his credit. Not long after one of his many victories, he had an engine quit on takeoff, and his plane hurtled at 200 MPH through trees, but the seat of his plane remained in tact even though the plane was junk. I had rushed to the scene in my jeep to find him, only to find the plane's carcass remaining. Apparently, he had escaped and was unhurt. He returned to the squadron headquarters before I did! A few days later his scalp was grazed by a bullet from a tail gunner of ME-110. But that didn't faze him. He just continued to be productive. There were other incidents, when the pilot just lost his nerve and had to be reassigned. Some pilots flew with fear."

May 11, 1944 Piacenza - Parma Area
Target Cover

"The P-38s were strafing one hour before us, & then our bombers were going to hit air fields possible after the planes had been scrambled originally. Well, the mission was a failure for weather was socked in tight as a drum with solid over east up to 10,000 & high around us but we had a tough day on losses. First, I leading the squadron, after rearrangement, had to fly through some clouds which I was trying to get under, and instead of being in there a couple of minutes, we were on instruments for close to fifteen to twenty minutes. Going on instruments Ralph McCubbin apparently got vertigo, got in a spin, & as far as we all know, went straight in with many a word over the R/T. Ralph was an old member having come in shortly after I, had a lot of combat time, was cool & level headed boy, and very likable, easy going fellow. He was being rather tuned up to take over one of the flights. He flew my wing for a many missions. The second loss was Hank Mann, who came in after me by a couple of weeks, who'd also had a lot of experience, was thought to be just about ready to take over a flight. He turned back today with Woody flying on his wing, because his canope had frosted over & couldn't see, so I said to them turn back & head for home–that was the last seen of them. A report from a bomber pilot said they saw a chute & single engine airplane spinning at 9:05 near Lake Elba, which was the approximately their position and time. "

A tragic day was when our great good friend Howard Baetjer was shot down. He was flying in my squadron and flight when he broke off and left the formation. After a short while, I spotted him coming out of a cloud above and to my right. I told him to form on the right of my flight (4 planes) when immediately not far in front, he spotted a ME-1O9 and went after him, even though I had said stay in formation. Unfortunately the decoy had some buddies above who immediately bounced on him and apparently disabled his plane. I saw the hits on his plane. I thought for sure his plane was finished, but I did not see or know if Baetj had parachuted, since I was being attacked myself. Apparently he did parachute and as he hit the ground a group of Serbian farmers started to pounce on him to destroy him. The local farmers were very unhappy about the Americans bombing their cities and wanted retribution. Quickly a command car filled with the Weimar soldiers jumped from their command car and riddled the farmers with their guns, captured Howard, and sent him to Stalag Luffte prison camp, where he spent the rest of the war. Quite an experience!"

Howard was a great fellow and we all loved him. Lots of fun, musical, great sense of humor, enthusiastic, optimistic, dreamer. Unfortunately, his biggest dream was shooting down some enemy planes. He struck out there. Our group of four (Fax, Murray, Baetj, and myself) was not the same after Baetj departed.

I was full of courage even though I was not a wild one, but, since I was not shot up, had good fortune with my plane, and handled the flying with ability, losing my courage never was challenged. I like to think that my courage would have continued even under terribly frightening situations such as Sam Brown's, but to be fair maybe the fact that I was unscathed is the reason my courage persisted. Maybe if I had been shot up or had a plane crash, my confidence would have broken also. Who knows?

May 24, 1944–Vienna

"Attacking the airdrome near Vienna, we again battled bad weather, & arrived at target area, just in time to see that some of Krauts were still around & so in we sailed. We were late in getting in the fight, mainly due to my fault for my radio was faulty & I never received the calls of other eyes behind us. I got into the fight, went down on two, MEs attacking bombers, drove up close to one, gave him a short squirt, & really knocked hell out of his cockpit. He fell over & fluttered down seemingly destroyed with the pilot dead. Not seeing results, I could only get a probable. Murray got shot up pretty badly by a P38, but managed to sneak home. "

Sometimes a little common sense or caution was pretty important to save your life. After landing in Corsica escorting another pilot home who had engine problems, when I was leaving the Airport, I could hear some pilot in a foreign language requesting takeoff from the opposite end of the runway. The Tower a bit confused had cleared both planes for "immediate takeoff" from opposite ends of the runway. Since the airstrip had a big rise at the mid point so I could not see the other end of the runway. I waited until the other fellow took off, then proceeded instead of having a head on collision.

I decided I had had enough and decided some others might take my place. I was getting tired of the flying both mentally and physically and probably not as an intrepid a flyer than I was a couple of years ago. So we received orders to report to Naples to take a voyage to the United States as soon as a convoy could be formed and launched. With no incidents on the seas, we arrived in New York City on July, 1944."

HEADQUARTERS
31st Fighter Group
APO 520 US Army

INDIVIDUAL COMBAT CLAIM FORM

Date: **3 July, 1944**

Claimant's Full Name Wilhelm, David C., Rank Captain ASN O-447454

Home Address 221 N. LaSalle St., Chicago, Illinois Crew Pos. Pilot

A/C No. 42-106551 Sqdn. 309th Date of Encounter 3 July, 1944.

Time 1205 B Place Near Bucharest Alt. 22,000 feet.

Type E/A Encountered ME-109's Claim: Dest 1 Prob Dam

```
            12
      11          1
   10                2

  9          .        3

   8                4
      7          5
            6
```

NARRATIVE: On 3 July Captain Wilhelm was leading the squadron on an escort mission to Bucharest.

At 1205 Captain Wilhelm saw 4 ME-109's at 22,000 feet between Bucharest and Ploesti going east. He attacked the last enemy aircraft on the right as it went on a gradual left turn down in a dive. He started firing from 200 yards, closing to 150 yards from 5 degrees deflection with a 3 second burst. Strikes were seen in the cockpit and fuselage and the plane did a violent flip and fell cartwheeling out of control. Lts. Bratton, Thompson and Sandler saw the plane going down in flames. One ME-109 is claimed as destroyed. Camouflage was dark blue.

DALTON SMITH, Captain, Air Corps,
Intelligence Officer
309th Squadron.

CERTIFIED A TRUE COPY:

DALTON SMITH,
Captain, Air Corps,
Intelligence Officer.

ALBERT D. LEVY, Maj. A/C
Gp. Intell. Officer

Approved as One E/A

(Dest - Prob - Damgd)

CHARLES M. McCORKLE,
Colonel, A/C,
Commanding

CONFIDENTIAL

Combat Award

HEADQUARTERS
31st Fighter Group
APO 520 US Army

INDIVIDUAL COMBAT CLAIM FORM

Date: 27 June, 1944.

Claimant's Full Name Wilhelm, David C.,   Rank Captain   ASN O-447454

Home Address 205 LaSalle St., Chicago, Illinois   Crew Pos. Pilot

A/C No. 42-106551   Sqdn. 309th   Date of Encounter   27 June, 1944.

Time 1030   B   Place NW of Budapest   Alt. 15,000 feet.

Type E/A Encountered   ME-210's   Claim: Dest   Prob   Dam 1

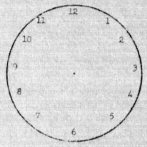

NARRATIVE: On 27 June Captain Wilhelm was leading Blue Section on an escort mission to Budapest. At 1030 he saw 2 ME-210's at 15,000 feet. The enemy aircraft immediately dived to the deck and Captain Wilhelm closed to 200 yards and fired several bursts and strikes were seen in the left wing and large chunks came off. This was seen by Lt. Bratton. One ME-210 is claimed as damaged.

DALTON SMITH, Captain, Air Corps,
Intelligence Officer
309th Squadron.

CERTIFIED A TRUE COPY:

DALTON SMITH,
Captain, Air Corps,
Intelligence Officer

Approved as One E/A

ALBERT D. LEVY, Maj. A/C
Gp. Intell. Officer

(Dest - Prob - Dams)

CHARLES M. McCORKLE,
Colonel, A/C,
Commanding

CONFIDENTIAL

Combat Award

HEADQUARTERS
31st Fighter Group
APO 520 US Army

INDIVIDUAL COMBAT CLAIM FORM

Date: __13 June, 1944.__

Claimant's Full Name Wilhelm, David C., Rank 1st Lt.   ASN O-447454

Home Address   221 N. LaSalle St., Chicago, Illinois. Crew Pos.   Pilot

A/C No.42-106551 Sqdn. 309th Date of Encounter 13 June, 1944.

Time 0940 B   Place Near Munich   Alt.   23,000 feet.

Type E/A Encountered FW-190's   Claim:Dest 1   Prob   Dam

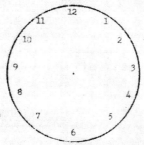

NARRATIVE: Lt. Wilhelm was leading Blue Section on an escort mission to
Munich. At 0940 3 FW-190's were seen flying close V formation attempting to attack
bombers from 8 o-clock. The e/a pulled up in a wide left climbing turn and Lt.
Wilhelm circled into sun and jumped them unseen from 350 yards. He fired a 4 to 6
second burst from 200 to 150 yards dead astern. Strikes were seen in cockpit area
and near tail assembly and many explosion s were seen. The FW flipped over on back
out of control and the tail section was apparently out of control. He was seen to
go down on fire out of control at 10,000 feet and this was seen by Lt. Bratton.
One FW-190 is claimed as destroyed. Camouflage was dark blue gray with a red emblem
in front of empennage.

DALTON SMITH, Captain, Air Corps,
Intelligence Officer
309th Squadron.

ALBERT D. LEVY, Maj. A/C
Gp. Intell. Officer

CERTIFIED A TRUE COPY:

Approved as One E/A

(Dest. - Prob - Damgd)

DALTON SMITH,
Captain, Air Corps,
Intelligence Officer.

CHARLES M. McCORKLE,
Colonel, A/C,
Commanding

CONFIDENTIAL

Combat Award

HEADQUARTERS
31st Fighter Group
APO 520 US Army

INDIVIDUAL COMBAT CLAIM FORM

Date: 10 June, 1944.

Claimant's Full Name Wilhelm, David C., Rank 1st Lt.   ASN 0-447454

Home Address 221 N. LaSalle St., Chicago, Illinois Crew Pos. Pilot

A/C No. 42-106551 Sqdn. 309th Date of Encounter 10 June, 1944.

Time 0950 B   Place Trieste, Italy Alt. 21,000 feet.

Type E/A Encountered ME-109's Claim:Dest   Prob   Dam 1

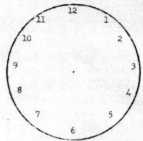

NARRATIVE: On 10 June Lt. Wilhelm was leading the squadron on an escort mission to Trieste, Italy.

At 0930 Lt. Wilhelm saw three ME-109's flying in a string at 21,000 feet attacking bombers from 6 0-Clock. He dived on the last enemy aircraft and followed him down to 7,000 feet. The enemy aircraft used good evasive action; climbing and turning and diving from split-esses. Lt. Wilhelm fired a 30 degree deflection shot from 200 yards and strikes were seen on fuselage. One ME-109 is claimed as damaged. Camouflage was dark blue, with white crosses on wings.

DALTON SMITH, Captain, Air Corps,
Intelligence Officer
309th Squadron.

ALBERT D. LEVY, Maj. A/C
Gp. Intell. Officer

CERTIFIED A TRUE COPY:

Approved as One E/A

(Dest - Prob - Damgd)

DALTON SMITH,
Captain, Air Corps,
Intelligence Officer.

CHARLES M. McCORKLE,
Colonel, A/C,
Commanding

CONFIDENTIAL

Combat Award

HEADQUARTERS
31st Fighter Group
APO 520 US Army

INDIVIDUAL COMBAT CLAIM FORM

Date: 24 May, 1944.

Claimant's Full Name Wilhelm, David C., Rank 1st Lt. ASN O-447454

Home Address 221 N. LaSalle St., Chicago, Illinois. Crew Pos. Pilot

A/C No. 42-106551 Sqdn. 309th Date of Encounter 24 May, 1944.

Time 1020 B Place Muchendorf, Austria. Alt. 21,000 feet.

Type E/A Encountered ME-109's Claim:Dest Prob 1 Dam

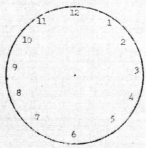

NARRATIVE: On 24 May Lt. Wilhelm was leading the squadron on an escort
mission to Muchendorf, Austria.

Two ME-109's were seen attacking bombers from 6 o-clock flying line abreast.
They broke off to side and flew straight and level. Lt. Wilhelm opened fire
from 200 yards closing to 150 yards with a 5-8 second burst from line astern.
Strikes and flashes were seen in the cockpit area; chunks came off the enemy
aircraft and numerous large flashes were seen by Major Warford and Lt. Thompson.
One ME-109 is claimed as probably destroyed. Camouflage was dark mottled blue.

DALTON SMITH, Captain, Air Corps,
Intelligence Officer
309th Squadron.

ALBERT D. LEVY, Maj. A/C
Gp. Intell. Officer

CERTIFIED A TRUE COPY:

Approved as One E/A

DALTON SMITH,
Captain, Air Corps,
Intelligence Officer.

(Dest - Prob - Damgd)

CHARLES M. McCORKLE,
Colonel, A/C,
Commanding

CONFIDENTIAL

Combat Award

CONFIDENTIAL

HEADQUARTERS
31st Fighter Group
APO 520 US Army

INDIVIDUAL COMBAT CLAIM FORM

Date: __10 May, 1944.__

Claimant's Full Name **Wilhelm, David C.**, Rank **1st Lt.** ASN **0-647450**

Home Address **221 N. LaSalle St., Chicago, Illinois.** Crew Pos. **Pilot**

A/C No. **42-106551** Sqdn. **309th** Date of Encounter **10 May, 1944.**

Time **1310** B Place **Near Zagreb, Yugoslaviat.** **18,000 feet.**

Type E/A Encountered **ME-109's** Claim:Dest **1** Prob Dam

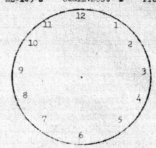

NARRATIVE: On 10 May Lt. Wilhelm was leading an element in Green Flight on an escort mission to Wiener Neustadt.

At 1310 he saw a lone ME-109 stooging bombers from 6 o-clock at 15,000 feet, just north of Zagreb. Lt. Ainlay attacked the plane first and overshot and then Lt. Wilhelm attacked from astern as the enemy aircraft went straight down. He followed the ME-109 down to 5,000 feet observing strikes in the cockpit, on tail, fuselage and engine as he fired for five seconds from 150 yards. Lt. Ainlay shot and strikes were seen on fuselage and Lt. Carey also had strikes in the fuselage. The enemy aircraft crashed, turned over and burst into flames. This was confirmed by Lts. Ainlay and Carey. One ME-109 is claimed as destroyed.

DALTON SMITH, Captain, Air Corps,
Intelligence Officer
309th Squadron.

ALBERT D. LEVY, Maj. A/C
Gp. Intell. Officer

CERTIFIED A TRUE COPY:/
Dalton Smith
DALTON SMITH,
Captain, Air Corps,
Intelligence Officer.

Approved as One E/A

(Dest - Prob - Damgd)

CHARLES M. McCORKLE,
Colonel, A/C,
Commanding

CONFIDENTIAL

Combat Award

HEADQUARTERS
31st Fighter Group
APO 520 US Army

INDIVIDUAL COMBAT CLAIM FORM

Date: **6 May, 1944.**

Claimant's Full Name **Wilhelm, David C.,** Rank **1st Lt.** ASN **0-447454**

Home Address **221 N. LaSalle, St., Chicago, Ill.** Crew Pos. **Pilot**

A/C No. **42-106551** Sqdn. **309th** Date of Encounter **5 May, 1944.**

Time **1505-1510** Place **Ploesti, Roumania.** Alt. **18,000 feet.**

Type E/A Encountered **ME-109's** Claim: Dest **1** Prob Dam

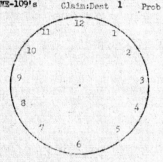

NARRATIVE: Lt. Wilhelm was leading yellow section on 5 May on a target cover mission to Ploesti.

One ME-109 attacked a bomber from the rear and Lt. Wilhelm attacked from 18,000 feet. The e/a broke right and started diving. Lt. Wilhelm closed to 150 yards before firing a short burst, and hits were seen in cockpit and on fuselage causing large explosion. The e/a then fell off more steeply and Lt. Wilhelm opened fire again and black smoke and glycol started streaming from cockpit. The fire around the cockpit and the glycol streaming out were seen and confirmed by Lt. Carey. One ME-109 is claimed as destroyed. Camouflage was dark-greenish black.

DALTON SMITH, Captain, Air Corps,
Intelligence Officer
309th Squadron.

ALBERT D. LEVY, Maj. A/C
Gp. Intell. Officer

Certified a true copy:

DALTON SMITH,
Captain,
Air Corps.

Approved as One E/A   (Dest - Prob - Damgd)

CHARLES M. McCORKLE,
Colonel, A/C,
Commanding

CONFIDENTIAL

Combat Award

HEADQUARTERS
31st Fighter Group
APO 520 US Army

INDIVIDUAL COMBAT CLAIM FORM

Date: 22 April, 1944.

Claimant's Full Name Wilhelm, David C., Rank 1st Lt   ASN 0-447454

Home Address 221 N. LaSalle St., Chicago, Ill.   Crew Pos. Pilot

A/C No.42-106551 Sqdn. 309th Date of Encounter   21 April, 1944.

Time 1205 B   Place   Ploesti, Roumania.Alt.   25,000 feet.

Type E/A EncounteredFW-190 & ME-169Claim:Dest 1   Prob   Dam 1

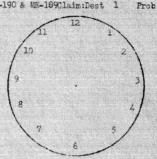

NARRATIVE: On 21 April Lt. Wilhelm was leading Yellow Flight on a target cover mission to Ploesti. At 1205 4 ME-109's were seen approaching the formation at 23,000 feet, and He led his flight down on them. Lt. Wilhelm closed from 400 to 100 yds, and observed hits in various places on the e/a and a concentration of hits in the cockpit. The entire canopy and side of plane disintegrated followed by a sheet of white glycol. The e/a then fell over on his left wing out of control toward the overcast. Due to the flashes in the cockpit, the thick black smoke, and the dis- integration of the plane which was streaming glycol; this plane is considered to be destroyed and the pilot killed. Lt. Carey, his wingman, confirms this. A few minutes later Lt. Wilhelm attacked an FW-190 and fired several bursts while in a turn and observed hits on the fuselage from close range. This is claimed as a damaged.

DALTON SMITH, Captain, Air Corps,
Intelligence Officer
309th Squadron.   ALBERT D. LEVY, Maj. A/C
                                                 Gp. Intell. Officer

                        Approved as One E/A   (Dest - Prob - Damgd)
CERTIFIED A THUE/COPY:

DALTON SMITH, Captain, Air Corps,
Intelligence Officer.   CHARLES M. McCORKLE,
                                                 Colonel, A/C,
                        CONFIDENTIAL   Commanding

Combat Award

16

RECREATION - AIR FORCE STYLE

ISLE OF CAPRI
(January 2- January 6, 1944)

"Murray, McCubbin, and I got the nod to have a few days R. and R. at Capri. After a couple of days of delay, we finally boarded the two and half hour boat ride to the island. We grabbed a taxi and drove as far as possible up the mountain side and then toted our bags to the deluxe Tiberius Morgano hotel. The assigned bedroom was complete with white sheets and comforters on the bed, our own bathroom and valet service. The view of the Tyrannium Sea was lovely. We relished in the comfort.

We spent our time break-fastening late, milk punches before lunch, wandering around the town until cocktail hour before an abundant dinner. In the evening pilots from bomber and fighter squadrons from the R.A.F. , the U.S.A.F. and assorted airmen from other allied forces gathered to tell their tall tales. It was evident that the American pilots boasted of their prowess, while the Brits modestly reported their experiences. As one fellow from our group extolled his achievements in shooting down four planes, a R. A. F.

flight spoke up modestly saying he had twenty f****** seven kills. The humility and restraint of the Brits was marked, and tended to restrain the Americans from their big boasts. All in all everyone enjoyed the various tales and lies as the evening usually lasted till midnight.

The island was active in many ways. The false nobility of Counts, Princes, and Marquises of Italy had taken up residence there after the surrender of the Italy to the Allies. Shops and restaurants were open and flourishing. We visitors enjoyed that civil environment and exchanged thoughts with the locals as we sipped our wine in the afternoon. One afternoon, at a small teashop, I joined a group consisting of two British sailors from Liverpool, an Australian lady who had retreated from Moscow, a local Prince and Murray and me. The locals were most hospitable and friendly with all. They were delighted the Germans had left.

In typical manner the Germans had sent their forces to the island as a rest area and had been greatly disliked by the Capricians. Besides their authoritive approach they showed their true self in vengeance by proceeding to destroy furniture, break windows and generally leave all that they could destroyed. In my experience, that is what they did in Morocco upon their defeat there.

The stay was a nice relief.."

"CAIRO AVEC PLEASURE":
May 25, 1944

"Only yesterday did we get the dope about going to Cairo and beyond. Since Murray didn't want to go this time to Africa, Hank Mann, George Loving and I wanted to go on this adventuresome trip. However, Hank had mysteriously disappeared en route home from our mission to Piacenza and was listed as a M. I. A. My recollection was as we crossed the Adriatic by Split, Hank did a steep turn to the left and his wingman pulled over him-that was the last that was seen of him. Hank has been pulling some odd ones of late, when it had been thought that he had been lost, but some way he always managed to turn up. So George and I were the two (from our squadron) who signed up for the venture... With our bags full of summer gear, clean clothes, and with our pockets loaded with $300.00, we set off for the Middle East.

David with old flying buddy General George Loving and wife Amber 309- Reunion.

Our conveyance was a stripped down medium bomber B-25- a perfect plane for the venture. Our squadron traded a Spit to their squadron for the B-25. (I have no recollection how this could have occurred). Major Stroshire was at the wheel with three of us crammed up with him and 6 more scattered in the Bombay, We zoomed off at 8:45, from Italy then to Bari to collect our orders "to take two pilots for gunnery training in Cairo". This was a lame excuse for the trip, but from the Air Corps standpoint, who cared. Next we took off at 9:30 to fly across the Mediterranean for 3 hours @ 200mph to Ben Ghazi; First, we landed at the wrong field, took off and found the right one; gassed up. Ben Ghazi still after fourteen months showed the signs of war between Germans, Brits and Italians. Wrecked tanks, planes, and buildings destroyed every where. The shadows of war still clung to this desolate dust covered steaming cauldron of a place.

We next landed at Payne Field in Cairo at 4PM, changed our money, and located ourselves at the National Hotel ready to see the town. The city was fairly western in appearance autos traveling at American speed. The entire higher standard of living reflects itself in the people and their actions. The streets are wide, trolleys, and kept clean. Night spots are numerous, American whiskey, British troops, professional women in all nightclubs. Well dressed, dusky girls with good looks and fine figures who work in the floor show plus others that sift around the tables dancing with those interested. They immediately call for a drink (orange soda) at $1.25 a drink. This was their way of getting to know their clientele?

The gals get 50% of the cost of the drinks. After a short while learning the intentions of their men friends, they either dance or drink more pop, or agree to further activity for $40.00.

For two days we ate fresh meat and veggies, drank our share of beer, and took camel rides to the Pyramids and the Sphinx. The temperature was steamy and hot. The flies were sticky and abundant. Early the next day we took off from Payne Field, buzzed the Pyramids and headed for Tel Aviv. Those few days were quite a change from Italy's closeness to the war."

TEL AVIV

"Even though we were told we would not be permitted to land at Tel Aviv, we knew "where there is a will there is a way. " After an hour flight across Suez, some desert, we came upon the modern gathering of buildings of Tel Aviv. Down came our wheels of the B-25, but up came RED FLARES to tell us "don't land here", so up went the wheels and around we went. Right near we spotted a small strip called Wilhelma Field(!) where we landed. We previously knew nothing of an alternate airfield but we were just sure there had to be one. After landing there, we tied down our plane and set off for the Yardin Hotel.

Tel Aviv was a city of 50,000. (1944). "The Hollywood restaurant serves Viener Snitzl and beer with German music. Everyone speaks English, Hebrew, Yiddish, German, and French so we were able to converse with many locals without difficulty. It was fun to talk to all these refugees from Europe, soldiers and locals. The food was fresh and wonderful. Not Arabic but clean and American like. This environment was certainly refreshing and a distinct change from war involved Italy."

ALEXANDRIA

"After a day we flew to Alexandria, Egypt. It turned out this was THE city of the Middle East... We stayed at the charming Hotel Cecil right on the Mediterranean. The weather was great with the Mediterrean's cool breezes making the temperature ideal. A favorite meeting place was the Cecil bar. The food was sumptuous with Quail, strawberries, Fresh veggies, milk, and ice cream all for $3. 50. per supper. I am sure we were so charmed with everything because of the contrast of not having to fly and to eat out of mess kits.

We stayed in Alexandria for a couple of days where we were charmed by the snake charmer in Hotel Cecil's bar where the Mediterranean lapped out side the open doors. We went to the Sporting Club to enjoy the pool and tennis. I found the tennis pro and he and I had a fun game. We did not have the time to enjoy the other attractions of this country club and horse racing track. Regretfully, we decided we had better return since the plane was leaving. So, we retraced our steps and returned to our squadron headquarters in drizzly Italy. We were promptly put to work flying missions over Europe. It was a great week that went well even though completely unplanned."

JULY 5- 1944
CAIRO-ALEXANDRIA

"Doug Gagwin, Paul Cooper (Supply), Murray and I hitched onto this trip back down again to Alexandria. Major Warford and Col. Daniels 'obtained our approval for this venture. Sixteen airmen from various outfits were given passage on this venture. The Bombay of the B-17 was jammed full with our passengers as we flew from Bari, to Ben Ghazi; then to Cairo at 5:30PM where we comfortably bedded down at the Savoy-Carlton Hotel. Clean sheets, private bathroom-all the amenities one would want. A little different from our tented camp. Before dinner I wandered over to Shepherd's hotel where I ran into George Seabury, a Yale friend. where we had a drink together. Rarely did I see someone from Yale, since most of the Yale's of my class served in the Marine Corps or Navy, and most of that service was in the Pacific theater.

Even though we arrived at the train station thirty minutes before train time, the coach car war jammed to the brim. Sitting on top of the luggage accompanied by two ladies, one of whom took a real fancy to Murray, we arrived in Alexandria in two hours. Unfortunately we could not get a room at the Cecil Hotel, but we did find a Pension which was cheap, clean, convenient and comfortable. In the evening Cag and I toured the Monseigneur, Union Bar, and then back to our lodging. In the meantime Murray met with his girl friend of the train and left us until we took the train back at the end of our stay.

For the next few days Cag and I spent most of our time at the Sporting Club. This was a true sporting club with a golf course, tennis courts, swimming pool/restaurant, and horse racing stable and race track. As we lounged around the swimming pool, we met some attractive, good looking, and intelligent W. R. E. N. S. members of the British Naval Service. We had a barrel of fun with them at the pool, luncheons, and dinners. Besides that enjoyment I located the tennis pro, Marook, and had daily tennis games with him. He was a far better played than I, but I was able to "stay on the court with him". I also played a round of golf on a green well taken care of 18 hole course. As a group we went to the horse races twice and enjoyed the Egyptian small horses running for their life. I regret I did not record their names or homes of those gals. However, it would have been unlikely to see them again.

After these five days of "playing", we caught the train back to Cairo to meet our B-17 plane and the others for our flight home. This was a fun stint. We felt familiar with Alex and we were able to transition into that atmosphere with no problem. This R and R was preparing us for our return to the United States!

We received our orders to be ready to move within a month. We will be ordered to the "Replacement Pool" in Naples(a tent city). During the wait Dalton Smith and I drove over to Bari to see and hear Irving Berlin singing "Over There", "White Christmas ", "YOU GOTTA GET UP" He was great and all the Gils loved it. Smitty and I made a few more little trips since I was no longer flying and just had to wait. After considerable time as we waited for a convoy to be put together in the Naples harbor and then finally we were delivered to the ship for the big trip! The ship still had to wait at its mooring for four days until finally we chugged off. For a little enjoyment the Luftwaffe dropped a few bombs toward us, but fortunately they missed. Finally the convoy started off and we slowly crossed the Atlantic and after a week we arrived in New York. The crossing had been without German attack.

17

FATHER'S DEATH
AND FURLOUGH

Before landing in New York, we were given strict instructions that we were not to bring any captured items into the United States. A doctor that I had met on board showed me a beautiful portable chest containing according to him rare and valuable medical tools. After carrying his prize all over Europe, he was so intimidated by the announcement that he threw the rare find over board into the New York harbor waters. He was crushed, and particularly when on disembarking there was no inspection and many others carried contraband with no problem.

Sailing into New York City, and drifting by the Statue of Liberty was a terribly emotional event. Just to see the Statue, the home land, the tall buildings of Manhattan, autos and America brought about the realization I was home after three long years made me break down in a wash of tears of joy and relief. To this very day I still have goose pimples and water come to my eyes remembering my feelings on that occasion. Surely the tension of warfare had been intense and it was not till that moment that I realized this was the end. AT LAST. I never felt that fearful or tense while the fighting was going on. I just blocked out those emotions. I guess I finally just relaxed and all of a sudden all that anxiety just overcame me. I just did not realize the strain that I had been under for two years of combat until that moment.

The joy was short lived for I went to a pay phone off the army post where we were disembarked and called home. I learned from my mother that my father had gotten word of my return and dropped dead with a heart attack. I was still on the Atlantic sailing home in the convoy at the time of his death. Apparently the shock of that news overcame him. Father was an earnest, hard worker, and diligent first Vice President of the Cudahy Packing Company. He did not return from work by the early train to Lake Forest to play golf as so many of his pals did. I know father was not in "good shape". He did walk either to the street car in the city or to the railroad in Lake Bluff on his way to work but he was overweight and smoked both of which did not contribute to good health. For sure he was not an "Ornish" diet advocate for my family ate abundantly of beef, pork, sausages, bacon, and all those other high fat plaque "goodies". Probably the combination of his life style in addition to the news of my survival contributed to his heart attack.

Life was sort of a blur for me when I arrived home at 735 Ravine Avenue in Lake Bluff. I don't recall where I disembarked from the troop ship, where I was processed, or in what manner I went from New York to Lake Bluff. Subsequently I don't remember the funeral or the condition of mother or Jean. I guess the whole change from the Air Corps to America and father's death was too much to comprehend.

I do recall an undertaker at our house trying to take advantage of mother by advocating an outrageously elaborate and expensive casket "to show your eternal respect". I was so irritated with him that I chased him out of the house. I have no recollection of the funeral. Father is buried at the Lake Bluff cemetery next to my mother and brother just to the left of the entrance to the cemetery off Sheridan road just south of the Lake Bluff boundary in Lake Forest.

When settling in with mother, I had little help from Jean (my sister), since she was living in Carmel awaiting Daggett's return from duty as an intelligence officer in the United States Navy. Mother and I were both saddened, so the home was gloomy and somber even though we tried to avoid that mood.

I spent three weeks helping mother get adjusted to her widowhood. I am sure that my presence was propitious at that moment and was a great comfort for her. We did the chores of giving away father's possessions, consulting with Mr. Fiske, the family estate lawyer, and attending to other affairs of father. Also, I observed that mother had given away all my polo equipment of mallets, britches, horse coolers, bridles, and saddles to my great dismay. I think she knew my polo days were over. She was right, but I thought her action was a little premature. I did spend a little time playing golf with Walt Taylor and Harry Wheeler both who were home on leave from the Pacific. Mother had her devoted two sisters Helen and Florence, who lived in nearby Lake Bluff and Lake Forest to console her.

During that brief stay I had dinner with Annie May Henry and Cy Manierre, who had just been furloughed from the OSS (the CIA of WWII) as he told us this story: Cy was parachuted into France to spy on the movements of the French Palou (the resistance French forces allied to the German occupation forces). The German Gestapo captured CY in plain clothes (rather than U. S army clothes) in Southern France, which in accordance with the Geneva Convention made him subject to execution. Subsequently, he was turned over to the Weimar to be shipped by rail to a Russian concentration camp where execution would be expected. On the prison train trip, he was unloaded en route east from their train into a large outside fenced combound for a brief stop before moving on. While milling around with all the other prisoners, he spotted on the other side of the fence that contained Air Force prisoners, his brother, Bill. He had been shot down in his B-17 on a bomber raid out of England and was being sent to one of the Stalag Luffte prisons. Seizing the opportunity CY engineered getting through the fence into the area where his brother was being contained. He subsequently posed as a member of the Air Force. With all the other Air Force prisoners, he was loaded on to their troop train and sent with his brother to spend his prison time for the rest of the war as a shot down Air Force person. So he traded death in a concentration camp for an Air Force Stallag Luffte camp-a comparatively comfortable prison. He was a POW and not a spy! With CY's humorous and modest way of relating the story, you would have thought the whole experience was a walk in the park.

After a couple weeks at home, I was transferred to Santa Monica, California for reassignment. We could try to choose our preference for our next duty (I requested duty in twin-engine A-26 night fighters and to return to combat), but my request was refused. Because of my experience in the Mustang, I was assigned to the Sarasota Advanced Fighter base to be an instructor in the Mustang. I am sure that assignment was logical and correct from the Air Force's point of view because of my past experience.

Typically the Air Force allowed an officer about three weeks time to travel from Lake Bluff to Santa Monica (to be assigned) and then to his eventual assignment (Florida), so I was able to spend some time with Jean (my sister) in Pebble Beach. We tennised, ate, drank and enjoyed a few days together. Jean and I had always been great pals and always enjoyed doing things together and being with each other, so this stay was fun.

Sarasota was a small attractive town, beautiful beaches, golf courses, and the Orange Blossom Hotel. Our airbase was a few miles out of town close to where we lived and played. We were there to teach young pilots the art of combat fighting.

My friend Dick Faxon was already stationed there, so that was a pleasure to reconnect with him. We both were assigned to teach budding fighter pilots all about combat flying.

Our schedule was to fly two sessions each day; one from seven to nine and the second from ten to twelve in the morning. I would meet five pilots and review what our mission would be. Usually, I would take them out and fly active formation flying. After a few practice sessions, I would form them up "line astern" and then have them follow me through acrobatics, such as Loops, Emmelmanns, wing overs, chandelles and anything else I could think up. The challenge for them was to see if they could stay in formation.

It was easy for the leader (me) to initiate these maneuvers, but it was more difficult for the followers to maintain their positions because there was lag by each following plane to the plane ahead. If I were to lead the flight through a LOOP at a normal speed, it meant that the followers had a harder time from stalling out at the top of the loop (since they would be moving more slowly). I had to be careful and not to slow down too much, or I would have my students floundering in the sky. In fact, I recall one time one of my students did get into a flat stall and spin and plunged down out of control to about 500 feet above the ground before he got control of his plane and flew out of danger. After that experience I was extremely careful to not make my flying dangerously difficult. However, this type of a problem might occur in a dog fight, so it behooved us to enlighten them of that problem.

When our flying was over, we would grab a bite of food and then we were supposed to report to ground school. Few attended those study periods. Instead we headed for our "homes", the beach, or the golf course. A famous ace fighter pilot (General Blakeslee) was assigned to our base from England and announced that he did not want the job of running an American based training school, but, since it had befallen upon him, he sure wasn't going to allow everyone to "goof off". "You will all move back on base (Surrender your living quarters on the beach or wherever) and attend ground school, effective immediately". You could have heard a pin drop. It turned out we did move back on the base, but only for two days. We felt ground school was what we did not need, so we gradually all disregarded his orders as he failed to enforce his edicts. We all returned to our pads "off base".

Mother someway made contact with Sissy Paterson, the owner and publisher of the Washington Post, and obtained a charming little house on Siesta Cay for me and my buddies to rent. It was the only house on the whole cay! There were no buildings on the entire beach except a small inn called Sand Away East (that is my recall). The house overlooked the Gulf of Mexico just a short stroll to the water for swimming. The house was furnished simply but adequately-it was sensational. Just sand and open beach. We of course made the most of it and hightailed it home to our retreat as soon as we left the airbase. Dick Faxon was one of the four occupants in our castle. We did our own cooking, and had more than one party with some of the lovelies whom we had gotten to know in Sarasota.

Mother in the meantime was preparing to go to Palm Beach for the winter. Her pals had all left a chilly gloomy late November Lake Bluff. So she was happy to head south. Since I was just across the boot of Florida from her, it was easy for me to obtain permission to use a PT-13 trainer airplane and whiz over in 45 minutes for the weekend to see her. I went out to dinner, played golf and was even a companion with her for some social evenings. That proximity in addition to having an airplane supplied to me by the U. S. Air Force made visits easy.

Under this environment I met Helen Doby from Stamford, Connecticut, known as "Apple". She was wintering in Sarasota with her four year old daughter, Julie, her sister-in-law (Emily Meyer), while their estranged husbands were still overseas in the Services. Apple and I became great pals. She had little use for her husband according to her own sister-in-law and was filing for a divorce. She was a 5'7" bouncy, effervescent, energetic, blond, fun loving girl. We would dance by the hour at the Lido (A pavilion at Clearwater Beach), enjoy dinners with her, swim in the ocean, watch Ringling Brothers trapezes around town, and spend many afternoons-evenings together. Our relationship lasted about six months. We became very close. I am sure we were both in limbo and unsure what was next in our lives. Neither of us knew what our future would be. We didn't care. We just enjoyed our time together. I do believe we thought that those days could last forever. However, when I was notified I was to be furloughed from the Air Corps and when she decided she must return to Stamford to proceed with her divorce, we tearfully said goodbye. Soon after she left Sarasota and temporarily went to Washington, D.C., I commandeered an AT-6 and flew up to see her in Washington for what turned out to be the last time I saw her. It seemed that the drastic change in both our lives put an end to the romance.

I left Sarasota for Lake Bluff and mother's adjustment to widowhood. Apple returned to Stamford, and I must come to a decision about the relationship between Diana Hill and myself, and I must face the decision of my future occupation. I just had to wait and let a few things settle before making some important decisions for my life. Later at a Yale reunion I learned from an old classmate and friend, Joe Mayer, who had grown up with Apple, that the end of my relationship with Apple might have been for the best because "David, you are fortunate that your relationship with her ended. She was no good. " Her husband and she were sailing when he mysteriously drowned. " You are fortunate. " Whatever the conclusions from that statement might be, I have fond memories of our relationship and I hope the same is true for her.

I almost killed myself on that flight back to see her in Washington. I commandeered an AT-6 (Advanced Training plane) to make the trip. On my return to Sarasota I picked up a Black Enlisted man who wanted to hitch a ride south. We loaded up, although I knew the weather was treacherous en route to Florida, but I thought I had to get back. Before long out of Washington, I ran into zero-zero thunderstorm weather that was so bad the FFA closed down the commercial airlines all along the East Coast. I got lost as I was flying VFR over the treetops in the fog, lightening, and downpours, and almost out of gas when I flew over an airfield- I did know not where (I still can't recall its location- maybe Georgia) when I made a sharp 270 degree turn and plunked the plane down amidst thunder, lightening, and a cloud bursts of rain. I was shivering from fright. As I climbed down from the cockpit, my passenger, who was perfectly calm and unexcited, exclaimed, "Sir, you sure are a good pilot". He never knew the real truth.

Prior to joining the Air Force, Diana Hill and I had been going together for a couple of years and had decided we would wait till the end of the War when I returned before we would get married. We were both very much in love. We had corresponded for three years while I was away, so we thought the love that we had was still there. With all the decisions that I had to make on returning obscured that decision. Gradually after a short reunion we both realized that marriage was not in the cards. Diana was a lovely girl- very feminine, non athletic, pretty, smart, alert, restrained, and charming. So our dream ended with warmth and regret. Years later I hired her to sell mother's house after mother's death. She met Anne and me at the Palwaukee airport where we had flown to in my plane. She was so attractive and so charming. She expertly sold the house. Diana apparently had a unhappy first marriage, but she remarried and led a happy life thereafter. She died in the early 2000s. She was a fine wonderful lady.

FURLOUGH
AND MY FUTURE

I was told after about a year to report to an Air Force base in Georgia (I can't recall)to be furloughed out of the Air Force. Since I had flown some 148 missions and two tours of duty, I had accumulated many "points", so I was given the early option of quitting the military or staying in. I did not hesitate. I jumped at the opportunity to retire. So I was furloughed from the Air Force in early May of 1945. Some stayed in with the idea of either Air Force careers or with some additional training to become a Commercial Air Line pilot.

I packed up, said good-bye to Fax, and headed for Lake Bluff. There I was welcomed as a hero (as was everyone else returning from the war). We were feted by the older generation many of whom were friends of father's that had been too old to participate in the war but who kept the industrial complex in America rolling along. I was asked more than once into Chicago for lunch with friends of my parents to relate the aspects of flying against the Germans. In the course of these encounters, I was offered enticing job offers with investment banking firms and banks. Good pay, Lake Forest and life style that had no appeal for me. I had no particular respect or interest for the investment banking business, probably because I did not understand it, or working for a Commercial bank on La Salle Street. I thought it was a non productive way of life. Many of the brokers and investment bankers that lived in Lake Forest seemed to return from work early in the day to play golf. With my father working till late in the day, I resented what I thought was too easy life for them. Obviously, I was naïve with some of these thoughts.

I had a vision that the financial world was one of manipulation and was basically not producing anything new. It was not creating. The growing of a calf or producing a corn crop was producing something new and therefore was actually creating. I am sure I did not understand the financial world. I could not see the tangible evidence of their efforts. It may have been naïve, but I felt it in my heart.

So I decided I had to get away to more open spaces and lead my own life and not be beholden to some senior officer in a big bank building in Chicago! I figured that I would forego the handsome financial offers to me for what I thought I could do my self.

I wanted to go some place new. The business life of La Salle Street did not appeal to me. I concluded I just might spend my life taking care of mother. My romances with both Apple and Diana were over. I had no demanding tie. Just mother, but I just had to leave. I was offered a job to go to work in the Stockyards in Denver for the Cudahy Packing Co. That's what I wanted: cattle, horses, small city, no commuting, new friends so I accepted the job and prepared to move to Denver. A new life.

18

GO WEST YOUNG MAN

After my discharge from the Air Corps in May of 1945, I returned to my mother's home at 935 Ravine Avenue in Lake Bluff, Illinois. Mother had lived widowed there since Father had died a year before. Jean and Daggett lived in Chicago, and so mother without any family nearby had lived alone during that period. Mother was trying hard to adjust to her widowhood by being active. But even with bridge, golf, luncheons and friends, the home was lonely. As a result she was overjoyed to have me home. We had always been close companions and had enjoyed many events together prior to the War. We had had happy dinners, golf games, and bridge games together. But I realized that I had to do my "own thing" which was difficult for me to be leaving mother behind. Most often in the morning I would be asked "David, are you going to be home for dinner tonight". I felt reluctant to say no that I was going to go out prancing with my friends who were starting to return from their war related duties. Life was celebratory for me. For many other returnees this was a period of cheer and rejoicing. However, I felt an obligation and desire to comfort mother which was quite incompatible with me seeing my contemporaries. Too frequently I was torn whether to stay with her or play with my buddies.

Within this environment I realized I must make a decision on my life's start and my future. What kind of work, what was available, what financial goals I might have, where I wished to live, what could I afford, what would happen to mother if I departed, and other questions all were churning in my mind.

I determined that, even though I had recently been offered a handsome salary to work for a large brokerage firm in Chicago, I thought that kind of work was not my cup of tea. I was enticed by the salary, but Chicago held no allure for me- inside at a desk on the 20th floor of a big office was even worse, and the idea of commuting on the North Western seemed like an awful way to spend two hours out of many days of my life. The Lake Forest social life had little appeal-the Onwentsia Club, same old friends, same dinner parties all seemed unexciting. I am sure I wanted adventure and something new. What did I want? What previous experience had I had that might be an aid in getting a good start and what would I want for my life? My Military flying had equipped me with ability to pursue a life in aviation and obtaining a lucrative job with an airline. Being an airline pilot did not appeal to me as I thought that would be nothing but being a glorified bus driver. My background with horses and cattle at the Arizona Desert School made a job with the Cudahy Packing Co. working as a cattle buyer in Denver just right for me. I could have a horse, work with cattle, breathe fresh air, live in a small city, meet new people, and be independent- that adventure was the right fit. There was little doubt what my choice would be. However, my main reservation was leaving my mother. After a considerable number of conversations between us, mother agreed that I should strike out. So strike out I did.

I got in the old Buick four-door sedan with all my duds and headed for the Mile High City. All I knew was there was a lot of outdoors, a small city, a new adventure, and a fun job all on the horizon. The only connection I would have in Denver was a certain Denise Barkalow who was a friend of my parents from their Omaha days. He and his wife greeted me kindly and immediately suggested that they give me a guest card at the Denver Country Club and I could lodge there. Upstairs in the main clubhouse were six or eight bedrooms (Now office space)- all of which had beds on rollers, which I could push out to a tiny outside, screened sleeping porch so I could enjoy the cool Colorado nights. Besides being inexpensive, I had the run of the club, which included the tennis courts and golf course. And of course with such amenities and being a participant in those sports, it meant I made many acquaintenances quickly and easily.

19

MARRIAGE

With a secure job and great place to live, I was ready to launch off on a new life. I would start work at 5:30 at the Stockyards and finish the day towards 4 P.M., so I would have time to enjoy exercise that I so desire. Since I had played lots of tennis in my life, it was often that I picked up a game when I arrived home. In time I met Anne Jackson by courtside and we sat and talked for quite awhile before we got into a mixed doubles game. What an easy way to meet someone. We seemed to enjoy each other and soon began seeing each other for dinner and other activities. We spent time dancing, talking, playing tennis and having a good time together. It seemed we just clicked right off the bat. She was the greatest dancer in the world and we enjoyed finding any place to dance. She was a top tennis player and we could have good singles or doubles games together even though her emotionless continence did not coincide with my often tempestuous manner. In a matter of a short time we were together almost daily.

Anne lived with her father at 935 Washington Street in a house too large for them. The Judge was the Chief Justice of the Colorado Supreme Court, a graduate of Harvard, whose long time home had been

Colorado Springs. Upon his appointment to the Supreme Court, he moved his two daughters, Anne, Jean and himself to Denver. The Judge was stern and busy and at the same time protective of his two daughters-more than I think they desired.

I felt not particularly welcomed because he had his reservations and suspicions about any new man on the block who was so attentive to his daughter. His formality rather overwhelmed me. Once when Anne and I were playing Bridge with Margaret (his future wife) and him, I answered his query of where I had gone to college to which I answered "Yale, have you ever heard of it?" He thought that was a rather smart ass way to answer as he gave me a stern glower. The lightness around the house

was not enhanced by the very seriousness of his to be wife. Margaret, who refered to her father in almost every sentence, and the judge invited us very frequently to "Waltz Night" at the Cosmopolitan hotel ballroom-an event we felt obligated to attend. Sister Jean and husband John would lighten up the evening along with John's enjoyment of a couple of cocktails before the music started.

Anne Jackson Wilhelm

Anne and Jean had lost their mother a few years ago and left them saddened. Living in this large home even after the Judge's and Margaret's marriage was not a lively place. Anne had great respect for her father, but at the same time had frequent severe disagreements with him. I know Anne was ready for a different life.

**Maid of Honor Jean and Anne
at our wedding in 1946**

Anne was tall, five foot nine (Without high heels), svelte, shapely, quiet, shy, Quakerism non-combative, reflective, intellectually inclined, frugal, beautifully dressed with a real appreciation of colors, and reserved. Her thinking was from her own mind, and not always of the often prevailing ideas. Her excellent taste was reflected not only in her clothes but in her décor of our homes. She was self sufficient which was shown in her six or seven year in the unfamiliar ranching or farming communities. She was even keeled so her temperament was consistently good with nary explosions of passion. She had great rapport with friends like Sheila Malo, Sidney Gates, Marcia Strickland, Ellen Embree, Nancy Dominick. She was an "out to lunch" auto driver who survived even though there were lots of dreams and thoughts as she drifted down the high ways.

Anne was a very assertive and opinuated mother. Even though devoted to her daughter, Jean received admonitions from her mother on her opinions and taste, which were not appreciated. Anne also had an unhappy time with Jeannie's husband John's and his lack of sensitive of the things that Anne liked (i.e. Anne liked a neat kitchen and was proud of it and her house). John Russell would come into the house or kitchen and toss his briefcase or coats wherever with no concern of Anne. Most often he would grab the telephone not even asking if someone else might want it. Not very sensitive. Anne did not blast out at John, but just seethed inside. Anne's displeasure did not please Jeannie. So that all led to all kind of difficulties.

I admire Anne allegiance to me. Moving to Fraser with no medical assistance and two babies might have raised objections from most mothers. Living in a small shack with rudimentary heating and plumbing and thunderstorms flashing lightening in the summer, having to help me rangle a horse in the morning-cooking three meals a day for the hay crew were all unfamiliar in her life. But she never complained and just tried to help me every inch of the way. What a girl. How lucky could a man be?

The Judge showed no emotion when I popped the question to him. My Mother was elated for she loved Anne and recognized her qualities. One of the Cowles family had told mother there was instability in the Jackson family which mother was mildly concerned about. I think the concerns were that some suicides in the family that hinted mental problems.

I had moved from the Country Club to the University Club (because Porry Robinson said I had overstayed my welcome.) Bill Embree was my close friend in Denver who then married Ellen Shafroth Alexander who was Anne's inseparable friend.

Jean and Daggett Harvey

My sister Jean Harvey
at Anne's & my wedding, Colorado Springs

Anne and DC after their wedding

The wedding took place at the Shove Memorial Chapel at Colorado College with a large pleasant reception at the Cheyenne Mountain Country Club. My sister and Daggett and many friends from Denver came to the wedding and everyone spent the night at the Broadmoor Hotel.

Anne and I went to the Horse races in Raton and then down to the La Fonda Hotel in Santa Fe. The city was crowded, but everything was beautiful and we were truly in love. We spent three great days there and then returned to Denver. We soon bought our little house at 627 Holly Street and life developed in great fashion from there.

20

STOCKYARDS

Anne and I bought a neat little two bedroom home at 627 Holly Street. Lots of social life along with hard work. I didn't have to fight for a job since I was the son of the Executive V. P. and nephew of the President of the Cudahy Packing Company. I went to work in the Denver Union Stockyards as a calf buyer. Started at 6 AM and usually finished by 4 PM. Anne would pick me up in our car at the plant on Brighton Blvd. I had major frustrations with Anne for the first few weeks, because Anne was always ten to twenty minutes late picking me up. I was a punctual type and I could not understand Anne's tardiness. I thought there must be some subtle motive she had. Showing she wasn't to be dominated? Just disorganized? Or was it just being late was in her blood? We would talk about the problem and she would repent and she would promise to be on time the next day but lo and behold the same thing the next day. As a new boy on the block, I was busting my gut and was anticipating a wonderful reunion with my new bride, only to be left standing on Brighton Blvd steaming. It seemed the problem disappeared only after I bought a second set of wheels.

Working was fun- learning about cattle-their habits, quality, weights, condition, health, and the monetary value of all the different kinds and weights within an active trading market. The Denver Union Stockyards was the marketing center of the Rocky Mountains and surrounding area where every week there were probably over 15,000 cattle were offered for sale at the Denver Union Stockyards by the cattle feeder. The cattle were then consigned to a commission man and placed in his pens. The cattle were watered, fed hay and then sorted for uniformity of weight and quality.

It was always exiting anticipating the market direction each morning. The packing houses buyers represented Swift, Armour, Cudahy, Wilson, Litvak, Capitol. Since a slaughter house carried little inventory of cattle for the start of the next day's day's slaughter (since cattle carried from one day to the slaughter next, shrunk and lost value), we were under the gun to get cattle bought immediately as soon as trading began so the plant could start the kill. It was a cat and mouse game testing each others outlook of the market at that time. The union workers in the slaughter house were paid whether there were cattle ready for slaughter or not, so it was a major loss if the packing house was without cattle to kill. The pressure was always on us to get the cattle bought.

My boss was Holly Blayney, a 65 year old pink faced old school Irish loyal devoted company man and stern task master. He was my mentor. He was haughty and superior to these young buyers-particularly those "Jewish upstarts". He felt he was the dean of the old school of cattle buyers. He was not one of those "miserable new Jews" representing the new packing houses. He rode a big roan horse, carried a long carriage whip, and expected to be treated with respect. He scoffed at the up and coming Jewish cattle buyers showing this by lashing his whip at them as they would peak their heads through the pen fences as they tried to listen to the trading conversation between Holly and the commission man.

The day would start at 6 AM at the barn where I would curry and saddle my little green mouse colored mare, ride down the hill to the stockyards and proceed to inventory some 80 separate pens of cattle as to quality, weight, breed, and finish and give this evaluation to Holly before the market opened. I and the two other cattle buyers for Cudahy would confer at the bulletin board prior to the market opening for trading where market quotes were being posted from the Chicago, Omaha, Kansas City, and Sioux City stockyards. We would read all the cattle market reports from the others markets so that we were prepared to give Holly our estimate what the Denver market would be. Holly then would give us orders of how many cattle of what type to try to buy and at what price. There were no intercoms so we buyers had to communicate by meeting around the yards as the morning progressed to see how our buy of some 1000 cattle and calves was being achieved. It was exciting, demanding and competitive. It was fun. The market could change as the morning went on influenced by the vigor of the retail trade in the beef markets of the whole country.

During the morning of buying there was lots of bluffing, anticipating the markets, the manner in giving your bid to the commission man, and ability to "make a deal". Each pen of some thirty cattle had a variety of good and bad cattle so I would for example say "25 cattle @$27.00 with 3 head @ 25.50 with one out entirely". I would then have to go through five more pens at that commission house and then repeat at possibly three more commission houses. In some cases the commission man would sell, sometimes not. I would either "leave the bid open till 10:15", withdraw the bid, or remember what I had bought. I would then have to keep that and subsequent bids in my mind with all the details of each bid. My buying would end when I had filled my order given me by Holly. Buying at stockyards demanded knowing cattle, good trading and having enough smarts to remember all the bids and the particulars.

After all our buying orders were completed I along with the other two buyers (Spud Shields and Joe McConaty) would "pickup" the cattle we had bought from the eight commission houses scattered round the fifty acres of pens and aboard my horse drive them down the fenced alleys through numerous gates to the Cudahy holding pens. At this point we would then sort all the steers, heifers, cows and bulls into separate pens each having uniformity according to weight, finish, and quality. This operation was done so that when a lot (pens put together) was killed and went to the coolers after slaughter that lot would all be similar hanging on the rails in the cooler and therefore facilitating grading by the U. S. government grader, who would them stamp each carcass Prime, Choice, Select , Good or Utility.

Holly did the sorting of the live cattle and this could entail two long tortuous hours as he carefully sorted, resorted and resorted the cattle. About 3 to 4 PM we would be released by Holly, and I would take the mare back for her rest and feed at the barn, and the day was over. Often on Thursday and Fridays, when cattle buying was greatly reduced, I the eager beaver would volunteer to spend time in the accounting department to try to understand what the business was all about. The stockyards job was great. The job seemed new and exciting. My background on horses and cattle at the Arizona Desert School made my new job easy to learn-Outdoors, horses and horsemanship, trading, competition- all right down my ally. Certainly more desirable than riding the 7AM train from Lake Bluff to a brokerage office in the Loop and returning via the North Western railroad at 5:10 PM to suburbia. It seemed to me just the right thing to be doing.

Often after hours I enjoyed a great association with Ben Duke, the head livestock commission man in the Rocky Mountain area. I would drop up to his office and talk cattle with him as I eagerly and interestingly was trying to learn. Ben became a close friend and a fun teacher. When Ben died his son, Ben, and I took Ben Sr.'s ashes, scattered them out of the window of my Cessna 182 over Northern Colorado where Ben had spent much of his recent time.

After six months in the cattle yards and a couple of weeks in the Hog yards with Frank Demetrovitch. (He was a Russian who said his father would hang him up in a tree by the thumbs to discipline him. Frank was so involved with the hog business that his nose looked exactly like a pig's snout! He was a loyal, expert employee for Cudahy.)

I was transferred to the killing floor of the packing house. This was a shock. Bawling cattle, bleating sheep, and squealing hogs in a steaming slicky blood stained killing floor was not for the light hearted. I was first given the shackling job on the sheep kill. I would have to go into a pen of lambs, grab one by the hind leg, put that chained limb on a counter clockwise turning wheel after which as you looked into those soulful eyes, you would then proceed to slit his throat as the blood gushed out all around you. I did the same job on the hog kill that might have been worse because a hog squealed so loud it was deafening. The regular crew that had worked on the "kill" was callused and went about their job like a secretary punching an adding machine. In 1946 the method of killing cattle was to lay the beef on their back on the floor after they had bled and skin them out. (Soon thereafter all cattle were put on a moving rail and disassembled with butchers using mechanical knives). The "floorsman" was a skilled knife man and one where I tried to help but the knife work was too hard for an inexperienced one like me. One had to skin out the animal leaving no fat on the hide and no nicks or cuts on the hide otherwise the hides would be harshly discounted in value. The three months on the killing floor was truly an experience but one that I don't think I wanted as a steady job.

I also worked on the hog kill moving conveyor line as a "gutter". You reached into the opened carcass of the hog, cut the guts from the interior lining of the body, and then slopped the whole heavy load onto a moving platform. I liked the killing floor because the process was a team effort and everyone had to keep up with the whole progression. The whole killing process was tough on one's humanity, but those six months were a maturing experience. I was glad when that experience was finished for me.

After that job I was shifted into the coolers and the dressed beef department. I became a beef grader, and head of the lamb and veal department. My tenure in Denver was obviously an educational experience with the thought that I might end up at the headquarters of the Company in Chicago. During this time I was even sent down town in Denver to the Denver National Bank where I was supposed to learn all about banking

in one month. I did not enjoy that month and I did not understand a thing that a bank did. I was too wet behind the ears to comprehend mortgages, loans, margins, liquidity, and such. I came away with little new insight on financing.

"Banker" Wilhelm 1955

At this early stage of my business career I did not focus on what was in store for me. I did not ponder what all this indoctrination might lead to. I was concentrated on learning my job and a good start to understanding all the details of the cattle business. Also Anne and I were starting and learning about married life. It was a great start.

21

OMAHA

The powers to be in Chicago decided that I should be given additional training in the Company and that the Cudahy Packing Company's largest packing house operation, was where the most could be learned. So I was moved to Omaha. Naively at that point of my life I did not realize that Uncle Ed was trying to groom me and his two sons for future executive positions in the Company.

It was a difficult decision to leave Denver and move to Omaha for Anne and me. We had a neat little house at 627 Holly Street, my cattle buying job was enjoyable, the tennis and golf fun, our social life active, and all her family close to Denver. There were reservations about moving but I was at this stage determined to learn all I could as quickly as possible. I think Anne was wonderful for she had no comittement there whereas I had my job. She agreed to the move, although I know it was a wrenching decision for her.

I give her my praise to sacrifice her happiness and security for me. She made no complaint and was a real scout to encourage me and go along with the plan. She was unselfish as always in this decision which I have appreciated always.

The United States restricted domestic home contruction during World War II so as to concentrate all efforts on building ships, planes, tanks and other necessities for the War. This concentration on producing war essentials created a critical shortage of housing for returning G. I. s. In their wisdom the government placed price controls on all new home construction. But since the prices so established were not high enough so that builders could "make it", there was a little new construction. Instead of creating more affordable housing, price controls aggravated the whole problem. The result was an extreme shortage of houses or apartments to rent.

In this setting Anne and I arrived in Omaha with Pinky our obedient cocker spaniel. We found a room at the Tower Motel expecting to locate an acceptable lodging soon. Neither the Cudahy Packing Co. nor Cousin Tony Cudahy, who was a resident of Omaha, made any provisions to assist our relocation. I would have thought he or they might have at least advised as to where to stay or given us a greeting or welcome. There was none of that. It could be that he resented the possible competition for a future position in the company or that he was an unthinking guy. At any rate that did not warm our relations for the future. The Tower Motel was dirty, noisy, and old. We occupied our one room along with a large family of friendly mice. Nightly we could hear them marching around our linoleum floor. Instead of a couple nights at the Tower, we found ourselves searching the FOR RENT ads for two long weeks. It was no joy.

Finally we spotted an ad and rushed from our mice invested motel and leased a one-room apartment from an old skinflint, Andy Knudsen. There were others waiting for the space if we did not accept it. If you ever saw a low cost construction and cheap apartment, that was it. Thin walls, hallways so narrow that we had to bring our furniture through the second floor window, 28 inch doorways, and leaky windows. But still a vast improvement-over our rat trap Tower Motel.

My Aunt Esther (My father's sister) and her husband Deen Cooper were our saviors. They were wonderful people. He was a civic minded businessman who ran Orchard and Wilhelm, a large furniture and decorating company. He was a 60 year old 6'3" serious, thoughtful, and a kind man. Aunt Esther was maybe 60 years old, feminine, thoughtful, assertive, intelligent, attractive, generous and jovial. We became close friends with them. They were very concerned and interested in our happiness and welfare in Omaha. They had two adopted children who were not in Omaha at that time so I think we satisfied their desire to have some young to be concerned about. Their daughter, Rose, was an erratic difficult girl who was away at school. Their son, Sam, was a good catholic boy who lived away from home. We rarely saw their children. At any rate it was within a short time that Deen found us a beautiful two bed room apartment with a large living room and dining room in a convenient and attractive neighborhood (The Knickerbocker Apartments) which we moved into as soon as we could leave Andy Knudsen. Anne and I felt elated with this find and Pinky was so well trained that he would trot down the fire escape from our third floor location, do his thing, and then proudly return up the fire escape stairs to our pad. So our living arrangements were finally happily finalized thanks to Deen and Esther's help.

I was an assistant beef cooler man grading beef in this highly unionized large meat packing plant. In addition I spent a considerable amount of time in the accounting department trying to analyze a hand inputted huge spreadsheet that had been compiled daily in the same manner for the last forty years. The purchasing numbers, cost, location in the plant, expected disposition, sale price and estimated profit or loss. It was a massive sheet of paper covered with penciled and corrected numbers. This was supposed to be a buying guide. The whole effort was imprecise and often inaccurate. Modern accounting had not hit the Cudahy Packing Co. Not even early computers were contemplated

The plant, an old Thomas Lipton tea factory, was the original killing plant of the Cudahy Packing Co in 1890. It had been modified and improved for 60 years, so it was a jungle and inefficient. The corridors around the plant were red brick wet walls with barely enough light to navigate. The union was strong and angry with management, and labor relations were poor. The old buildings sprawled over three square blocks during either the nasty winter weather or torrid summer was inhospitable, somber and antique. It was not a cheery place to work.

My work was impersonal and uninspiring. I would drive my Plymouth in 6 A. M. morning darkness often in fog or ice to start the day. Cousin Tony was a brash exMarine Cop, who was no inspiration or terribly friendly. He was brusque and opinionated with little reason. Quite quickly I could see that I was being groomed for a job in the executive offices in Chicago which held no allure to me. I did not like Omaha, the job and certainly did not look forward to moving eventually to Chicago.

One of the more unpleasant events was the United Packinghouse Workers strike that took place while I was employed in the beef coolers. Crossing the picket line one day a big black 270# man struck me in the back of the head and knocked me cold. At the testimony before the National Labor Relations Board, Mr. Goodman stated that I had struck his wife and he was merely defending her. He won the case and was not fired. This event had much to do with my dislike of the labor unions. They spent their time roughing up women office workers, tossing bombs into houses, and turning over non union employee's autos (Including mine). With the Omaha police force members of the C.I.O., there was no police protection. Two people were killed in the riots. It wasn't exactly fun going to work which I did all through the strike.

As it turned out Cudahy's financial woes were mounting because the company and its leadership did not see the change in the industry. Outdated physical facilities, relocation of slaughter plants to be near source of feed growing areas, the changing from rail to truck transportation of moving feed, meat and live cattle all contributed to the obsolescentence of Swift, Cudahy, Wilson, and Armour-the BIG FOUR. New companies with new plants in new locations such as I.B.P. in Iowa and Texas, Monfort in Colorado, and others took over the slaughtering of cattle and distribution of beef in the United States. Management of Cudahy failed to foresee these changes. Cudahy was on its way to liquidation some thirty years hence, so my decision to leave the sinking ship saved me from participating in the liquidation of the company.

Anne had made friends with Coppy Ramsey, my Aunt Esther, and a few others, but life was not joyous for her. My particular friend was Jack Kennedy whom we both liked tremendously. I played squash at the Omaha Club, but since I went to work at 5:00 A. M. and worked late and since we were new in Omaha, we generally did not have much of a social life.

Anne contacted pneumonia during the nasty winter weather and was pretty much bummed out for about a month. Her sister Jean came out to help her recoup and that was a great solace for Anne and me. She added cheer and reassurance for Anne and I think she hastened her recovery.

So there we were after ten months both of us disenchanted with Omaha, a probable executive business future in Chicago, and the possible liquidation of the company. I liked the financial security of my job but I felt I had to forget that and strike out to do something that interested me. I had $47,000 of Red Wing stock so I was not broke, and I thought I could with that asset and borrowed money get into the ranching business and get out of Omaha. So I quit to the joy of Anne and my self and headed back to Denver. If I had stayed on, I would have been involved with the deterioration of the company and its liquidation, which would have been uninspiring. So I was probably fortunate that I left when I did.

22

RANCHING IN
FRASER, COLORADO

Returning to Denver was a breath of fresh air after those ten months of Omaha. Blue sky, good weather, friends, family made the return joyous for both of us.

We stayed for a few weeks with Margaret and the Judge at 935 Washington. They were most hospitable, but this was not a pleasure for either of us so we were ready to move on. No place for a young married couple!

Since Guilford Jones was married to Anne's aunt and since he was a ranch realtor, the easy choice for me was to engage him to help us locate a cattle ranch. Since I knew little about Colorado ranch country, I wanted someone with experience to guide us. However, I later realized that Guilford did not know beans about ranching. He, for example, never discussed the economics of plains ranching as opposed to mountain ranching where the former was more fitting to run yearlings (my bent) and more profitable than the mountains. A good realtor would give his opinions even though the advice might be counter to his client's. It could have been that we indicated our preference being in the mountains that deterred him from offering his opinion. I am afraid he was after the commission and that was it. But a little fatherly advice might have steered us differently and where ranching would be more profitable. At any rate he drove us around Colorado to ranches at Gunnison, Telluride, and other mountain towns. I am sure the proximity to Denver and medical facilities would have been important considerations in our final decision anyway. Since we planned to have a family, we both were interested in medical availability. Even though not as remote as other spots, Fraser was within an hour and half of Denver and emergency aid within 30 minutes. Also touring around in the early summer, mountain country was beautiful and such a contrast to flat old Eastern Colorado country. So Fraser, Colorado was our choice.

We agreed to buy Pat and Lillian Lucas's ranch between Fraser and Tabernash- located contiguous to Highway #40 on the west side of the D. R. G. railroad. Coldest spot in the US. 53 below one night. (The bottled gas distributor, Pellini, read and turned the temperatures in from his backyard gauge to K. O. A. radio station which thus got national recognition for Fraser). I ran about 400-500 yearlings on the ranch. Put up hay from July 20 to Labor Day (when it might snow again). Then after grazing the cattle till the snow got too deep for them to graze, we fed the hay on the snow covered meadows, and after the snow melted away by May 15, we grazed the cattle on our land and US Forest land in the summer. The weather made for difficult ranching, but because of the mountain runoff of irrigation water and 18 inches of rainfall, we were not subject to droughts to the same degree that would affect plains ranching. So ranching might be safer in the mountains, but it entailed more work and expense.

Fraser was a timber and ranching town population 200, dirt roads, an old fashion Mercantile store where Frank Carlson sold screw drivers, clothing, and grocery items. Across the dirt road was the "hotel" and active bar that was frequented by railroad workers, timber men and cattle ranchers. Ivor and Bob Florquist ran the Conoco gas station and auto repair shop, Pat Coleman was the drug store owner and operator. Apparently his love jilted this NYC musician so he emigrated to Fraser to become the veterinarian, doctor, and pharmacist. Everyone knew everyone. Anne and I were looked upon with suspicion because there were limited tourists or recreation ranches in the vicinity at that time- there were few newcomers to the area. Most of the ranchers and woodsmen had come from Sweden or other cold countries and had been there for a long time. We were city slickers. I was pretty good hand with a horse and knew cattle and cattle markets from my stockyards experience and worked like a peon, so I passed their scrutiny.

Seventy years old Frank Carlson, who became a consular to me and a good friend had lived all his life in Fraser, so he had tales going back to 1880. He started his day with a shot of whiskey "to get things going", ran the store, operated a ranch, and told old tales of Middle Park. One that I recall was his story of a large two story log building that was on our ranch that was THE HOTEL at the time of the building of the Moffat Tunnel. Frank maintained it was better known as the best whorehouse in the area. Those lovely ladies occupied that beautiful two story square logged building which burned to the ground not long after we left Fraser.

Our house was a summer uninsulated one story shack with a wood stove for cooking, a primitive bathroom, an oil heater, two tiny bedrooms, and a screened porch looking out at 14,000' mountains. It was an icebox in winter but beautiful in the summer. It was a rugged little place particularly when Jeannie and David arrived on the scene. We would put Jeannie in her crib on top of the oil heater to keep her reasonably warm, even though oil heaters were notoriously subject to uncontrolled explosions!(There was a Forest Rangers house that had just burned to the ground in Winter Park).

I usually hired one man in addition to the hay crew in the summer. My first employee was Chris Cristiansen who really thought I should work for him, and resented this green horn telling him what to do. I gave him the gate after about six months and hired Mutt Briggs as my helper. He was 6'2" lumberman, kind, and warm smile, willing, reliable, honest and able. He didn't know much about cattle, but he could fix anything and he was right at home with the cold and freezing winters. He was born and raised in Fraser, so he had an edge on me as far as understanding and adjusting to the area.

About the middle of August haying would start. I was the stacker- the one who would with pitch fork in hand build about 70 stacks of hay. It was a dirty hard working job. After the horse drawn mowers would mow the grass, the hay would be windrowed and then "bucked" to the slide stacker. Two horses would then propel a long ram that would push the hay up the inclined rails of the stacker to its top, where it would then drop the hay onto the stack (Or on me, the stacker), It was always hard to hire a crew. Once I had four boys from an eastern prep school, another time some drunks from skid row in Denver, and other times some itinerate help. It was hit or miss and made it difficult because of their lack of experience. That ordeal interrupted by rain showers and hired help problems usually limped along till mid September when snow was in the offing. The only fun of that experience was its completion.

One summer I hired four young eastern prep school boys to come to help the haying. One of the boys was Gene Tunney (Grandson of the ex Heavy Weight boxing champ) later to become Senator from California. They started out with great enthusiasm, with varying abilities but soon palled with the vigorous schedule. By September 1 a cold drizzle settled into the Fraser valley, the haying stopped as we waited for hay to dry, and the boys got itchy to go back to Long Island, parties, and girls. One approached me to say they were quitting and going home. I bristled realizing we had lots of hay down and more to do. I said "you signed on and you're not quitting". They were staying in an unheated bare cabin where they retreated, conferred, and returned to me and said "OK, we'll stay". After three days of more drizzle and no sign of let up in the weather, I relented and told them they could leave. Within minutes they were gone, probably muttering "that old son of a bitch". Mutt, his father, and I finished haying in late September. During this entire haying season Anne was feeding three meals a day to those four boys in addition to me and Jeannie and David. That was tougher work than haying

The 900 tons of hay that were harvested would then be fed from early fall till May to the calves that I would buy each fall for growing till sold as yearlings in the following fall. In the winter each morning we would harness up our team of frost covered horses that had grown long heavy coats of hair to protect them from the cold. The leather harness was stiff and frozen and the buckles ice cold. I was a real sissy for my hands and fingers seemed frozen, whereas Mutt acted as if he was in the warmth of Palm Beach. After that chilling ordeal the horses would pull the empty sled down through the snow covered meadows for maybe twenty minutes to break through the drifts around the hay stacks to load hay onto the sled. Often these four foot drifts around the stacks took some hard lunging and pulling by the horses to get the sled into a position to load the hay. As we would plough down through the snow covered meadows to load the hay from the stacks in the field, the weather usually was brutally cold. I was bundled with everything I had, but Mutt just would say "nice morning, eh?" After pitching hay from the stack onto the sled, we would scatter the hay on the snow for the cattle and horse's daily feed. The cattle and horses adjusted to the cold and relished our arrival with their daily feed. We fed every day except when a howling blizzard kept the cattle back in the woods and when we probably could not have gotten to the hay stack.

During the summer after the cattle were turned out on the National Forest for grazing, I would load up old faithful Tango, my faithful bay Morgan gelding, onto my pickup and travel to where the cattle were supposed to be. This would entail keeping track of some 500 head of yearlings as they grazed over 10,000 acres of mountain stream bedded meadows high up in the mountains. I would look for foot rot, brisket, and bloat to doctor them to forestall sickness or death. Since these yearlings are not sedentary like mother cows, they liked to wander and stray. As a result I had a continual job trying to keep track of the numbers and their whereabouts. At the end of one season Peter Dominick came up in his little airplane to Granby where I would meet him and we then would comb the valleys from his airplane looking for my strays. We found some 15 head about 25 miles away in the Williams Fork one time, which I then went down in my truck and rescued.

I rode all day for at least three days a week trying to keep my herd together. I shared the Forest Permit with Jimmy Murphy and Bill Daxton so I spent many a day with Bill riding. They were true ranchers and wanted nothing more (except better cattle prices). Some years before Bill had been driving a wagon hauling logs when he had a runaway and was entangled with the timber that broke his leg. Having no medical assistance the leg healed, but he had a big limp on a leg that bowed like the letter C. He had a very small beautiful ranch nestle in the mountains, lived in a bare dirt floored log cabin with his PhD educated wife and sons. He lived on what he raised and the few cattle he sold. I know he was offered a large sum of money for his property, but he turned it down. "What would I do with a lot of money living in a city? I'll stay here till I die" and he did.

In retrospect the country was too cold and high to ship cattle into the area. It was not possible to produce sufficient weight gains on light yearlings to make the operation but barely profitable. There was too much of an adjustment for them. The ranch should have been operated as a cow/calf outfit, and it would have made more sense. I was green as a gourd, and I had little experience in running a cow-calf outfit so I chose running yearlings. I thought my knowledge of markets would make this a better way for me to operate the ranch.

We did have an apt rented at 22 S. Downing in Denver that took some of the heat off the grind at Fraser. Anne bore Jeannie and David in Denver and did convalesce in one of those one-bed room apartments. I would dash back and forth to visit them. It was a good place for Anne, but not a very satisfying arrangement for me.

Anne was terrific. She had no social life except elderly Swedish rancher's wives, had considerable apprehension while helping me wrangling horses in the A.M., no medical care within 90 miles, had to cook three meals a day for five weeks each summer for the hay crew, and had the care and upbringing of two bustling active babies and me! She did not complain, and I believe she enjoyed the challenge and experience. But I am also sure that she was happy "to move on" when we left Fraser

Jeannie and David were old enough so the whole family was together the entire summer. The kids loved the outdoors, the diphtheria cow (from whom we drank her milk for two years before we knew her to be diseased), and the rubber swimming pool. They received lots of attention from our visitors who were usually weekend friends from Denver, Aunt Edie Jackson or other members of Anne's family. Daggett and Jean Harvey visited us, even though Dag almost froze his ears when it hit 53 below zero. The summer was great but it only lasted about 75 days, when again the cold temperature would limit the enjoyment.

David and Jeannie in Columbines - Fraser

We experienced many unwanted and exciting events during our three years in Fraser. The time that I pulled a thirty-foot log across the main line of the railroad and got it stuck thereby stopping a freight train. We eventually pulled the log from the track and the freight went happily on its way to Denver.

Just in Time

Once I had a heart stopping emergency when all my cattle were grazing on a lush pasture 5 miles from home back in the mountains when a 3-½ foot snow storm isolated the cattle without feed. A D-8 Cat from Koppers Co. bulldozed the three foot snow to make a trail home. On the way home I dropped my D4 CAT through the ice crossing St. Louis creek, and feared I would freeze the final drives and therefore ruin it. Jr. O'Neil however built a huge fire in a barn so we could save the tractor. It was a long day that seemed almost insurmountable at the time and one of disastrous financial implications. At first I had no idea how to get the cattle home or feed to them. In the end it turned out OK.

David J., Jeannie, Peter & Andy - My children

The time a water fight with our guests the Dominicks and Haskells necessitated a new paint job in our house.

The time my Sister Jean insisted wearing her Mink coat to our branding when I was trying to convince locals I was just a humble young poor kid trying to make it in the cattle business. I certainly did not want them to know I was connected to the Cudahy Packing Co. -a well-known name to every cattleman.

Then there was the time I was delivering some 500 cattle to the Fraser stockyards for shipment to Denver. With a raft of horsemen we picked up the cattle from our ranch and started a two mile drive across country to the rail road stockyards. All went well as we drove the cattle slowly and carefully through the edge of town. We had put hay into the entrance of the stockyard to coax quietly the cattle into the pens. The lead steer just cautiously poked his head through the entrance gate when all of a sudden two young lads popped up in front of the lead cattle, spooked them and the whole herd bolted so that we now had cattle all over the town and in everyone's backyard. After four hours of preening the town of cattle, we pushed them into the pens for shipment the next morning. I was cringing at the weight loss of the cattle. But we survived.

Financially, we lived on nothing, and the sales of our cattle and the operation paid for our existence.

Embree, Westfeldt, Dominick, Haskell, Ellen, Jean, Nancy, Eileen with Wilhelms, 1947, Wyoming

I worked like a slave, and after three years realized that I could not make a living and that my talents could be used otherwise in the cattle business, and that Anne would obviously be happier in another environment. I liked the life but also found it not challenging and not the road to riches. I sold the ranch at about what I bought it for ($78,000.00) and moved on. (In 2010, the ranch would be worth at least $10,000,000.00 next to the ski slope in Winter Park). It was a great experience; Anne was superb and I greatly admired her as an enduring, loving wonderful wife. If nothing else we formed a loving bond in our hardship.

23

LONGMONT FARMING AND THE START OF THE CATTLE FEEDING BUSINESS

We packed up our little furniture, horses, dogs and family and moved to Longmont, Colorado to a farm seven miles from that farming town 60 miles north of Denver. Our new house was a palace compared to our mountain home. It had been owned by a Long Island man who modernized an attractive one story farm frame house shaded by huge cottonwood trees and surrounded by a white pickete fenced yard. We had a neighbor across the road. We were close to civilization with the amenities (hospitals, supermarkets, entertainment) close by, so this made life more civilized and comfortable for Anne and me.

Andrew Fiske Wilhelm (3/15/53) was born in Denver after we had moved to the farm in Longmont. He was an easy young man, so we were delighted to have him join the family. David and Jeannie played with young Andrew and life was quite peaceful and enjoyable.

To add to this menagerie was Nell Cornell, a crusty determined opinionated old doll who was Anne's helper and nurse. Nell not only had her own ideas on the children's upbringing, but also was not reluctant or shy in correcting Anne and me on our ways of raising our children.

We ate most meals together – it was complete togetherness. I would trudge back from my inexpertise in farming for lunch with the group. Anne and I did not dare to admonish or correct her ways because she might quit. She had no problem doing all the dirty work and preparing food so we were grateful for the help and we plugged along and refrained from offending her. Her presence was a mixed blessing.

Jeannie treated Andy as a doll, which was convenient and helpful for Anne. David had become old enough to think I was worthy of emulating, so he would follow me around in the pickup as I did my chores. Of course, he still carried his "blankey" around with him even as he dragged it through the manured cattle corrals. He also would accompany me into the Longmont grain elevator and then to the local café where I would coffee with farmers, truckers, and the like. He would sit attentively as we gabbed about things that did not interest him.

Even though the house was shaded by huge cottonwoods, the days were hot in the upper nineties and the unairconditioned house was stifling. Often at the end of many days, Nell and Anne would prepare a picnic dinner and then all of us would drive up to the North St. Vrain mountain stream and have dinner by the cool rushing waters. The kids loved it and we enjoyed a drink and a picnic away from our rather stuffy hot home. We enjoyed dinner as the children played by the running stream.

I am sure that both the children and we benefited from those ten years of ranching, farming and rural living. We all lived in harmony and the seeds of family closeness were originated and developed during those six years. I feel sure Anne and I had realized we did not want to live in Longmont or any other farming Northern Colorado town, and that I could see that financially I could not support the family from the income of farming or ranching.

I had become greatly involved in cattle, cattle feeding, and markets but not it farming, so I saw no reason to toil on the farm breaking my back and not seeing any financial future. I did learn that dealing in cattle themselves in a more efficient manner and not trying to raise cattle or feed was the way to go.

When we first moved to Longmont, I brought a small cow herd with me. Since we had to have a branding each spring, it was necessary to gather a crew to throw calves, help in castrating, dehorning, adminstering injections and brands. I realized that I had a lot of eager would be ranchers in Denver who were practicing law or doing some other sedentary job, and who might be available for a branding and champagne barbeque dinner. So we asked some twenty people including the Dominicks and Haskells to participate. They exerted extreme inexpertize effort in manhandling the 200 lb calves, and in so doing inflicted considerable harm to their own bodies. Peter D. put dehorning paste on his shin which developed into an open sore for months and Floyd H. pulled his back so he walked with bent over angle for as long as I remember. Since the two became US Senators, I do not think those injuries deterred their accomplishments as Senators.

Later, I decided to sell my cowherd. I advertised the sale and agreed with a Wyoming rancher to a favorable sale price. The following day, I found a dead cow in the pen and others that looked badly and ill. Regrettably, I called the rancher and cancelled our deal. As is the custom in the cattle business, I shipped the cattle to the Denver Stockyards where the cattle were sold to a Denver cattle trader. I collected my check of some $45,000 for the sale. However, the buyer of the cows had two cows drop dead after they were delivered to him and paid for. He immediately cried fowl. It turned out the cattle had a disease called antiplasmosis which, if known by me previous to shipping could not be shipped for sale at a public stockyard. Since I did not know that, the Administrator of the Packers and Stockyards Act absolved me and I was able to retain the check. That incident gave me a few heart palpitations!

Farming and I did not get along well. I didn't enjoy sitting all day on a tractor. I didn't know squat about machinery. I didn't see any prospect of making enough money to support my family, unless I bought a large farm which I could not afford. I had to take a turn in my agricultural quest.

My cattle experience at Longmont had wetted my interest in cattle feeding, but, if I were to continue that my effort in that direction, I had to conduct the feeding and finishing of cattle in a more efficient manner. I had wasted time and effort in Longmont because of lack of modern equipment and facilities. I needed an elevator to receive and process feed ingredients so I could formulate the feed rations in the correct proportions and at the most advantage cost. If I bought feeds from a commercial elevator, I was paying for his services. Additionally, I needed farm equipment to harvest, load and haul the feeds I raised to the elevator for mixing. Also I needed equipment to dispense the rations to the cattle and corrals and feed bunks to hold and feed the cattle. To justify the investment to modernize cattle feeding, I must increase the size of the operation to justify the capital investment. Just think of a Yale graduate spending his life doing backbreaking physical labor for no benefit except staying in shape. Certainly I had to find a better answer.

During my many visits to the Denver Stockyards to get "posted" on the markets, I met George Mancini a respected farmer/feeder in the Brighton, Colorado area. George, who farmed a 200 acre farm, was of Italian decent, 30 years old, and knowledgeable in farming and cattle feeding. After discussing our inefficient feeding practices at our respective farms, we recognized how we should join forces and build an efficient cattle finish feeding operation. We would have to raise capital to construct pens for the cattle, an elevator to receive, store, process, and mix feeds rations and provide office facilities and finally provide working capital for the operation.

The first move was to set up a Limited Partnership. The General partners were George Mancini, Bill Carey, and myself.

Jean and Bill Carey - Mexico

George owned 20 acres of land suitable for the Yard which he contributed for his third interest. Bill Carey, a recent friend and acquaintance of mine, was a Notre Dame and Harvard Business School graduate whom I had recently met in Denver. He was unmarried, entrepreneurial, and ready to take a ride. He knew nothing about the business I was proposing but was ready to invest along with me. We both contributed $50,000.00 to the partnership and obtained a one third interest. All three of us put up unconditional personal guarantees for our borrowings from the bank. George and I took a very meager salary for our management services.

Next we raised additional capital with the addition of some Limited Partners such as Fred McLaughlin, an investor, John Matthews, a rancher, Bob Flanagan, investor, Malcolm Stewart, rancher, Stanley Livingston, investor, Sandy McCulloch, investor, Jim Lewis investor and few more all advanced cash for their limited liability interest. They were all loyal and stood by our company for many years. In all we were able to capitalize the "Wilhelm-Mancini Feedlots" adequately to satisfy out lenders.

I had difficulty obtaining the loan because "you don't have any experience", "your plan of a commercial feeding operation is not proven", and "I don't know enough about you" Finally, after a great effort I obtained a line of credit and we were ready to start construction. Those early bankers were not very enthusiastic or encouraging. We opened the feedyard in 1956 ready for action, but a little bit apprehensive of our future success.

Our plan was to build a yard with a capacity of 5,000 to 6,000. We would purchase all the feeds and other ingredients and mix them in our elevator and then deliver with automatic delivery trucks to the segregated pens of cattle.

Since we did not have sufficient capital to own the cattle to fill the yard, we solicited investors, ranchers, meat packers to let us buy cattle, feed, fatten, and sell their cattle for their account. They provided the money to pay for the cattle and pay their monthly feed bills. We then sold their fattened cattle hopefully for a profit. We managed the entire operation. For the services of buying, fattening, and selling their cattle we were paid a fee.

We filled the yard with cattle quite quickly. George supervised the operations of the feed and elevator whereas I "rode" the cattle for their health and happiness, managed the partnership financial affairs, and solicited most of the Custom feeders. George and I on our meek salary worked seven days a week from dawn to dusk. We started making a profit quite soon after opening.

Bill Carey was a good partner for the next 30 years. He was honest, smart, loyal, gutsy, intelligent, personable, patient, and someone with whom I valued his opinions over those years. He was a good friend. He died having never married at Johns Hopkins Hospital of cancer in 1997.

George was an experienced respected Brighton farmer involved in cattle associations and Brighton organizations. He knew cattle, marketing, farming, local suppliers of feeds, and understood machinery and how to make the operation work.

George was a small town man who liked operating in his local environment and had no particular desire to reach out. So when Bill and I saw opportunities with larger operations and wished to buy another small farmer's operation in Rocky Ford to build another feed yard in 1957, George did not wish to be involved in a larger show. He was uncertain of added debt, felt Rocky Ford was too far from home, and was uncomfortable about taking in additional unknown partners. We could not expand the Brighton yard because of limited land, so that was the only manner I could see to expand the operation.

Unfortunately, while this discussion of expansion was going on, I found out that George had "borrowed" without authority money from the Wilhelm Mancini Feed Lot operating account. Our account was not so large that we could stand $75,000.00 withdrawal. Furthermore, George's action was totally illegal. He apparently had been speculating in the Futures Market and was trying to cover his losses. His action was unacceptable to me and Bill so that we terminated the partnership and relationship with George immediately. It was not a pleasant event. We liquidated that partnership.

We then established a new Limited Partnership with the same Limited Partners and bought a farm and old feedlot in Rocky Ford in 1957 with the idea of expanding it to have a capacity of 20,000 or 30,000 head. We now had confidence that we had a solid business idea. We settled our differences with George by deeding him the Brighton yard and we used our cash from the old partnership to obtained ownership of the Rocky Ford farm/feed yard.

I spent many hours rebuilding the Rocky Ford operation.

The "Curve Court" motel was my many nights home in that poor desolate little dry sun baked town on the Arkansas River in Southern Colorado. We built a new feed mill, many yards of concrete feed bunks, new corrals, a deep 1000' well, office, 60' scale so that we had capacity of about 20,000 cattle in addition to 1000 acres of good farm land. The area had little farmer feeding, so we had little competition for our feed purchases from local farmers, and we were close to an American Stores meat packing plant that meant low cost in delivery of our finished cattle. I hired Jack Anderson who was a nice fellow but not very smart or quick on his feet.

But we filled our yards, built more pens for a capacity of 25,000. I spent many hours in New York, Chicago, Colorado and Texas with ranchers, oil men, meat packers, investment councilors, and bank trust departments to try to tell them the advantages they would reap by feeding cattle for their own account or for their customers/clients. Included in my travels was a trip to Dallas to meet the mysterious and dean of the early oil "wildcatters", H. L. Hunt. He looked with some question at this young whippersnapper asking him to feed cattle. H. L. was rarely photographed, but was known as the "Warren Buffett" of his day. He was the dean of Wildcatters. He had been a riverboat gambler, who made his first bucks in cards. He was a gentle white haired man who looked as if he had never exercised in his life. But he was soft spoken and courteous to me. I was very impressed with his private elevator, his phoning around the world as I sat patiently in his office. This was a rare visit for the word was that "no body ever got an appointment with H. L. Hunt". (Bill Carey knew his accountant who made the meeting for me). Finally after I had given my tentative presentation, he pulled out a large yellow spreadsheet and said "Son, you can see by this summary that this year I fed 50,000 cattle (in Omaha), and lost $49.85 per head or about $2,500,000. I don't think I will feed with you. I don't think I will feed with anyone again. " Even for the richest oilman in the USA $2,500,000 in 1957 was a bit of a hit.

Our company kept an office at the Denver Stockyard sitting a floor above the greasy Picador Café. We were quite apprehensive that the cowboys and cattlemen who had a beer or two after selling their cattle or truckers having hauled in the cattle would burn down the building and our office. But the rent was cheap and it accommodated us. (The National Western Stock Show now occupies the location).

The office was manned by my faithful and able secretary, Betty Hemmingson, and Mary Jackson, bookkeeper. Both worked for me for 25 years! Betty was most capable and it soon became known by cattle buyers, purveyors, and meat packer buyers, bankers that the best answers came from Betty and not from me. I gave her tremendous authority so she made decisions without my constant supervision. I do not recall ever having seen her make a mistake of any substance. She had had no formal accounting background, had never been around agriculture, and handled telephone calls to me with great diplomacy. She took care of all my personal affairs even one time correcting the public accountants of their significant error in computing my income tax. At the time when we sold our business in 1985, I was adrift and lost in my own personal affairs. She helped me understand my own affairs. We never had harsh words, never any disagreements of salaries or time off. She was a gem. Now in 2008, I see or exchange Christmas cards with her yearly. She was wonderful, and I was lucky to have someone so loyal, intelligent, and contributive. Mary too was able, loyal, and a very good substitute if Betty went on vacation. I am indebted to both of them for their help.

I ran the show. I directed the cattle buying and selling, negotiated with all customers, handled the financing related to the Limited Partners, supervised the accounting, and set the policy for our risk management. We made money and our customers were making money or accomplishing their goals related to their taxes. (Sometimes different).

Many of our customers fed cattle with us to avoid taxes.

We financed the 90% of the cost of the cattle and the cost of feeding. Upon signing the feeding agreement with us, the investor would put up $50.00 per head in cash. If the cattle lost $50.00, the customer lost his $50.00, but he would have a tax loss of $350.00 (money he borrowed from us plus the $50.00 per head). Any loss of the cattle over $50.00, we assumed the loss. We experienced profit of feeding and care of their cattle (about $20.00 per head). So we were out of pocket if the losses on a group of cattle exceeded $70.00 per head-a rarity . Since we hedged our risk by selling futures contracts on the Chicago Mercantile Exchange on the Live Cattle Futures Pit, we basically protected ourselves from the wild swings in the cattle market. Clients with large income could thereby write off the loss against other income. As a result our customers were clients of banks who managed accounts of wealthy clients (U.S. Trust, Chemical Bank Trust department clients), Hollywood actors or producers, cattlemen, local high-income executives, and accountants representing affluent individuals. This scheme was legal from about 1957 till 1970 when the IRS decided they would close those tax advantages. **When they did our playpen changed dramatically**. While it lasted we profited handsomely.

After seven years of success at Rocky Ford, we were exuberant enough to think we should expand our success. In 1964 we bought 900 acres southwest of

Fort Morgan a farm. On open land we built pens for 32,000 cattle and filled them with customer cattle. Even before building this new facility, we had strengthened our financial strength. We thereby strengthened the financial position of the company, reduced our personal risk, and had limited guarantees from our financially substantial partners.

During this time we of course expanded our office and son David came into the operation. It wasn't long until he took overall the hedging operations, the actual operations of the two feedlots, whereas I continued with customers, the bank, and partners. I really believe except for my relations with our partners that David took over the management of Wilhelm Company. Of course, I had the experience in the markets and controlled the general policy. I am sure that he managed the feed rations, the hedging, and the personnel better than I had been doing. I launched the new ideas, expansions, and overall supervision. I was flying around trying to make deals with customers or bankers to such a degree that the careful details had to be dealt with and that's what David did so expertly. We had bought a 100 Section ranch in Cheraw, had leased two backgrounding feedyards in Sugar City and Swink besides running feeder cattle in Texas and Oklahoma, and even became involved in a small meat packing plant in Denver (Adams Packing Co.), and even some farms in Nebraska. All this meant I was flying around like a crazy man and David was certainly running the day-to-day operations.

To expand even more we entered into the feed manufacturing business (PURINA-like) where we would make pelleted supplement feed for rancher's cattle and poultry operations. We established a sales company (Wilgro Feeds, Inc with equal partners Jack Malo, Bob Schmidt who ran the company, and Walnut Grove, a large feed manufacturer in Walnut Grove, Iowa.

This business was conceived because I thought we could manufacture this kind of feed along with our cattle feedyard feed thereby utilizing our feedmills 24 hours per day. Theoretically it was a good idea but the FDA was so strict about contamination between the two feeds that we had to take costly building moves to insure there was no cross contamination of different ingredients. We soon recognized our liability if we either violated the regulations of the F. D. A. or caused damage to the animals that consumed the feed. When the FDA scrutinized more and more and we could see potential law suits. (Once we were sued because a poultry raiser's chickens lost all their feathers because we had mixed the feed mistakenly with too much salt). The risk was larger than the potential profit so we then ceased making animal feeds for hogs, range cattle, and chickens and sold our interest in Wilgro Feeds.

So this was our peak of profitability and the point at which our exuberance had overtaken our wisdom. We ploughed every earned dollar into expansion after giving yearly distributions to our partners.

To rationalize our enthusiasm I felt a totally integrated operation would be even more efficient. If we could control the slaughter and distribution of the beef, we could capture the packer's profits, eliminate marketing expenses, and control the flow from range to the retailers of beef. So let's build our own meat packing plant.

We built a slaughter house by borrowing more money from the banks and investing some $2,000,000 of cash from our working capital. We were full of hope and optimism as we started our new operation, but within another five years our dreams turned sour and we sold our company to Amfac, Inc.

24

Home Base in Denver

After I sold the farm in Longmont in 1952, I bought our first house at 490 Williams Street. After ten years we had at last settled on our mode of life and style of living. A nice quiet street, convenient to Graland School for Jeannie and Mrs. Van Brat's play school for Andy and Peter. The house was small with lots of small rooms. Anne with her Midas touch of decorating spruced up the house so our family of five had barely enough room, but it was made attractive with furniture of our families, a cozy backyard and a quiet neighborhood. I was commuting to Brighton leaving at dawn and returning after dark as George Mancini and I were getting our business going in 1955. Jean and John Emery (Jean's sister and brother-in-law) lived in the house the summer of 1952 as a temporary home as they moved to Denver from Fort Morgan.

Peter arrived on the scene in 1959 when we lived at 490 Williams Street. Jeannie was now 10 years old, David 9, and Andy 6. The older ones were all running around immersed in sports and school, whereas Peter was spending much of his time at Mrs. Van Brat's babysitting house just down the street from our house.

Because of this age difference, Peter found himself excluded from most of our trips to Europe, Mexico, and other spots where often the three older children would come with us. I think rightfully Peter has regretted being "left out" of so much that went on in the family... Not having contemporary brothers or sisters to play with, Peter became friends of a whole different age group, including his cousin Charles Emery. At that time Peter also came under the wing of Jean Emery who used to take him to church every Sunday. So Peter grew up separated from his siblings. By the time Peter had graduated from C. U. , the age difference between them was insignificant. And even a few years later all chose different directions for their lives. Eventually Peter chose to live in Arizona and Oregon so the communication between us was more difficult than the others who lived in Colorado.

I was gone early in the morning and not returning till dark, since I was operating our Commercial Feed yard in Brighton, Colorado and starting a new one in Rocky Ford, Colorado. This was a distinct change in our family life style. I no longer was home for lunch, left early before everyone arose for breakfast and barely home before bedtime. This led to a different relationship with the children. I was so occupied with business that I missed much of that growing up time of their lives. That was too bad, but I felt I had to put my all into the formation of my new business. Anne spent more time organizing, caring, and nurturing the children's development and I was not as much of an asset as I might have been. Anne very dearly put her heart and soul in being a wonderful mother and handled things perfectly well and lovingly. She was always home to greet the children when they returned home from school so home was a true home for them.

In about 1962 we moved to a larger home at 740 High Street over looking Little Chessman Park. It was a rather unattractive 1920 home, but it had lots of room and all kinds of hidden assets, such as the downstairs "hockey rink", the Mile High Squash court, the pool room, lots of rooms and baths. In due time Anne's gift of making the interior attractive with Japanese Silk screens, "modified "library", and attractive upholstering and curtains. Many fond memories at this spot. Jeannie was now just beginning to attract boys; David and Andy were involved with their cousins (Matt, Willie, Steve Jackson and Jake Emery at the DCC in ice hockey and tennis).The park offered plenty of room for our own playground. Easter time we had joyous base ball games with many of the neighbors participating, such as the MacMillans, Jackson's, Balls, W. S. Jackson SR, , John and Jean Emery, H. J. Jackson, Edith Jackson and Margaret Jackson, Frank Kemps, and more.

Lest we not have enough livestock at our house, we provided the home for four dogs; Rip, a little nondescript dog was David's pal, Andy laid claim to Max, a smart but nippy Aussie shepherd who nipped David III in Aspen-which was a pretty scary event, and Tulip, a golden retriever who had a hard time doing anything but sleep. Tulip was Peter's pal. So with four children, four dogs, a nurse (usually), and Anne and me, we had a full house.

The 740 High street house was surrounded on the

west and south side with a covered porch and underneath was an unfinished basement that had a cement floor, plaster walls, no windows- so it was indestructible. It became the home of a "shinny ball" ice/field hockey arena where afternoon games continued after school, when everyone should have been studying. But everyone had fun and it became a Mecca for many friends.

I briefly established an office on the third floor with a Mrs. Organ. An old faded blond bombshell (she thought) as my secretary. She tried hard, was inept, the third floor cubicle was inadequate so we closed that office, before buying with Andy Brown (A builder) an old post office building for an office at 4700 North High Street. So both family and I were now located in Denver.

Andy Wilhelm - 1953, Longmont

Another extra curriculum feature of the home was the Squash Court. Behind the house was a garage that formerly had been a stable, where the straight stall and water trough still remained. Andy and Bill Toll decided that there was a fine hidden retreat to go upstairs and silently smoke their cigarettes. Unfortunately they started a fire in the upstairs closet. Apparently the boys flew the coup and it wasn't till Sweetie Askew(our faithful black cook and helper) noticed "sure is a lot of smoke coming from the garage" that she alerted me. The fire engines arrived and put out the fire, but the interior was burned and gutted. Of course Andy and Bill denied any knowledge of the problem, and it was only when a fire investigator put the pressure on the two boys that the truth finally came out. Andy looked pretty humble after his admission. I do not remember what punishment was given-Probably only scowls and a few harsh words from me.

After some reflection I decided to make a Squash Court out of its ruins. The walls were in tack and the dimensions were a couple inches more narrow than a regulation court, so for $7,500.00 I proceeded to have the garage converted. There were very few courts in Denver at the time; the demand for squash was considerable, so I founded "The Mile High Squash Club". I enrolled about 40 male members and 10 female squashers. Initiation fee was $10.00. Each player put in $. 50 to play. All reservations were telephoned to Betty Hemmingson (my secretary). A Key to the court was left out doors, so there was no disturbance for our home. It was a great success for a rather active "membership". There were a few problems with the facility- heating was nil so we had to keep extra balls in a hot plate, because the ball in play would get so cold, it would not bounce on those sub zero days. Under rare high humidity atmospheric conditions, the whole court surfaces would "sweat" so it became so slippery, you could not stand up; a center point where the ball continually hit wore away the plaster / concrete surface thereby causing an often-repaired surface. When we sold the house, the buyers thought the space was for storing squash and veggies! All in all I played a lot and we had great sociability and enjoyment. It was a great success.

One incident that caught everyone's attention was the time that I bought two pigs and built a pen for them. The kids thought their arrival was great. The following morning after their arrival lo and behold no pigs! They had decided to take a stroll down Seventh Avenue where someone captured them and forthwith called the Denver Post. The paper sent out a photographer who then had the paper print a front page picture and article captioned "Any one Lost a Pig?" I found out who had retrieved the pigs, but, after calling him, he reported he already taken them to an abattoir.

We had a visitor for a few months- Patrick Westfeldt. After a legal trip down to Rocky Ford, as he approached his automobile loaded with an abundance of person clothes, he said "Betty and I are separating and I am headed for the University Club. " I said no way, you are coming to stay with us. That he did, and we enjoyed his stay that lasted a few months.

Jeannie and David were attending Garland and Andy was at play school. Peter was in the hands of our wonderful Negro cook/maid/companion, Sweetie Askew who came upon the scene about 740 High Street days, someway adopted Peter. "Sweets" and Peter became a close and loving pair. She loved Peter, even though she had some nine children of her own. Peter of course reciprocated with her. By the time we were living at 740 High (1970), Peter at 11 old was confronted with siblings of high school and college age.

Anne was able to hire various attractive and able help. She employed a Japanese/American girl (Emma) who was just marvelous with Peter and Jeannie. Jeannie adored her. Her life was snuffed out in an auto accident on a visit to Kansas. This untimely event shocked and grieved our family for it seemed so unfair for this twenty five year old to lose everything so unexpectedly. Anne also had a Swedish lady who dressed as well as Anne, was mature, responsible, and handsome and a pleasure to have around. And lastly I remember Anne Baxter, a red haired eastern 22-year-old girl who was a fine companion for all the kids. Anne did a wonderful job in finding and working with these ladies.

Once again the urge to move. We relocated to an absolutely beautiful house at 101 high and eventually moved there about 1975.

HIGH 101 STREET
DENVER

Burnham Hoyt, an architect, designer and planner of many civic and other buildings in the Denver area drew up the plans of this handsome home. It was a dream home that satisfied all the tastes of Anne. We had a huge living room, dining room, pantry, small library, a garden room, 5 bedrooms, a large yard, and a north and south patio. The home had style. It was located across the street from the Denver Country Club, which was convenient for ice hockey in the winter and tennis in the summer. The proximity to the club saved Anne from lots of carpooling.

As scholastic students Jeannie always had good grades, did her homework dutifully, and just cruised along easily. David had a reading problem (dyslexia) so that he was working hard to get C and B- grades. Often times even these marks were not achieved. But with that disability he had to work harder and often surpassed by harder application. Anne and I made more than one visit to Chuck Froelicker, the headmaster of Colorado Country Day to discuss David's scholastic difficulties. Andy went to Andy Black's Colorado Academy where he did not require us to visit the headmaster regarding Andy's progress except for his non-scholastic conduct. At one celebration Andy guzzled excess amounts of the hard stuff, so when Anne and I went to pick him up from a school party, no Andy. He had passed out and we found him by the side of the road asleep. Peter always had acceptable grades if not outstanding. Unfortunately, Peter continued to be left out of the family fun which was similar to Jeannie's cousin, Melissa where her brother and sister were considerably older than she. As a result she almost became adopted by our family. She and Jeannie formed their lifelong friendship at that point. Peter also being the same age as Charles Emery meant that those two had good experiences together growing up.

I was kidded years later (by my children) for my trying to impose my idea that dinner was "not a filling station", but an event where everyone at the table should contribute some of their thoughts or ideas for the benefit of those around the table. Dinner conversation should be lively, informative, and fun, I thought. As soon as I tried to worm words from a quiet one, I would be given the deep freeze and passive resistance would emerge around the table and silence would descend around the table. Obviously, Dad was a little heavy handed, but with Anne's urging, I would lay off and the meals would attain what I wished in the first place. I was a bit of a clod.

Tennis, Dale Lewis, DCC, Easter parties, Birthday parties, social functions, soccer games, carpooling, baby sitters, etc. -that was the life. There was little church going or religious involvement. Anne and I did not attend church, and so our children received no religious training. Only Peter went to church because of Jean Emery's generosity and influence in escorting him each Sunday. (That training did not rub very deeply, because I do not feel he has since attended a church). Jeannie, David, Andy and Anne were all baptized at St. John's cathedral, a place very unfamiliar to Anne, the children and me. Only did Jeannie reluctantly become a church member after she was married. And that move was dictated by John Russell's strong devotion to the "Christian" Church. Jeannie was having a hard time accepting the principles of the church. Baptism of our whole family took place because my mother threatened Anne that if she did not get on the stick, she (Nana) would have them baptized in the Catholic Church. That was all it took so, since Anne's abhorrence to the Catholic religion was so intense, we quickly accepted the Episcopal rights. Anne felt that Catholicism was too severe, too dogmatic, and unable to adapt to life necessities (abortion).

Since Anne and I both enjoyed tennis tremendously and played as often as time allowed, we quite naturally interested our children in the game. Since we were both relatively good players, we would rally with the kids and eventually play what became competitive family battles. At the same time the Denver Country Club was within walking distance. The DCC had an inspiring tennis pro (Dale Lewis) who charmed the kids. At the club there was a large group of our children's age so they made many friends and spent many summer hours on the courts. No summer camps or foreign study groups- just competition and tennis tournaments. They became either intermountain or state champs. They may not have learned much of the bible, but they benefited from the value of competitive sports, i. e. how to lose with understanding, how to win graciously, how to be honest, how to understand the meaning of hard work, how to handle pressure, and how to help your health and how to have fun.

At the same time I was also playing competitively. When I was 65 years old I decided I would try for a National Ranking, so I went to work and played every second I could. I entered the four National Tournaments that were required to be ranked in California (Indoor and Hard Court), Tennessee (Clay), and Long Island (Grass). Anne accompanied me and gave me valuable practice and warm-up times before all the tourneys. It was very helpful to go out for half hour of warm-up before facing these aging warriors. I got to the quarterfinals (that meant winning about four early matches) of all the tournaments and as a result I was ranked 18th in the country. It was a big effort, had good fun with Anne and with the competition. During that year I won about five tournaments in Colorado and New Mexico.

This was the period in the family's life when the children now were young adults and that meant great changes in their aspirations, conduct, and activities.

Jeannie now had graduated from Garrison Forrest, Wheaton College, Boston College, and Colorado University so she had a pretty good taste of various educational institutions of the United States. Now at home she was attracting flocks of male suitors. I as the grumpy old Dad was of course very suspicious of them. Some infuriated me such as Craig Skinner who would wave to me "Hey" as he lay prone on the couch of the living room, where as the polite young men such as Billy Gerber would stand up and great me with "Hello, Mr. Wilhelm." Of course, I favored the latter. (As it turned out Craig turned out to be a great lawyer). But I guess I was not rational - just a protective father.

And then there was the time Daggett Harvey and I were both attending different Amfac meetings in Honolulu. Jeannie at the time was going very STEADY with Willie Draper. He and some pals had resurrected an old sunken scow, were going to refurbish it and make it sea worthy to sail around the world! Jeannie was part of the act. She I think prepared the food as the boys mainly smoked pot, played the guitar, and did little work on the boat. At any rate Willie and Jeannie picked Daggett and me up in their beat up pickup allowing Daggett and me to ride in the back of the truck. They sped through Honolulu ignoring traffic lights and other regs as they laughed. Meanwhile Daggett lawyer background made him furious about their irresponsibility. The evening ended with us wondering what kind of life this was and what is to become of daughter Jeannie. (The Monsoon was never made sea worthy).

I had built a small hot house off the side of the kitchen. I devised a rather unique irrigating system where automatically the water would flow down rows to nourish the plants as they were growing. I raised all kinds of garden vegetables and gardenias for the benefit of the household.

David also set up a test to see the value of adding protein to the diet of chickens. So one room in the basement was involved in the chicken business. David would feed those chicks morning and night and proved by their greater growth that it did pay to supplement their feed. The only problem was that our kitchen smelt like a chicken house as wafts of chicken odor came up the back stairs. And chicken odor is stronger that cattle's aromas. No one was too sorry to see those unappealing birds going down the road.

25

WILHELM FEEDLOTS COMPANY

I found out quickly that I was no farmer. I didn't know squat about machinery or farming techniques. I needed to make enough money to support my family. I realized that my Longmont operation and my ineptitude would not contribute to achieving that end. I could see how cattle feeding on a commercial basis could be a profitable business, if I could form a company, raise some capital and operate the business successfully.

Also it was obvious that cattle feeding in that manner required a large volume operation because per head profit margins were small. Cost of inventory (cattle and grain), capital improvements (pens, elevator, equipment), and working capital required capital that were substantially beyond my means. I also planned to feed cattle for customers such as meat packers, cattle feeders, ranchers, or investors.

I knew many of these potential customers personally. By attracting individual people to feed cattle with us, I could increase the volume while having our risk reduced.

Therefore, I decided to form a company to raise the necessary capital.

Our company was formed as a Limited Partnership. One of the three General Partners was George Mancini, a long time farmer from Brighton, Colorado, who I had become acquainted with at The Denver Union Stockyards, had the same realization of the need to concentrate on building a commercial feedlot. George was widely known in cattle circles, well respected, and knowleable about the farming products available and fat cattle marketing. Bill Carey of Dallas had become a friend of mine in Denver who was intrigued with our concept. Bill was a Notre Dame, Harvard Business school graduate who had been successful in the oil business and was interested in an additional investment.

Bill and I both put $25,000.00 in the company and George put in $15,000.00 and we agreed to all become equal General Partners. With this $65,000.00, I proceeded with great difficulty to obtain a long term capital loan and a working capital loan from the Colorado National Bank. In addition, I sold Limited Partnership interest to additional partners in amounts from $25,000.00 to $450,000.00. Jim Lewis investor and Centex Executive and interested in cattle, Fred McLaughlin, an investor, John Matthews, a Texas rancher, Bob Flanagan, investor-rancher, Malcolm Stewart-rancher, Stanley Livingston, investor, Sandy McCulloch, Investor and Inter Ocean Oil CO-NY Investor. They all provided cash for their limited Partnership interests. They were all loyal and stood by our company for many years. In all we were able to capitalize the "Wilhelm-Mancini Feedlots" adequately to satisfy out lenders.

So we were on our way. We bought 40 acres of land near Brighton, started construction of the physical necessities, bought equipment , began buying or contracting for feeds, and started buying cattle for ourselves and our customers. We were in operation within six months. George and I took a very modest salary, worked from seven AM till seven P. M. George bought the feed, and supervised the elevator operation and the maintenance of the facilities. I handled the cattle buying, the care and doctoring of the cattle in the yards, customer relations, and the business end of the company.

Our plan was to build a yard with a capacity of 5,000 to 6,000 head. We would purchase all the feeds and other ingredients and mix them in our elevator and then deliver with automatic delivery trucks to the segregated pens of cattle.

We filled the yard with cattle quite quickly. George supervised the operations whereas I "rode" the cattle. I worked seven days a week from dawn to dusk. We started making a profit for the company soon after opening the yard.

After three years we were feeling our oats and thought we should expand. It seemed that northern Colorado was becoming over saturated with cattle feeding operations so it was becoming more difficult to buy feeds. In addition we were hemmed in and could not buy more land for expansion. So I explored other opportunities.

I visited the Arkansas Valley in southern Colorado where there was abundant farming with very few cattle feeders. It seemed there was a good opportunity for purchasing feeds, an important ingredient for a profitable cattle feeding operation.

I proposed buying a farm at Vroman Colorado, near Rocky Ford and build a feedyard on that property. Bill Carey fully supported the expansion, but George was reluctant. George did not wish to be involved. He was uncertain of added debt, felt Rocky Ford was too far from his home, and was uncomfortable about taking in additional unknown partners.

Unfortunately, while this discussion of expansion was being discussed, I found out that George had "borrowed" without authority money from the Wilhelm Mancini Feed Lot bank account. Such action was tantamount to thievery. He did not have the financial resources to repay the "borrowing" since he had lost the money on cattle futures speculation. George's borrowing from us was totally illegal. He was trying to cover his losses. His action was unacceptable to me and Bill, so that we terminated his interest in the partnership immediately. It was not a pleasant event. We liquidated that partnership and folded our Limited Partners into a new Partnership. We settled our differences with George by deeding him the Brighton yard and transferred our cash from the old partnership to a new partnership which was augmented with new limited partners.

We then bought the 1000 acre farm with a small old feedlot in Rocky Ford in 1957 with the idea of rebuilding the old lot and expanding it to have a capacity of 25,000 head. We had confidence that we had a solid business idea, good financing, customers, and an excellent location.

Subsequently I spent many hours building the Rocky Ford operation with the faithful, willing, and able Mexican help... The "Curve Court" motel was my many nights home in that poor desolate little dry sun baked town on the Arkansas River in Southern Colorado. Anne and I regretted my frequent absences from home with four young children back in the nest in Denver. However, flying my own airplane did reduce that absence. I supervised all the construction of a feedmill and new pens for the cattle.

The location of the lot was good. We could purchase feeds at favorable prices, and the area was drier and warmer than northern Colorado. The new Lot would be the closest feedyard to the large meat packing plant of American Stores in Pueblo thereby giving us a freight advantage over other feedyards. Also only ten miles away were the two large sales Rings in La Junta that gave us favorable opportunities for buying replacement cattle for the lot. We were pleased with all the benefits this area offered us.

Henry Mancini, brother of George, who was a nice fellow with feedlot experience and knowledgeable in construction of the lot, was our first resident manager. He however was a poor manager of the business, so after a short period I was forced to replace him. Jack Anderson who had spent his life in the feedlot business was an improvement but Jack did not represent our company well. He had poor repore with the community and lacked initiative in the daily problems that arose. He lacked respect from the farmers with whom he dealt with in buying feeds or with local merchants with whom we traded. I handled all the cattle sales by establishing a continual favorable relationship with American Stores.

Quite quickly we filled our yards with customer cattle and a few of our own, built more pens for a capacity of 25,000. I spent many hours in New York, Chicago, Colorado and Texas with ranchers, oil men, meat packers, investment councilors, and bank trust departments to try to tell them the advantages they would reap by feeding cattle for their own account or for their customers/clients. The result was our capacity included many non cattle people who fed for profit motive or tax benefits.

Included in my travels was a trip to Dallas to meet the mysterious and dean of the early oil "wildcatters", H.L. Hunt. He looked with some question at this young whippersnapper asking him to feed cattle. H.L. was rarely photographed, but known as the "Warren Buffett" of his day. He was the dean of Wildcatters. He had been a riverboat gambler, who made his first bucks in cards. He appeared as a gentle white haired man who looked as if he had never exercised in his life. But he was soft spoken and courteous to me. I was very impressed with his private elevator, his phoning around the world as I sat patiently in his office. This was a rare visit for the word was that "no body ever got an appointment with H.L. Hunt." (Bill Carey knew his accountant who made the meeting for me). Finally after I had given my tentative presentation, he pulled out a large yellow spreadsheet and said "Son, you can see by this summary that this year I fed 50,000 cattle (in Omaha), and lost $49. 85 per head or about $2,500,000. I don't think I will feed with you. I don't think I will feed cattle with anyone again. " Even for the richest oilman in the USA $2,500,000 in 1957 was a bit of a hit.

Our company kept an office at the Denver Stockyard located a floor above the greasy Picador Café. We were quite apprehensive that the cowboys and cattlemen who had a beer or two after selling their cattle or truckers having hauled in their cattle would burn down the building and our office. But the rent was cheap and it accommodated us. (The National Western Stock Show now occupies the location).

The office was manned by my faithful and able secretary, Betty Hemmingson, and Mary Jackson, bookkeeper. Both worked for me for 25 years! Betty was most capable and it soon became known by cattle buyers, purveyors, and meat packer buyers, bankers that the best answers came from Betty and not from me. I gave her tremendous authority so she made decisions without my constant supervision. I was gone from the office about half the time in my airplane contacting customers, selling cattle, thinking up new opportunities for our business or appeasing bankers. Betty was innovative and authorative in making decisions in my behalf. I do not recall her make a mistake of any substance. She had had no formal accounting background, never been a business woman, had never been around agriculture, and handled telephone calls for me with great diplomacy and authority. She just was a natural. She also took care of all my personal affairs, even one time she corrected a significant error by our National public accountants who were responsible for our yearly audits significant.

At the time when we sold our business in 1985, I was adrift and was lost in my own personal affairs without her help. We never had harsh words, never any disagreements of salaries or time off. She was a gem. Now in 2008, I see or exchange Christmas cards with her yearly. She was wonderful, and I was lucky to have someone so loyal, intelligent, and contributive. Mary Jackson, Betty's assistant was able, loyal, and a very good substitute if Betty went on vacation. I am indebted to both of them for their help.

I ran the show. I directed the cattle buying and selling, negotiated with all customers, handled the financing related to the Limited Partners, supervised the accounting, and set the policy for our risk management. We made money and our customers were making money or accomplishing their goals related to their taxes. (Sometimes different goals).

Many of our customers fed cattle with us to avoid taxes.

We financed the 90% of the cost of the cattle and the cost of feed and care. Upon signing the feeding agreement with us, the investor would put up $50.00 per head in cash. If the cattle lost $50.00, the customer lost his $50.00, but he could generate a current year tax loss of all the loan money (borrowed to pay for the feed and care) in addition to his initial cash deposit. If that loss against his ordinary income reduced his total income enough to reduce his income tax, it was a worthwhile investment. In the event of a loss of the cattle over $50.00 per head, we assumed that loss. We experienced profit of our services of feeding and care of their cattle (about $20.00 per head). So we were out of pocket only if the losses exceeded $70.00 per head-a rarity. Since we hedged our risk by selling futures contracts on the Chicago Mercantile Exchange on the Live Cattle Futures Pit, we basically protected ourselves from the wild swings in the cattle market. As a result of this investment many of our customers were clients of banks who managed accounts of wealthy clients (U. S. Trust, Chemical Bank Trust department clients), Hollywood actors or producers, cattlemen, local high-income executives, and accountants representing affluent individuals. This scheme was legal from about 1957 till 1970 when the IRS decided they would close those tax advantages. **When they changed the law, our playpen changed dramatically**. Our customer base disintegrated. While it lasted we profited handsomely.

After seven years of success at Rocky Ford, we were exuberant enough to think we should expand our success. In 1964 (before the changes in the tax laws) we bought 900 acres of land southwest of Fort Morgan, a farm, and made a working agreement with a feed mill in Fort Morgan. On open land we built pens for 32,000 cattle and filled them with customer cattle. Even before building this new facility, we had strengthened our financial strength by admitting new limited partners. We thereby strengthened the financial position of the company, reduced our personal risk, and had limited guarantees from our financially substantial partners.

During his time we of course expanded our office and son David came into the operation. It wasn't long until he took overall the hedging operations, the actual operations of the two feedlots, whereas I continued with customers, the bank, and partners. I really believe except for my relations with our partners that David took over the management of Wilhelm Company. Of course, I had the experience in the markets and controlled the general policy. I am sure that he managed the feed rations, the hedging, and the personnel better than I had been doing. I launched the new ideas, expansions, and overall supervision. The careful details had to be dealt with and that's what David did so expertly.

We also bought a 100 Section ranch, the Timberlake Ranch near Cheraw, Colorado, the Owl Creek Ranch in Walden, Colorado and leased two backgrounding feedyards in Sugar City and Swink. We also leased ranches in Oklahoma and Texas and ran feeder cattle in Texas and Oklahoma. We also became involved in a small meat packing plant in Denver (Adams Packing Co.), and bought some dry land wheat ground in western Nebraska. All this meant I was flying around like a crazy man and David was certainly running the day-to-day operations. I was uncontrolled without a leach around my neck. In retrospect, I was like a chicken with its head just cut off. I had lost all control.

Peter at branding time at Timberlake Ranch, 1965

To expand even more we entered into the feed manufacturing business (PURINA Like) where we would make pelleted supplement feed for rancher's cattle and poultry operations. We established a sales company (Wilgro Feeds, Inc with equal partners Jack Malo, Bob Schmidt who ran the company, and Walnut Grove, a large feed manufacturer in Walnut Grove, Iowa owned by W. R. Grace and ourselves.

This business was conceived because I thought we could manufacture this kind of feed along with our cattle feedyard feed thereby utilizing our feedmills 24 hours per day. Theoretically it was a good idea but the FDA was strict about contamination between the two feeds that we would have had to take costly building moves to insure against cross contamination of different ingredients. We soon recognized our liability. When the FDA scrutinized us more and more and we could see potential law suits. (Once we were sued because a poultry raiser's chickens lost all their feathers because we had mixed the feed mistakenly with too much salt)! The risk was larger than the potential profit so we ceased making animal feeds for hogs, range cattle, and chickens and withdrew our interest from Wilgro Feeds.

So this was our peak of profitability and the point at which my exuberance had overtaken my wisdom. We ploughed every earned dollar into expansion after giving yearly distributions to our partners.

I did not see the wisdom of some restraint.

26

SALE TO AMFAC

With my exuberance of prosperity I now took a step to expand our companies' operations by building a meat packing plant. My vision was that we could control the production of beef from the live animal until that animal was fattened, slaughtered, fabricated into primal cuts, cooked products and ready for the consumer (Wilhelm Foods, Inc.) We would control the weights and finish at the feedlots, deliver the finished cattle of desired weight and finish to the packing house after their most efficient time on feed. Sounds absolutely great. The challenge was to make all the links synchronize so that the flow of cattle to beef worked as planned.

We bought five 18-wheeler cattle trucks to facilitate the transport of finished cattle from the feedlots to the packing house. We would load 5 trucks from Rocky Ford, drop the cattle off at the Denver plant for slaughter, drive on to our feedlot at Fort Morgan and pickup another 190 finished cattle, return to Denver, unload, return to Rocky Ford and repeat. Since we billed the PUC Interstate trucking rates on these shipments, this high usage of the trucks was extremely profitable.

Our first glitch on the grand plan was that we were unable to time the finishing of the number of cattle to the exact numbers of cattle that the packing house demanded. In the event of shortage of feedlot cattle, we were forced to go to the public market to buy third party cattle. Being spasmodic "fat" cattle buyers at the stockyards, we were treated as occasional supporters of the market so that the dependable daily buyers were given preferences. So, our fat cattle bought very often were costing more than our competitors.

Another part of our overall integrated plan was to buy light cattle(from Louisiana, Texas, Oklahoma, Mexico, Mississippi) graze them on grass, wheat or oats or leased ranches in Oklahoma, Texas, New Mexico and Colorado until they were of desirable weight for the feedlots. We employed a manager who would locate ranchers who leased their farms or ranches upon which we would deliver our young cattle for growing. Our manager would be responsible to evaluate the owner's and operator's ability to manage his operation.

We were dependent on favorable weather(no blizzards, adequate moisture etc) for the cattle to attain the weight demanded by the feedlot. If our contracting rancher turned out to be inept or dishonest or if the natural forces turned against us, our goal of having suitable and cheap replacement cattle for the feedlots failed. On the whole the results of this operation were mixed. Sometimes the cattle had to be shipped to the feedlots at undesirable low weights, or at times when the feedlots were full, there was no room for them. When we were in need of cattle at the feedlot and we had no replacement cattle ready, we were forced to buy "replacement cattle" at inopportune times at unfavorable prices which added to our problems. It was almost impossible to schedule the flow of cattle as desired.

We constructed a small meat slaughtering and meat processing plant on the north side of packinghouse area in Denver. The plant was designed to process approximately 300 cattle per day. After slaughter we would sell part of the kill in carcass form and "break" up the much of the rest of the carcass into primal cuts for shipment and sale. We then dropped the trimmings from the kill and fabrication to our large kitchen where we cook and pack frozen ready to eat products. (The trimmings or to supply our large ready to eat cooked products kitchen.)

Theoretically it was a great idea. Total vertical integration. No middlemen. Scheduled supplies. Total control. No waste. Highest Quality. Efficiency of the utmost.

However, I found that everything did not work as smoothly and as easily as I anticipated. There were many unforeseen factors that prevented the integrated grand plan from working. Some of problems were as follows:

Lack of Capital- Inventory cost: Carrying as many as 200,000 cattle and beef products for almost a year created a huge inventory. To accommodate this need, we were forced to acquire short term borrowing at damaging high interest costs.

Construction cost: The packing house cost us about $2,000,000.00 with some 40% of the equity coming from Wilhelm Company's working capital. Because of limited capital, we did not build all the necessary required essentials of a slaughtering and processing plant (i. e. A Rendering Facility or a modern Hide Cellar).

Operating Expense: Labor expense of 350 employees plus other operational expenses were in excess of our planning. With a 30% annual turnover and many of the lowest quality workers, our productivity was poor.

Good or bad weather that affected the performance of the cattle made timing of cattle deliveries erratic. We either had too many cattle ready for slaughter at one time or two few at other times depending "how well" the cattle did in their different environments. If we were short of killing cattle, we were forced to buy cattle on the open market. Our irregular supply of beef for the retailers did not sit well with scheduled buyers (Safeway). They wanted a constant dependable number each week. Our relatively small kill made this demand difficult to fill. Our Labor contract required minimum hours per week. If the plant was short of cattle to kill and the kill was suspended, we were forced to pay the employees their guaranteed time.

At he end of the week on Friday if we had unsold carcass in the coolers , we were forced to sell to some of the THEIVES (local butchers)who usually scammed us. (We could not keep carcasses or cuts over the weekend because of shrink in weight or "going out of condition" and condemned by the U.S.D.A. inspectors.)

In our enthousiam we bought and operated a **ranch in Walden, Colorado** that required a capital investment and more borrowed money to own the ranch and stock the ranch with 1500 yearlings. The ranch operation did not justify the investment and only added to our increased debt burden.

We borrowed money irresponsibly from Arizona, Colorado, and Omaha banks. We showed poor judgment in obtaining loans and spending instead of reigning in our expenditures. All of the loans were guaranteed by David and me and to a limited extent by our stock holders.

The **interest expense** from our highly leveraged position became an impossible burden.

The packinghouse lost money almost continually (except for a brief period when price controls were imposed on beef and we profited handsomely for about two months). Even if a slaughterhouse runs at its greatest efficiency, profit margins are usually less than 1% on sales. We also were "new guys in the park", so buyers of our beef or cooked products made it hard to dislodge established relationships. The result we had to sell often to buyers who were trying to "pick us off".

Art Sigman was in charge of the kitchen operation, and his sales and profits never materialized to the extent he or I anticipated.

Harvey Yoakum was the packinghouse manager. He was a tough Okey who could handle the labor force and oversee the operations with ability. He also partly handled the beef sales, which he conducted marginally well, because of his minimal experience in sales.

With small margins on sales we needed to have additional size to warrant our overhead. **We were just too small.** With the construction of huge packing companies such as IBP, Conagra, Farmlands Industries that killed 20 times more cattle than we did, our unit costs were uncompetitive along with our inadequacies mentioned above. So the concept of the integrated beef plant was theortically correct, but I did not understand the needs of capital and did not see the operational problems.

So after two years of torturous operations with mounting losses and with banker's hot breath upon our necks, it was necessary to sell both the Wilhelm Feedlots and Wilhelm Foods. With huge indebtedness and bankruptcy close by and David and me facing the majority of the liability, I decided to sell everything if we could. After many attempts to interest other food concerns in purchasing our companies, I finally interested Amfac, Inc. a New York Stock Exchange diversified conglomerate, to buy the Wilhelm interests.

Amfac was originally a land owning company in Hawaii with a very prosperous department store in Honolulu (Liberty House) and owners of valuable real estate in the islands. They decided to diversify the company and one of those new branches was a food division. They proceeded to buy Lamb-Weston (a potato manufacturer (McDonalds etc.), a cheese company, a fish company, a mushroom operation, and finally the Wilhelm operations.

I don't think that Jack Baxter, the head of the Food Division, knew in what hot water we were or he could have bought us for much less than he did. In the negotiations, which lasted four months, I put up a good front and tried to sell them that with proper financing and better management that our operation would be just the thing for them. I offered that our prepared and ready to eat division would be a gold mine if they would only integrate those products with their potato merchandizing expertise and their established distribution system. It was a natural all that meat and potatoes under one roof!

I finally obtained a good sales contract from them. What a relief. Soon after we were set to close the deal and had signed a Letter of Intent, we experienced an unfortunate event. We recently had sold to a certain Bernie Scheib, a New York wholesaler of carcass beef, seven rail cars of carcass beef worth about $280,000.00. We sold the beef on the agreement that each load would be paid for upon receipt ("Sight Bill of Lading"). Upon the first few loads we were told by Scheib's bank (Bank of Americas) that the cattle were received in acceptable condition and the payment was its way. With said assurance and the remaining sales of additional carcass beef already loaded on cars in Denver and on their way, we released the cars for shipment to them. The bank claimed the delay of payment was due to a "change in management" and that the funds would now be sent promptly. By then the other cars had arrived at Scheib's. He immediately sold the beef, collected the money from the sales and paid off his loan with the bank (with our money). We sent demands through our factoring lawyer (Walston and Co.) and were told that Scheib had no funds in his account and had paid off his indebtedness with the sale of our cattle. Walston and Co. on our behalf filed suit in New York City against the bank for misappropriation of funds. Apparently their lawyer lost his cool in the courtroom in exasperation, and was expelled from the courtroom, and the Judge dismissed the case. If ever there was a greater travesty, I would like to know. I flew to NYC with Peter and Anne and went down to a dingy warehouse in New York's west side to meet that sniveling, fat, little schmuck Jew where he kindly offered 10% of the total $280,000.00 as settlement. The bank by all rights had an obligation to pay us- not credit Sheib's account. I about had a stroke at the time because Amfac had a right to cancel our purchase agreement right then and there. I looked at the cancellation of our sale as ruination for David and me. I called Jack Baxter and told him the facts. He said, "We won't let that happen again, will we?" Meekly I said, "We surely won't." Jack is and was a good New England gentleman whom I have respected always and this proved his metal. Case closed. Close Call?

Well we prevailed and we sold both companies at a price sufficient to clear out all our obligations plus giving us a comfortable profit. What a relief! That was a tough journey!

At this point the Wilhelm Foods, Inc. was totally owned by Amfac. All our original stockholders were paid back their original investment in addition to a considerable profit. Some of us retained Amfac stock, rather than selling it promptly, which we received from the sale.

So I went to work for Amfac. David was dismissed because of nepotism policies of Amfac (Even though Henry Walker's (CEO) incompetent brother was on the payroll)! David's departure was a blow to our efficiency because he was running the feeding, ranching, and grazing operations (with about four qualified assistants) and he was doing a superb job. So with him gone I basically had to run the entire operation. I had no qualified assistant. I worked my butt off to try to make things work, and Amfac took over the management of Wilhelm Foods (the processed food division).

I for the first time had someone "coaching" my every move. Jack Baxter's assistant, Bill Deshler, was Jack's hatchet man, so I weekly had a visit with "suggestions" on what, how, when and where I should do what. That coaching and the continual monthly and quarterly forecasts and budgets were new to me and not only very time consuming but also reasons for many real blowups I had with many of the Amfac "superiors". However, since they knew nothing of the feeding business, the customer relations, or the operation of a packinghouse, they were stuck with me. I realized that, but I was so exasperated by their harassment that I wanted to quit, but I felt that I had committed verbally to Jack that I would run the company so I dug in and did everything I could. I swallowed my anger and tried my hardest to do them a good job.

During this time the two feedlots were completely full of investor owned cattle. With Amfac financial backing, we were able to carry cattle on grass, wheat, and warmup yards to supply our feedyards. That meant we would have a total inventory of 200,000 cattle. To keep the yards full, it entailed frequent sales trips to New York bank's Trust departments and corporate leaders to entice custom cattle feeding. So besides managing the slaughterhouse, the futures hedgings, the feeding operations in addition to the many tax oriented and feeding programs, I had my hands full. I had hired some good assistants in the cattle purchasing, grazing, and feeding ends of the business. Harvey Yoakum(whom New England Jack Baxter disliked thoroughly) was my slaughterhouse manager and I believe did a good job managing the packinghouse, if not the sales.

The first year of total operations we made Amfac a $16,000,000.00 profit and they thought I was their fair-haired boy. I was welcomed in two divisions of the company (the cattle company and the investor financing company).

They became so enamored with our operation that they sent me to Australia to investigate the idea of buying some of the vacated Swift Packing houses and establishing some large feedlots in Australia. I finally vetoed the plan even though the arithmetic was excellent, because the sale of cattle from Australia was totally dependent on the approval of Japan to allow the admittance of the cattle/or beef into their country. If the Japanese embargoed beef, we would have no outlet for the beef (Aussies only eat grass stringy beef) and would be forced to dump the fattened beef. My advice was good, because within a year, Japan closed the door for all imported beef.

The following year we lost about $16,000,000 so Amfac really got spooked. Because the cattle business is highly leveraged, Amfac had huge Current Liabilities on their balance sheet because of all the short term borrowing for the inventory. Wall Street did not condone large short term liabilities because they feared risk.

Anne and I were cruising with the Davis's and Livingstons off the Virgin Islands when we stopped at

Puerto Rico. I called the office only to hear an urgent message for me to get my butt to Honolulu pronto. We had many short contracts hedges on our cattle inventory which resulted in some $11,000,000... in margin calls. They were frightened with this position even though I pleaded with them that those positions were a protection against a falling cattle market. They disagreed with me and ordered me to remove all short positions. Within a few months the market took a dive and now their unhedged cattle lost almost $16,000,000.00. Had they stayed with their hedges , their losses would have been insignificant, if at all. They just did not understand the cattle business and how we were running it. As a result of this sudden turnaround they concluded the cattle business was too volatile for them.

Old pals Otis Carney & Dap Lamont

I stayed on to help liquidate their holdings. I sold one feedlot, farm, feed mill, packinghouse and every thing except the Rocky Ford lot, which they had been pricing for sale at $1,500,000, which I could not sell. After two years Jack Baxter telephoned me while I was visiting the Lamonts in Florida and said "what did you say you would pay for Rocky?" I said "$650,000.00". "You have just bought yourself the feedlot". I then went to the bank and borrowed $750,000.00 with the feedlot as the sole security for the loan. (No personal guarantees were required).

So David rejoined me as a General Partners, along with Bill Carey and Neal Kottke and Jim Lewis who became new Limited Partners. (The other partners had departed after we sold to Amfac.) For better or worse we were back in business. I had to be dumb, stubborn, or stupid to go into business again after our rather formable financial problems just a few years ago. However, we knew this end of the business, so we knew we would do well. And we did.

27

BACK INTO THE FIRE

After a couple of years after assuming our own management after the buy back of the Rocky Ford feedlot from Amfac, we operated that profitably with everything going well. We concluded that we knew what we were doing and why not expand again if only in the feeding business. It came to our attention that the Sonnenberg brothers in Sterling were in deep financial trouble. They had over built a feedlot with all the bells and whistles that one could imagine. They had spent all their money on an elaborate setup and woke up out of money. How could we turn down an offer to investigate the possibility of buying the installation? Our requisite was that we did not have to come up with any cash?

We did our due diligence of the feedlot and realized the location was superb. Nearby packinghouse, abundant corn and alfalfa because of the good irrigation water and therefore cheap feed, decent weather, good feed mill, superb construction on pens and working chutes, remote location, excellent sloped pens (drainage) - all the necessary physical attributes one could want. It was a better plant than our Rocky Ford operation.

We still had to make the decision whether we should take on this additional burden. We were doing very well at Rocky, so we should do even better in Sterling, we reasoned.

David and I proceeded to Sterling with lawyer Whit Wagner to try to make a deal. The Sonnenbergs were going to take bankruptcy, if they did not make a deal with us. After an all night negotiating session, we agreed to assume most of their debts in exchange for getting title to the property. No cash, just the assumption of debts. We concluded a deal (10/3/1983). No cash. Now of course it was essential that we operate profitably so we could service a very sizable debt load.

To fill the new feedlot we appointed a good manager (Bill Morgan), made a deal with Agra Tech (a cattle owning company financed by Mr. Chillowitch, the largest exporter of cattle hides to the USSR and friend of Commissar Brezhnev) to guarantee us a constant volume of cattle for the feedlot. In addition we had a good reputation in the financial world, so we continued to have large volumes of customers. We did not see dark clouds ahead.

Suddenly and without any warning, the Department of Revenue and in particular the Internal Revenue Service in 1984 decided that the cattle feeding by investor feeders was a tax dodge. The New York investor could show a large taxable loss in one year and offset that against large taxable income thereby avoiding paying taxes in that year. For example, if a baseball player who was given a monstrous signing bonus in one year, he could show a large paper loss in cattle feeding in that year that would offset his signing bonus income and therefore reduce his income tax. That income "rolled over" could then be spread over subsequent years at lower tax rates. The IRS issued a directive that said unless a taxpayer was a true cattle feeder, he must go on the inventory (accrual) accounting system. That stopped the "tax feeders".

We immediately lost many customers. Volume dropped at the lots. And we had to hustle to try to fill all those empty pens. We made a deal with Simon Chilawitch, to feed a large number of cattle with us on a year around basis, but that still was insufficient to keep the hotel full.

To alleviate our oncoming problems, we sold our Rocky Ford lot to Bob Josserand of the American Cattle Co. thereby realizing some immediate cash. At the same time we gave them a guarantee of keeping so many cattle in the Rocky Ford lot. Since we could not sustain that guaranteed number, we subsequently soon suffered a substantial loss.

High interest and principle repayments and low volume at the lots translated into losses. With loans from the Omaha National Bank, Valley National Bank, Federal Land Bank, plus our continual fixed costs spelled double trouble in old river city. To top it off David and I were guarantors for any debts that the company could not pay.

I went to work to wiggle out of this monstrous problem. We hid under the argument that David and I had lost everything and that our guarantees would give them nothing if they pursued us to collect their loans. After months arguing with the Land Bank, they dropped their suit against us as we deeded over the fixed assets to them to absolve us from out indebtedness.

We pursued the same tack with the Omaha NationalBank. left after a tumultuous all day meeting in Denver when we told them to take a walk. We can't and won't pay you zip. They were furious, but did not pursue us.

We settled with the Valley National Bank of Phoenix amicably even though they took a big hit and did not try to pursue collection.

Finally, we settled for twenty cents on the dollar with American Cattle Co. on the volume guarantee. So we escaped personal bankruptcy, but it was a tough nerve racking seven months for David and me. Anne and I talked of moving out of Denver, selling what we had left (mainly hers), and settle in a small town where we could live on very little. Anne was great showing little fear for the worst. I survived barely. We survived to live another day.

Now I had had all I wanted of feedlots. That was the end of many years in a business that had been a roller coaster financially even though I came out a lot stronger financially than I was 30 years before. I liked working with cattle, enjoyed the thrills of the market, working for myself, with all the ranchers, farmers, investors and even bankers and especially enjoyed working with David and having his expert help. I am not sure I liked the financial insecurity at the time and I am sure that I did not like being away from Anne and my children as much as I did.

28

ANNE EMERY

In May, when Doze and I were visiting the Charles Emerys in Columbus, Ohio, Anne Emery had also come over for a family get together. I recall her having trouble sleeping because of an ache in her back. I recall proposing that maybe she should use my bed to which she refused. No one thought anything about that incident at that time.

In mid August Doze and I flew out to Portland to see John Kyllo and Anne because Anne was now feeling punk. She by now was on Chemo for an undiagnosed cancer problem. My recollection was that there was conjecture what type of cancer had invaded her. At any rate Anne by late August had gone to the Willamette Hospital because of dehydration. She responded quickly after some intravenous injections, but the weakness and fatigue was apparent as she seemed to desire to only sit in her chair in their house. She had little energy. Her health deteriorated until she died of ovarian cancer on September 30, 1988. I am sure she went out of this life happily with her three brothers, her husband John Kyllo, and Doze all by her side.

I am inadequate to try to describe what a wonderful girl she was. She was tall and handsome with a warm understanding smile. She was a positive person as she broke down barriers that others could not. When she came to Denver to visit us, she would go into Doze's secret space (her refrigerator) and immediately dispose all of those antique saved things in the frig. Very few people had the courage or the ability to accomplish that. Most were prohibited to touch objects in that private place. She would accomplish her mission and Doze would not lift a finger in opposition.

Anne had great enjoyment and talent with her violin. She was beloved by her participation in the Oregon Chamber Orchestra. She had a great ability to have fun and laugh. She was devoted to her brothers and of course John and her mother.

She had care and love for the children upon whom she practiced her music therapy and earned respect from the staff she worked with.

I quote from my diary of October 1: "Doze is a brick. She is devastated by the loss of her only daughter with whom she shared her inner most thoughts- a relationship that only a mother and daughter can have. Doze looks tired, but is indominable. She has not outwardly shown despair, and has kept a smile on her face. She has kept herself busy regarding Anne's affairs. I trust there will be no relapse when the busy lessens. I give her an A+ for her courage. "

The boys were crushed for they all loved her and had a superb fun relationship with her.

Jean and Anne Emery Kyllo

Anne K. also was very supportive of me. We had a loving relationship. When Doze, Anne and I tripped to Ireland together we all had a wonderful time. Anne was so much fun, generous, imaginative, and thoughtful that made the whole trip great.

We all miss her and hope that she is strumming her violin to all her admirers in heaven.

29

1988 AND
ANNE WILHELM

In 1987, I was ready to change directions in life. I would not reenter the cattle business or any other total economic involvement. I would forever stay out of debt, incur no borrowing, take a deep breath and not worry about creditors. Jeannie, David, Andy, and Peter had left the nest so Anne and I were ensconced in our small one bedroom but attractive home at 3130 East Exposition. We played tennis together at the Denver Country Club, enjoyed our time together without me chasing to work, and enjoyed our small Townhouse at 2600 Skyline in Tucson(Bought 1/27/83). I played golf in US Seniors Association in New Jersey and Connecticut with D. B. Lamont, fished in Alaska with Jim Lewis on Salmon River, and visited the Carneys in Cora, Wy. It was a complete change in my life style. It was a year of fun with no worries- we thought!

The following year of 1988 however things changed. Peter and I stayed at Polly Kemp's house in La Jolla prior to watching the Broncos get pummeled in San Diego by the Washington Red Skins in the

Super Bowl. Anne and I went to Tucson that spring and Anne started experiencing some back pain. Mac Clayton, a well know orthopedic surgeon from Denver, stopped by our house on Skyline to check on Anne's discomfort. After getting her to lie down on her back and do some exercises, he advised just keep exercising and things will be ok. No question in his mind that maybe something other than orthopedic problems. (What a one-track narrow vision person!). So Anne exercised as she always did and seemed to feel all right but not great.

Soon afterwards Anne and I went to Florida and visited Donald and Louise Lamont at their oceanfront home in Hobe Sound. While I played golf with Dap, Anne played tennis with some ladies. The first day she tried to play, Anne had to quit because of pain in her back. To have Anne stop playing tennis, there had to be a problem. A couple days later we drove to Epcot in Orlando where Anne would have to rest as we walked around the lake from one ethnic exhibit to the next. The distance between stops was short, but she still chose to rest repeatedly. As strong as Anne was, these two incidents in Hobe Sound really signaled that something serious had developed.

Anne still wanted to keep going thinking nothing disastrous was happening. I guess until that time I felt that when we got home we should certainly see Dr. Bob McKenna and Dr. Mason Morfit. In the meantime Anne and I went to Chuck Spalding's 75th birthday celebration in San Francisco. She danced around merrily, looked beautiful in her brown gown with feathers on the skirt but said "my back hurts, I have to go home". That once again was out of custom for one that loved dancing as she did. All these events happened in a two-month span. I question now why did we not go to Denver in February instead of waiting till May whether any difference in the outcome of her cancer would have occurred. I am sure not. Anne certainly did not suggest any investigation on during that rather active spring in the manner she did.

Then the chronology of the next six months:

5/25/88-Dr. McKenna blood test does not look good.

5/27/88-McKenna and Morfit consultation. There opinion things did not look good.

5/31-Anne goes into hospital

6/1- Oncologist Garfield

6/7-14-Chemo therapy at hospital

7/12-Jeannie, Anne, and I fly to Rochester Mayo's in Gates Co. plane. Anne exhausted. Had to rest before going to see Doctor. Diagnosis very negative, but solace to Anne because she understood the hopelessness of her life which was eloquently explained to her by the Mayo doctor.

7/15-Peter arrives for visit

8/2- Andy arrives for a visit

8/6- John Donaldson arrives "What a lady"

8/15-New X-ray not good; Donna helps in house

9/28-Teddy Carney visits

10/12-Fred Kents visit

10/16- Nancy Dominick visits

11/24-DCII, DCIII, Andy, Sylvia, Donna dinner at
    Doze's house

Anne continued walking in our backyard as many as
50 times around a circle she had made. She was
determined to make life as good as possible right to the
end. She had quit the Chemo and was not in pain, but
often tired and exhausted. I cooked good dinners for her
which we nightly ate together. Those were warm
wonderful dinners that I savor. She never expressed
despair, never suggested life was unfair to her, and never
complained - she just carried on with her head up.

12/18/1988 Anne died at 3:37 A. M. at 3130 East
Exposition with all the family except Peter there at
her sad death. He arrived a couple hours later from
Ashland.
    I was most overcome when the funeral attendants
arrived to pick up her body. Seeing her being wheeled
that was the end and it brought deep sorrow and tears
as she was being wheeled away. Someway that said she
is gone forever.

12/19/- The next day I played some tennis to help
my despair and afterwards Doze comforted my sorrow
and had dinner for my grieved family and me. What a
kind and thoughtful relief that was. Soon afterwards it
was lonely at 3130 so I welcomed Doze's kindness and
turned to her to assuage the pain. My children were
back home with their families and responsibilities-
Andy to Grand Junction, Jeannie to Aspen, and Peter
to Tucson. Only David remained in Denver.

1988 was a year that started out with great hope for Anne and me, but ended disastrously!

Goodbye, my love, what a wonderful person you are. I will love you forever. David

30

NEW LIFE AND
JEAN EMERY

After Anne's death, my children returned to their homes in Aspen, Tucson, and Grand Junction with Jean (Doze), Anne's younger sister and me being the two mourners remaining in Denver. Dose owned her Townhouse at 3333 East Florida where she kindly invited me for dinner during the Christmas holidays. My house at 3100 East Exposition was very vacant as I spent some time at home but soon I was asking Doze out for dinners at night or eating dinner with her at her house. Soon I was seeing her every evening. Things seem to gallop forward and we were being asked out to some of our pals for dinner. Friends seemed to be aware that we were seeing each other continually. Chat; chat; chat!

In February I asked Doze how about coming to Tucson for a brief relief from the Denver routine. I had the Condo at 2600 E. Skyline just waiting for someone. We both hopped onto United and flew that hour and half to the "Old Pueblo" for our stay. Doze had visited us a few years before, so the surroundings were not foreign for her. We walked, hiked, went to movies and plays, ventured around and met John Donaldson again, and generally had a joyous time together.

The death of Anne certainly preyed on my mind, but I saw no reason to sit around and grieve-I preferred to try to divert my attention of her death from my mind. Certainly the companionship of Doze helped me accomplish that.

By the end of our two week stay together, a spark had been lighted and I knew there was something developing between Doze and me. I had realized something in Doze that I had not known in all the years I had known her. I was being entranced by a wonderful caring, compassionate, spunky lady. Subsequently as things progressed, I realized our relationship had developed into real love for each other. I suggested that we solidify our bond with marriage, but I ran into resistance. She thought we had to think about it. "Don't be so impetuous. " "You are on the rebound". I kept after her with as much pressure that I thought was productive. It was still "time settles everything". To be a good suitor I had to agree- for awhile. I was not deterred or discouraged for I thought I knew the Jackson temperament. Don't make decisions too quickly. By April of 1989 either because she too was in love or because she became tired of my relentless pursuit, she gave in and we decided to get married. I was for getting married right after we decided to marry, even to get a marriage certificate in Nogales right now.

But she convinced me we should wait till summer. She, I think, was motivated by the soonest to get married for a grieved one should be six months- then it would not be a rebound. So we finally concurred. The green light went on and we proceeded to announce and plan for a wedding.

It was April that we made the announcement of our prospective wedding date. Most of our friends were not in the least surprised of our plans for they had witnessed our constant companionship. Doze and I celebrated our decision and announcement by taking a trip in early May to Tucson for a trip to visit the Missions that Father Kino, the 17th Century itinerate Jesuit priest, had established. The 100 degree weather was no surprise and we welcomed the commodious air conditioned bus as we took our seats in Tucson in the bus as we looked forward to a nice cool trip with our Arizona unknown fellow travelers. After we crossed the border at Nogales, we were transferred to a beat up Mexican bus. We were seated next to the inoperative toilet where the hot temperature did not improve its odor. The seats were so worn that one felt they were sitting not on a toilet seat but a donut. To add to our premarriage honeymoon, there was no air-conditioning to combat the 105 degree Sonora weather. But we did not seem to complain. On we went in that dilapidated bus under the guidance of Jim Officer and Jim Griffith, Arizona Professors, to Caborca, Piticitto, Magdalena, and then Nogales. We had a fun and informative trip without any objections to the frequent discomforts.

Our wedding was planned and developed to be a family affair at Rand. The Reverend Kenneth Burton drove up from Colorado Springs to perform the ceremony. We chose an aspen grove about 125 yards south of our house as the chapel for our wedding. Bales of hay became the seats for the family and two bales of hay stacked one on top of the other with pine boughs adorning the alter. In the middle stood a cross made from branches of the local Aspen trees. It was a lovely little quiet amphitheater that comfortably accommodated all of Doze's and my family.

**DC & Jean's Wedding
in Aspen Grove at Rand Ranch**

The wedding took place on August 19, 1989 during the late afternoon as the billowy cumulus clouds were just building up for their afternoon of rain showers, thunder, and lighting. The good but rather stout Reverend Kenneth Burton cloaked is his flowing ministerial robes began his walk across the meadow through the tall grass towards the chapel only to be met by thunderbolts and rain sprinkles thereby forcing him at a difficult jog, back to the house for shelter. This little drama repeated itself three times till the skies subsided and the good Lord decided that the wedding ceremony should proceed. Our Shakespearean actor reverend performed the ceremony with his usual brilliant oratory. Very soon thereafter we retreated to the house to celebrate. Great wedding, slightly unusual but so fitting for a second wedding ceremony for both of us. Simple, beautiful, families, loving, and calm.

Many Happy Days

Our marriage has been very successful if not for a few rough spots along the way that have gradually been adjusted. Doze had been married to John Emery before his tragic death in Bermuda after which she lived as a widow for some eight years. I had lived a happy married life with Anne for some thirty years. Both of us had developed habits that had been formed over the years that were hard to alter. Different opinions on minor physical functions such as locking the front doors and car doors, peaceful cocktail hours before dinner, tardiness, kitchen participation and procedures, hiring kitchen or garden help- all very minor but still causing irritations for both of us. There were more habits that had to be adjusted, but after some quarrels and even pretty good verbal fights, within five years most everything had been compromised between us and life no longer had these irritants. We had adjusted to our own personal habits and life was joyous, loving and happy.

I am very lucky to have Doze as a wife and companion. We have had many interesting and exciting trips together, many lovely and peaceful days at the ranch in Rand, and fun in Tucson with new friends and our many pleasant dinners together. The moving between three homes has been a challenge for her but she has worked hard to the necessary adjustments and I think she has enjoyed the three spots. She has made me happy and contented with life. She has been a great mother-in-law (and aunt) for my children.

In addition she has had to cope with her own discomfort from her Steniosis while at the same time being patient and caring with my health problems (heart attack, teeth, back and hand operations, back operation; broken ribs all in 2008-9). She has been a constant caring person for my discomforts and immobility and always ready to give her consul on what my conduct should be. (Maybe sometimes too often?). Through those difficulties we have enjoyed life and coped well with our problems thanks to her.

Now that I am healed, even though strength and mobility have been diminished. We are ready to trot ahead with my hair showing the first signs of graying, our pace slower, bed time earlier and Doze's Steniosis, because of her daily exercising, improving her back. We are interested in new instructional courses at the University of Arizona (literature course, drawing, astonomy, religious study plus golf for me up to twice a week).

We are both grateful for our "good health".

31

MY EXTENDED FAMILY

I have not provided a capsule of my family in these memoires so it seems appropriate to look at what this expanded family is up to. Some are at Kindergarten, quite a few instructing, some in the corporate world, and some involved with the financial sector. All seem to be plugging along with exciting plans, thoughts and Ideas.

Jake Emery is the head of the History Department at Fountain Valley School while Lisa has continued her 5 AM departures from her home to her Air Force Academy Public High school and teaching French literature and Spanish language. She is also teaching at Colorado College Jake I think is looking forward to retirement within the next five to eight years, but in the meantime has become a multilevel gardener in their new home?

Patrick is giving his all to make Balarat a fulfilling and contributive place for young people to expand their knowledge of nature and hopefully show them their obligations to preserve the environment in the world where we live. It's my impression that he is not being recognized for what a unique and good job he is doing. Cathy's continues spasmodically her architectural job and is a full time soccer mom. What's she going to do when Lin leaves the nest? This is the same challenge that's gone on for centuries... Elle endorsees the Block Plan and likes C. C. Lin at East after a exchange student trip to Slavia this past summer, is a little bit lost with her sister gone but looking forward to Western State University near Durango next fall.. Her big interest this year is singing in the choir at St. Thomas.

Charles is enmeshed in Ohio State University in the Gerontology Psychology dept. teaching and researching all the problems we oldsters are facing. Edith continues her writing producing another book after losing her father, selling a home and reestablishing in a new one. Their house has become somewhat vacant with Vida starting at CC, so their life is now different. Will they be more drawn to the West as a result of Vida's moving west? I think not since they have become Ohioans what with the proximity to Chicago. It wall depend on where the remaining families after his retirement (mothers, children)will be after ten or fifteen years.

Kate & John Russell

Jeannie Russell, while becoming a NIA teacher and real estate landlady, has, after some soul searching, become a resident of Aspen. John is pretty much a Big Island man. They have decided to get a divorce so I feel Jeannie, although admiring John, feels free. I think it's great and Jeannie will find happiness now that the two are able to go their own way. I pray so. I fully endorse their decision. Kate is in Santa Barbara at Westmont College, Lyza and David moving from Santa Barbara to Shingle Springs, a new challenge in life with job responsibilities and a growing family. I am going to be on a panel this February month in Sacramento, so I hope to see them. Andy studying cooking in NYC, outdoor survival school, piano and more. Many dreams and adventures in his mind. Still soaring around.

Peter has proceeded well after getting his divorced from Linda. Peter working for a church and also landscaping jobs. He is a wonderful father and spends many hours helping them become wonderful children. He's involved totally with Tia and Luna, so his life, I think has opened up being on his own.

Andy Wilhelm is trading on the Board and playing pretty good golf and skiing. A good contributor of ideas with "our investment" portfolio decisions.

David Jr. , after finally moving his office away from me after more than 25 years, has become the leader in family affaires- legally, financially, and planning. He has taken over from me and my inadequate records, the straightening out our family legal affairs, and initiating and controlling the family financial affairs. He continues to help me in my every little problems for which I am forever grateful. Since his pop corn business in declining, he is still looking for new challenges. He has become well known in Denver venture capital circles as he studies prospective investments for the family. Marsha has gone through a tough health year, but with her determination and guts has continued her wonderful recovery. Her nest has also diminished with Polly just back from L. A. and looking for more. Marsha shall receive his law degree and is practicing as defense attorney in the local court room and Izzie, the dynamo, after being a member of the East U. S. winning debating team, starting at Lehigh University with enthusiasm. Lots going on with this family. Marsha has reassembled all her brood back closer to her nest.

David III life with Bristol Myers moving from Princeton to the L. A. beaches is committed to his pharmaceutical company. Aislin has her hands full with two youngsters. David getting to know about the 2 AM shift. Both are to stay west and not desiring a potential move to the East.

Ali and Mike are moving from Perth and Kansas. He was ensconced in Kansas after finding Perth employment not easy. Ali after returning from Perth is now moving to Toronto to contiue her good and respected work. Coco is being one of the greatest, caring for Reece with her blood problem. Coco is tough, resilient, and loving and giving all the attention necessary for Reece. Jason experienced and able to cope with the world.

Andy Wilhelm has showing thoughtfulness and original balanced thinking as he works with David and me on the family Investment Portfolio. He has been most contributive, although he has left the grunt work up to his brother. His trading success is a mystery to me. Gotten pretty good at his golf game. Sylvia teaching and arting and painting and gardening with determination and success. Lyla graduated from Conzaga, teaching art, getting ready for law school after a stint in peace corps. She is loaded with thoughts and opinions.. Mia transferred from Montana Sate to U. of Colorado and seems to be searching for some exotic and challenging life in some overseas location. She spent a venturous summer month in Casas Grande where she saw a new different life, before escaping to London for Christmas.

Grandchildren: Luna and Tia Wilhelm

Family is growing so fast I don't now if I have left anyone out. Luckily Doze have healthy children and all with their sights on the future, even though times are most difficult during this recession.

Daughter Jeannie - Hawaii - 2004

32

THE RAND RANCH

In the seventies, I bought a ranch in Rand for my own account located a couple of miles from the town of Rand, Colorado, population 20, twenty nine miles from the nearest store in Granby or Walden. The ranch was initially used as the summer grazing ground for the Wilhelm Co. yearlings that were wintered at the company ranch, the Owl Creek Ranch, in Walden. After the company sold the Walden ranch, I operated the Rand ranch as a cow and calf operation. It was a low cost operation that made a few bucks. I had no employees, but contracted all the work out. Verl Brown (a wonderful neighbor) was paid so much per head per month to manage the cattle during the summer. In November I loaded the cows and calves up and shipped them to Sterling (Frank Waitley) for winter grazing on corn stocks. In the spring after Frank calved out the herd in Sterling, the cows and new baby calves were loaded up (separately) into trucks to spend the summer at Rand.

After the cows and calves arrived in Rand, after their six hours haul, we unloaded the cows and calves. We usually had a rodeo as they were unloaded. The calves would be separated from their Mommas at Sterling into different trucks so after the six hour truck ride, both Momma and babies were bawling and crying to be together. When the gates of the trucks would open at Rand, the cows would descend down the ramp of the truck slowly and wondering where their babies were. The bewildered and scared calves would bolt out of the trucks and take off running in all directions like Secretariat. We would all be on horses to try to calm the frightened babies and keep them in the area and eventually coax them to pair up with their mamas. Usually within three hours we would have them quieted down and together. But there was a lot of galloping and shouting before the day was over and until things calmed down.

DC with Emery "Golfers" at Rand, 2008

On June 20, 1990 Emco Cattle Co., the Partnership of Jake, Patrick, Charles and Anne Emery, DBA Emco Cattle Co. bought 160 acres of land from the Comanche Land and Cattle Company Co (DCW). Jeannie, David, Andy, and Peter Wilhelm formed a LLC and bought 120 acres contiguous with Emco's land. Quite immediately Andy and Peter bought out Jeannie and David. Emco bought 2. 5 c.f.s of the JAY water rights and Paco bought 2, 5 c.f.

In addition Emco purchased 2. 5 c.f.s and 1. 0 c.f.s. in the Ivey and Jay ditches respectively plus ½ of the existing minerals for a cost of $40,720.

I then sold the main part of the operating Ranch to Verl Brown, so we now had a recreatonal country spot with a touch of the ranching (hay meadows and irrigating)remaining.

Andy and Peter (PACO) owned a neat little cabin on their land, but Doze and I wanted our own pad. Paco's cabin was built by Peter and Andy about 1970 with the help of Burt Shilling and his father. (Their "guest house" was originally the horse barn.) So Doze and I investigated buying at some other location for the Emco home looking in southern Colorado (Cuchara), the Poudre River, and Kremmling. Soon we decided that right there at Rand was a great building sight overlooking an expansive meadow with Jack Creek and the Jack Creek valley (the Lower Riddle) with a background of the Never Summer Range. There are spectacular views in every direction of 14,000' towering mountains. The house is at an altitude of 8900 feet, so we have cool summers and very cold winters. We have always felt our choice of location for the house and environment was absolutely correct. Also Rand was two and half hours from Denver, neighboring to Paco's land so the location would be conducive to the togetherness of the Andy Wilhelm familys and ours. Emco, the owner allowed us to make the initial home building choice.

Peter, Andy, Jeannie, David with me - 1995

Doze and I looked over plans of a log building company in Fort Collins, and, after studying those plans and visiting other log houses around the state, we drew up our own architectural plan. I hired an overseer (Randy Nicholson) to help me in the construction, purchasing and labor availability details as I decided to be the General Contractor. We had hued round logs hauled from Majestic Log Homes in Fort Collins, where the frame of the house was put together, logs marked, disassembled, trucked to Rand, and reassembled. We had the house completed for our occupancy for Thanksgiving of 1990.

Except for a lawsuit brought by a fraudulent casual worker, everything worked out within our budget and the house was built expertly. (Cost of building $260,000.00). In the law suit the claimant (Stevenson) asserted he was totally incapacitated by a fall from a ladder, but fortunately I photographed him from the upstairs bathroom window at a later date carrying a 50# Aspen tree to its planting location in front of our house. This evidence proved he was not incapacitied. (Stupidly he was assisting a friend and did not know I was perched ready for the kill!). That evidence presented to the judge at the trial was sufficient to dismiss a potential large disability award.

In 1996 I sold all my cattle and the ranch to Verl. Emco now had land that was still termed a ranch since we did take in cattle for grazing and did put up about 100 tons of hay. The sale reduced the responsibly of owning a cow herd and the sorting and culling of them each spring and fall. We still retained what we wanted sin vacas.

In 1993 we engaged in extensive discussions concerning building a pond with objections from Doze because of flood risk (?). We persuaded her to agree to the construction and we proceeded with a difficult bulldozer contractor (Huey Thompson) to build our pond. After difficulties with construction were concluded, he bailed out and quit, so we hired Sessions (Todd Verhill) with his large backhoe to finish the job.

The Extension Service of the Colorado Department of Agriculture gave us their engineering assistance in establishing and locating water level control boxes, and emergency over flows. The expertise was very questionable, for we were forced to overturn some of their decisions. We had extensive discussions and negotiations with the Soil Consevation Service to convince them that we were not destroying wetlands, but were actually creating more. I had to convince a Mexican lady, who was an employee of the S. C. S, of that fact. I do not think she had ever been in the field before so she accepted my argument and gave us approval to proceed. After much paper shuffling and numerous trips to the their office, I finally received their office's building permit to proceed. The pond has been an aesthetic jewel, an ice hockey rink, a fishing pond, a beaver and muskrat home, a restng spot for geese and a habitat for a new growth of Lodgepole pines. All our families and friends have enjoyed their swims, fishing, ice hockey, and walks associated with it.

Over the past 30 years I have enjoyed developing the grounds, planting trees, repairing and building irrigation ditches, maintaining fences, irrigating, developing an extensive lawn, improving the plumbing and sewer, developing and filing with the State engineer for the Emco #1 water right, maintaining the overflows, building a ditch to carry the water to the pond, establishing haying and grazing agreements with Verl Brown, contracting the construction of our "shop/ garage", maintaining the "Ranching Status" of the lands for beneficial real estate taxes, maintaining the access road to the house, providing easements for Emco thru Paco's land, maintaining the good condition of the house including the removal of one billion dead flies, establishing friendly contacts with neighbors and contractors, protecting legal rights of unfenced owned property, maintaining status of water rights (Particularly the Ivy), and more.

Challenges lie ahead. The Beetle killed forest, the cleaning and deepening the pond, the repair of both the Ivey and Jay headgates, the reroofing of the house, and more. It will just need attention so not to let the ranch deteriorate.

It is interesting our pond is loaded with Rainbows and Brookies even though we have never stocked it. Ben Duke advised me not to buy and stock it-just wait and fish will work their way up or down the inlet or outlet and they will be stronger and more durable than if you stock it. His advice was correct.

I have had an extensive involvement with horses. Our two oldest inhabitants were June and Boni Sadr. June was put in her eternal resting place in 2002 after 34 years of loyal service. She was a sprightly, good gated, handy, good-looking chestnut lady that carried many visitors and children around the ranch. She became very thin at her unusually old age, so that, even though the day before her demise, she led the other horses on a dash across the meadow. It was hard to have Doc. Weddie put her down when her spirits were so good. She rests in a grave on the hill to the south of the woods. Boni was a big common bred quiet old horse with a canter that would jolt your teeth out, untrained for anything useful, but just quiet enough for little kids to ride. He basically was a wimp for every horse chased him away from their own proximity. I don't think he ever thought of biting or kicking any other horse. He was a big gentle teddy bear with a good soul. He reached 28 in 2003 so I put him to rest beside his pal, June, of 20 years.

Other horses at our rancho included two obstinate Shetland ponies that were soon shipped out, a rodeo mule that tore down our fences and was quickly removed from the ranch, a big roan (Morrie) barrel racer who unloaded a few visitors and was therefore banished, a strawberry roan pony that was cut "proud" thereby thinking he was a stud. (He spent most of his time trying to breed June or chasing big Bonnie out of his view). He was quickly returned to his former owner. The horses were left outdoors with the mosquitoes, deer flies, rain, and snowstorms. They huddled in the lodge pole pine forest of Verl's when the blizzards hit. They wintered on the same feed grounds as Verl's cattle. It should be proof that box stalls, horse blankets, and pampering is not the solution for equine old age. Their hair was so long in the winter they looked like bears but they stayed as healthy as any horse could.

I rode my horses happily till about 2003 with Bonnie, Sadr and June my mainstays. Bubba was a four year old with too many bucks for me. When left unused and filling his belly with all that good grazing and energy, Bubba proceeded to buck Andy off causing some pretty good bruises. It was getting tough for me to get my leg over the cantle, easier to get cramps in my groin, and hard to open and close gates. I realized I did not wish to get bucked off by him and end up in traction for the rest of my life. Basically I got chicken (or was it wise?). So I gave up riding and horses at Rand. I felt happy just to have those guys around so I could feed them corncobs and provide and care for them. Bubba would always greet me when I arrived in the pickup so that was like having a friend waiting. However, I decided in 2003 to send him down to Roy Waitley to sell. It was a tough call for me, but the move made sense.

Rand Ranch with Elle Emery

The Rand ranch was the occasion for many visitors. The Patrick Emerys were frequent weekend visitors and even sometimes had big groups of their friends up for a tent city party. We finished the "Meadow Level" into an apartment with kitchen, two bedrooms, and living room mainly for their benefit for their winter excursions (Hockey on the pond, skiing nearby, snow shoeing, and other winter activities). The Charles visited every summer for a week. With Vita, Elle, Lindsay, Mia, and Lyla present it made for after dinner games and theatrical production by those budding thespians. Doze and I also had visitors often on the weekends when we came up. In addition Andy and Sylvia, and family and friends also spent many days enjoying their cabin and exchanging meals with us.

Jean Emery Wilhelm

Jean, Jeannie

Wilhelms

Emerys

Lisa, Jeannie, Sylvia

Mia, Elle, Lyla, Lindsay, Vida

Rand Ranch Family Shots

Little did we know that Rand would be the location of three glorious weddings, a big birthday bash and other festivities. They were all different with charm for each.

The festive marriage of Peter and Linda's wedding took place on June 15, 1996. Many of the seventy or so guests were housed at the King Mountain Ranch where we had the rehearsal dinner. Bob Kinney, Linda's father, gave a humorous speech insinuating that Peter should not avoid bathing. (He had been aware of something in his times with Peter). The following day Peter and Linda had an Indian type sit down around in a circle smoking Sage as a slow rain descended. (The spot where Peter's sauna is located is now where the ceremony took place). But the band and liquids soon raised the celebration to a high pitch ceremony.

The second event was Anne Emery's and John Kyllo's wedding, August 16, 1996, just two months after Linda's and Peter's. Most all the guests were gathered together in front of the old log Homestead down in the Riddle Meadow by following a Scottish bagpiper through the path cut through the tall grass, where John's nephews handed us programs and verses. We sat on hay bales as we awaited the procession. We were greeted by Anne's and John's minister from Oregon, and he and they created the service. I walked Anne from behind the Homestead. She was radiant and splendidly dressed in the same dress as her mother and Anne Wilhelm had worn in their weddings. Jean and I presented her to John. At the end of the service, each received a rose and then everyone followed Anne and John and the bagpiper back to the Emco house for celebratory lunch.

I have already written in this book of the great wedding Doze and I had in our "wedding chapel" in the Aspen grove not far from our house.

In 2010, Doze with the help of Jeannie Russell and her siblings threw a big bash for me on my number 90 birthday. A big tent was erected on the lawn in front of the house, tables , chairs buffet serving tables, hot plates, Mexican delicassies, deserts, wine and beer all greeted some 45 guests. Many of our ancient (Contemporary) friends declined attendence because of the distance from Denver and because the altitude was too much of a burden on their old hearts. Jack Malo, Knickrehns, Daggett and Ellie Harvey, Hagertys, Owens(day early), in addition to many of our children's ages made up the participants. The neighbors Elizabeth and Mike Schleppy helped supplying food and tables for the affair. Traditional Toasts were offered in good cheer and fun. Even the mosquitos enjoyed the party, even though they were unfriendly.

There is no question that activity changed after fifteen years after the building of our house. Both Doze's and my families had grown up and were either in college, going to work, or overseas, so the youngsters had disappeared.

We had turned off the top floors from water and heat, so that the garden level could be operated without concern of frozen pipes or heat upstairs. Cathy and Patrick enjoyed their winter excursions with friends occupying the "garden level" thereby easing the warming of the house in the sub zero winter. Patrick and his family would drive up in the winter with their friends to enjoy the snow and ice for games and hockey. They had a good wood stove, kitchen, bed rooms so they were cozy downstairs. Andy and his family lodged in their warm little cabin frequented the ranch often in the winter so they contributed hockey players and friendship. Mia, Lyla, Elle and Lindsay often with friends completed the winter fun. Doze and I abandoned Rand after Thanksgiving till the following May.

Andy and Sylvia with Mia and Lyla were great and often visitors in their cabin, which was a five minute walk from our house. Andy spent probably more time in Rand than any of us. He controlled and managed the irrigation from the Jay Ditch, cut and supplied much of the fire wood, helped me attaching different tools like the rotary mower, back blade, and other attachments that I no longer could handle, negotiated cattle grazing and haying contracts with Verl Brown, maintained his internet connection to continue his commodity trading business, and generally helped me with many of my efforts. Sylvia also loved the ranch and when she could free herself from her teaching and art combined with Doze with many fun cocktail and dinner exchanges between the two homes. Mia and Lyla added freshness and fun whenever they could join the group. My enjoyment of Rand would not be the same without their companionship and help.

In 2008, I asked Patrick Emery to take over management of the Emco Cattle Co. ranch. ("Rand"). He is very busy and occupied with his managing and directing the the outdoor educational facility, Balarat, for the Denver Public Schools. I know that his allegiance to that operation is paramount in his thinking. Charles Emery is also completely involved with his teaching and research at Ohio State University. Jake Emery also has more obligations at the Fountain Valley School than he would like, so his time is limited. It could be that Doze and I may continue to help until those three might find enough time to devote to the management.

With everyone growing older and their interests and abilities changing, the usage and enjoyment of the ranch is changing. My only hope is that all of us can find enough time to maintain Rand in its present state. I believe in another twenty years this property could become an even greater jewel. Mountain property with a view, a stream, a pond, some grazing land, an attractive home that is not too large and does not demand a cattle operation will be in great demand in the future when the economy has recovered.

The responsibilities are many and, if not hard, they include attentiveness and implementation. The maintaining fences, irrigating, caretaking and watering an extensive lawn, maintaining the current legal and effectivness of the head gates, ditches and condition of the Ivy and Jay ditches, improving or rebuilding the necessary changes in the Jay and Ivy ditch headgates, maintaining the overflows, maintaining the pond and its tributaries, the legal requirements relating to water rights, establishing the annual haying and grazing contracts with Verl Brown, maintaining the "Ranching Status" of the lands for beneficial tax treatment, maintaining and repairing the fences and the access road to the house.

Certainly, the upkeep of the house and continual operation of the liveability (Linens, furniture, windows, cleaning)of the house is vital for the general condition and operation of the property so that it continues to be a benefit to all of our families and for its future value. Doze's contribution to maintain the home is very important and I am sure she will contribute her energy and efficiency to achieve that end. Between the two of us and the Andy Wilhelms we will carry on.

Doze and I both loved the mountain country and the ranch, and enjoyed ourselves by ourselves or with friends. Our interest has diminished when the snows and sub freezing weather arrives. I enjoyed time fishing, reading, doing office/computer work in peace, irrigating, ditching, mowing the Rand golf course, watching the wildlife and being with Doze. However, I did miss not having my horse friends around. It was wonderful enjoying the 70 degree weather rather than facing crowds, traffic jams, pollution, noise, and heat of the city-just being away from the hot cement city.

33

FLYING IN BUSINESS

From my experience in American Fighters in the Air Corps, civilian airplanes were a piece of cake to fly. The planes I flew for business and pleasure were not as "hot" as the military planes and therefore they were a breeze to fly. I could get into little airstrips or rough ground so they were very suitable for me visiting feedlots, cattle sale rings, remote ranches or fishing lodge strips. The one disadvantage of these planes was that I could not cruise above 22,000 feet, which meant more flying close to thunderstorms, since I would have to fly through or around them instead over them. And that was pretty hairy with lightening, big turbulence, and inundations of water onto the plane. Of course, the engines having 350 horse power instead of 1800 H. P. meant that gas consumption was low enough to make their use feasible and economical. At the same time I had planes that I could carry at least 3 passengers and even some that would carry 5 passengers so that I could fly the cattle buyers, the family for small trips or accommodate the Wilhelm Air Lines (see below) travelers.

I seemed to trade airplanes frequently with Harry Combs, who owned the "Fixed Base Operation",

Combs Aviation at Stapleton Airport, Denver. Trying to save a buck and still have a good plane under me, I would buy used airplanes that had been traded into Harry. For example, Peter Kiewit and Co. , an international construction company amongst other things, would trade in their Executive planes when they had flown 900 hours, even though the manufacturers warranted the engines for 1500 hours. I could buy this "luxury" plane at a bargain and still have a good sound plane with 500 PLUS hours left on the engines. So from about 1955 to 1987 I flew about 5000 hours owning a bevy of different airplanes, including Cessna 182, Cessna 210 B and C, Beach Baron two models, Piper Twin Comanche, Travelair, Twin Bonanza A, C, and D, AeroComander 580E and maybe some I have forgotten.

One of my favorites was the Beach Twin Bonanza that had a couch, television, and two lounge chairs besides the pilot's seat. The big landing wheels gave the prop high clearance so that landing in the prairie over cactus or other obstacles made it a versatile vehicle. I even slept over night in it at some airports. It was no rocket ship for it would cruise at an indicated airspeed of 125 MPH.

The Travelair was a small twin Beach plane that was vastly underpowered, so one time when I was leaving John Matthews's ranch in eastern Colorado, I had trouble getting the plane off the ground on takeoff on a 100-degree hot day so I barely missed flying through a barn at the end of the runway. That got my heart beating! I just kept urging it for more altitude, which it barely did. I turned the plane back to

Harry immediately. It turned out that the maintenance log had been falsified and the plane had not had that major overhaul that the log represented. I should have sued him for excess stress!

The other poor plane was the Twin Comanche. Piper Aircraft decided they would put two engines on their single engine Comanche fuselage to appeal to those who liked Twins. However, once on the approach to the Aspen airport I almost lost control of the plane. There was a 20 MPH right (west) wind blowing off a 200' mountain some ¼ mile from end of the runway. For some reason, the "wheel" (controls ailerons) became completely vapid. There was no response to my efforts to stabilize the plane. For probably only 15 seconds(even though it seemed many minutes), I had no control of the plane as it started to drop one wing and headed for terra firma. Finally, control returned and I regained control of the plane, straightened out the glide and landed without incident. I flew it back to Denver and got rid of it pronto. I understand that Piper discontinued manufacturing that plane for obvious reasons.

The single engine plane that I liked the best was the Cessna 210. Speed 170 IAS, Richardson short field landing kit, 4 comfortable seats, and economical to fly and maintain. I flew many times to my strip at the ranch at Rand with no problem, even if 35 MPH crosswinds confronted me.

Even though flying was exhilarating and fun, sometimes the inevitable unexpected happened. I took Vic Neet, the Connecticut General Insurance agent, to Crookston, Minnesota for an inspection trip for the loan we had on the ranch. Flying home in that same Comanche plane that I had had previous problems with, we were happily chatting and viewing the green farms below us when all of a sudden the plane started shaking so violently that I could barely hold onto the wheel. I throttled back to decrease the shaking at a speed just above the stall speed. Apparently something had happened to the right propeller, so I shut the right engine down. I had no control of the prop so it just "wind milled" thus offering resistance ("feathering the prop would allow the prop to knife through the air and thus not create drag). In this distressed situation I called Fargo radio to give them a "May Day" in case I went down before I reached the airport. I still had the left engine, but I could not maintain my 5,000-foot altitude. I was about 40 miles west of the Fargo airport, losing about 500' per minute so (without a computer), I figured I could just make it to the airport. I limped over the boundary of the airport and landed on the runway. I found out that the prop had broken with a piece about 10" off its end. It had just sheared off. This imbalance created the violent action. We grabbed a Commercial airplane and flew home as they repaired the plane. Although Vic Neet was visibly shaken, he did approve the loan!

Sometimes our trips were not entirely pleasurable. David, Jeannie, and I set out for Palm Beach for their spring vacation in about 1964 to stay with my mother (Anne took the airline). I removed the back seat of my single engine Cessna 210, spread blankets and pillows to make a comfortable bed for those two trusting souls. After 4 hours of flying we ran into a wild SE line of Thunderstorms, so we put down in Greenville, Mississippi in the black dark of the night. We ate a fun dinner at "Doze's" café (must have been propitious) before our next day's leg to Palm Beach. The following morning the weather was still so bad that we could not fly, so we went to a morning movie ("Horse with the Flying Tail"). The weather in the afternoon looked somewhat better so we took off in the afternoon. We penetrated a series of Thunderstorms as we pitched and lurched through lightening and rain until we finally landed at Jacksonville, Florida. On our approach we landed in a cloud burst with wind and lightening pitching us around like a kayak in a wild stream. It rained so hard I believe we were in a waterspout. We were all pretty shaky as we exited the plane. I think Jeannie was so shocked that she was reluctant to fly even with an airline for quite awhile. She never requested another flight with me. I don't know about David. He took flying lessons some years later, got his license, took his cross-country required flight (Denver- Amarillo-Denver), and then never flew again. I don't know if the Jacksonville landing haunted him. So Florida was fine, but that flight was a terror.

The "Wilhelm Airlines" flew from Stapleton Airport to Aspen and left late Friday afternoon and returned Monday at the crack. Tom Hilt, Pat Westfeldt, Gus Ball and others would fly with me in my Twin Bonanza. One-way ticket was $10.00 which paid my gas bill. A bargain. One evening as I took off from Stapleton field on runway 35 and climbed to two hundred feet, I lost the left engine (the prop gear box sheared) so with five people and hot 100 degree air, I had to make a 120 degree left turn at a speed barely over the stall speed with a big load to try to get back to the nearest runway. (Old runway 12 at Stapleton Field). That was my best option rather than landing on an oil refinery in north Denver. That was asking a lot for that strong old plane to keep flying for another three minutes. I fire walled the right engine and barely made a safe emergency landing (with all the fire wagons waiting for my arrival). That right engine that carried us around that three-minute flight was ruined because of that full power and full prop speed I had to give it. That was two engines gone in three minutes! That was white knuckle time. I think everyone was happy to fly Aspen Air Lines after that. That abortive trip also was the final flight of Wilhelm Air Lines!

There are as always many more tales of flying. Possibly because there is a danger flying a small plane, there are many "interesting tales". Flying was great when everything went alright. Very occasionally everything went wrong, so it behooved a pilot to keep on the alert. After flying those many years, I was getting tired of the thrill and beauty. In addition with my active management of the cattle business finished, it was not economical to fly just for convenience (and fun). As Commercial Aviation expanded in the US, flying regulations became more demanding with airport ground regulations and directives, with ATC airways control and procedures more exacting, with private corporate jets pushing my type of plane into the background, and preparation for flying became more time consuming, everything was building up to complicate flying. So in about 1980 I sold my Aero Commander 58E to Amfac and hung up my togs. So after forty years of flying, I figured I did not need to fly any more.

I was getting physically tired from flying. It meant I was on a speeded up time clock. Hurry, Hurry. For example, many days I would leave the Denver office, fly to Sugar City on the way to Rocky Ford, then fly to Fort Morgan and then to Sterling then onto Rand and finally end up at Aspen at sunset. That journey might have taken four long days by auto whereas I could do it in 12 hours- but at a price of fatigue.

Quitting left a void in my life. It had been an important absorption for some forty years. However, I felt relieved and happy that I had finished flying. No more thrills! No more excitement. No more fatigue. No more scares. Flying had been a great part of my life. I had been a good safe pilot with never a blemish caused by me on any plane I flew. So as they say "A good pilot is a live pilot. "

I took a trip with Tony and Kit Marrs in their Stinson in 2007 to La Paz from Tucson. Because of its slow speed of maybe 90 I. A. S and small gas carrying supply, we flew many circuitous ways to obtain gas or to avoid cross winds on landing (Loreto). The plane's cabin was not airtight, so even at 1500 to 2000 feet I thought I might freeze solid. The temperature in my backseat was just below freezing and we were not equipped with winter gear. That little trip made me recognize that I was delighted I did not have to fly a small plane around any more.

34

Second Home
Tucson

Anne and I had flown on United Air Lines to Tucson in 1978 staying at the Arizona Inn as I attended the Cattleman's convention. The meeting was as usual pretty dull and uninformative. We both had visited Tucson over the years and loved the area. Rather spontaneously we decided we should investigate the idea of buying a pad. We looked around one Saturday and the next day we decided to buy 2600 East Skyline- a very attractive old condominium. We did not come to Tucson contemplating purchasing a home. The Condo at 2600 East Skyline, Unit #6 was a 1000 square foot home opened upon a beautiful landscaped swimming pool and garden. The interior was planned with imagination with diagonal halls and walls that made the interior unique and interesting. It was small, inexpensive, easy to keep up and just the ticket for brief sojourns. Since I was still working full time and trouble in Sterling had not developed, we used the condo for brief stints from time to time.

Eleven years after its initial purchase, and after Doze and I had stayed in Tucson more and more, we realized it might be smart to sell this town house and move to a larger home and one that would not be gobbled up by expanding Tucson. New condominiums were being constructed nearby, Skyline drive was being expanded to a four lane freeway, a new school was being constructed, and a new bank across the street, the Westin Hotel a block away, and future major plans of expansion all would make the corner of Campbell and Skyline a major intersection. Noise and confusion was beginning. And our Condo was right next to that intersection. We could see that we better get moving. Our prophecy of the future was correct. Now in 2010, a major shopping center has developed, numerous restaurants have located there, and the corner is the busiest intersection in the Foothills of the Catalinas.

On June 16, 1993 after two years of searching for a three bed room townhouse with a south view, a quiet spot, and a location that would not be encroached upon, we found what we wanted- a 1900 square foot Town House at 5865 Placita Del Conde. The house has a spectacular open vista south over a wash that cannot be built upon, a mile from Sunrise Blvd (Quiet), close to Paloma C. C. , tennis court and pool next door, small garden areas for my herb garden and citrus trees, and a grass side yard. Just the ticket. The house had been purchased by a father for a daughter who preferred New York to Tucson therefore the house had been abandoned for two years. The yard was unattended with trees untrimmed and bushes growing wildly, the kitchen antique and dark, the tile floor unattractive, the deck in total disrepair, and other problems. We proceeded with a new satillo tile floor in kitchen, skylight in kitchen, new deck and more. Upon the renovation the townhouse fitted our ticket to a tee. Since we bought the house at a deep discount ($152,500), we could afford the renovation to make the house well valued after its completion. (By 2003 eleven years later the house had doubled in market value to $300,000; probably by 2010 $200to 250,000.00 the Crunch!).

While Anne was alive we visited Tucson, but did not spend much consecutive time there so we did not become well acquainted with many locals or "winter birds". Since I was pretty well retired by the time Doze and I were married, we began staying for longer periods of time until we became true "snow birds". We would spend a week before Christmas and then from January 1 till May 1. As a result we became more involved with the Arizona Theater Co. , St Philips church, Paloma Country Club, University of Arizona, golf, bridge, walks and hikes, car exploration, other snow birds and locals. We both became close friends of many new people. Brays, Weeks, Boerners, McKnights, Jordans, McConnels, Sam Ward, Haits, Robinsons, Bugdons, Murrays, and others. Many were from the Milwaukee area. The Harpers were snow birds for quite awhile, but sold their house and came back for a short spell at the Arizona Inn. All in all I have more friends in Tucson than I do in Denver. The environment made it easy to meet friends. Many people in the foothills were retirees so golf, tennis, church friends, and Denverites all had the leisure time to pursue that which they wanted to do. For quite awhile the Wallin Fosters were our closest old friends from Denver who wintered yearly in the Old Pueblo. Unfortunately, Wallin died of Parkinsons in 2001. His widow Marylyn however soon visited sparingly. Soon thereafter Paul and Cooey Harper (sister-in-law to Doze) bought a house in Tucson and they were great friends, frequent movie and dinner companions. However, they too put their house up for sale in 2008, so they were mostly gone. Bob and Joan Johnsons were friends on the golf course and bridge table. Unfortunately, Bob died in 2007. Of course John Donaldson was an old pal from the days of the Arizona Desert School with whom I had played polo in 1934. By 2009 he was suffering from Parkinson's and had taken a nasty fall breaking his hip. He died in November of 2009. Our pals in Tucson were disappearing one way or another.

Garden of the Gods Club
Return from Tucson

Quite often one or more of our children would visit us on their vacations. So we had enough room for all and were able to get accommodations at a hotel or at our neighbor's for their stays. We also bought season tickets to the Arizona Theater Co. , Tucson Symphony and the Invisible Theater, attended classes in Spanish, Russian politics, writing this autobiography(!), spiritual classes, drawing, astronomy, book club and more.

Christmas Group - Tucson

Golf and tennis once or twice a week for me. I thoroughly enjoyed my life there. After I broke three ribs playing very poor tennis, I decided this was not the game for one that had lost much of his balance and whose "wheels" just did not function well. Playing tennis at the age of 90 was hardly tennis-if the ball came to you, you hit it, but if you had to chase it, forget it. It was a game of mobility and that was gone. I hated to quit, the exercise, the companionship, the competition I am leaving behind with regrets.

The formative years at the Desert School became part of my mind and body. The dry weather, the eternal sun, the hot weather (not summer 105s), the occasional cloudbursts, the ever changing sunsets, the purple mountains, the picturesque Saguaros, the spring dust storms, the cooing of the white wing doves, the cackling of the Gambil quail, the unwanted visits of the Javalinas, the circling of the Red Tails all are part of the Tucson Arizona scene. It was familiar and comfortable for me.

Doze did not have that background, but to her great credit she became occupied and interested in people and activities. She joined a book group, became friends of Ann Baldwin, Joan Johnson, Shirley Bray, and others. She taught Indian and Mexican children at a public school. All enjoyed her as an interesting good friend. Even though she missed seeing her children, I believe she too loved the beauty of the desert and overall loved her stays in Tucson.

I had a heart attack January 1998. I drove myself to Heart Hospital after I felt the pain in four minutes. Immediate attention. All recovered by summer time. It is a lesson that when you have a heart attack be sure to be within minutes of a hospital!

35

ASPEN SUMMERS

In 1958, Frank Shafroth, Gus Ball, and I bought a house in Aspen at 334 Francis Street. We paid $18,000.00 for the house with a $14,000.00 mortgage. Wonderful location-a simple two-bed room house-Two blocks from Tent. We would rotate the use among the owners and rent it the rest of the time. Even though we rented it almost continually when the owners did not through Kay Reid, we made little money by the time the real estate company took its fees, the capital improvements and the thievery. We owners and our wives' were socially compatible, but their tastes were decidedly different. Even though Anne was known for her Jackson paucity, the thrift of Frank and Gus was too much. If there was a thought of colors or décor, everyone had a different idea so there was no action. Even though Anne and I were thrifty, our partners had less desire to spend any money for improvements or upkeep. Anne certainly was not charmed with the Shafroth idea of décor. I think Pat Ball, who had beautiful taste, would agree with Anne, but Gus was ready to veto any spending. It was quite apparent that a continuation of the joint ownership would soon lead to an unhappy relationship. So it was mutually agreed that we should break up the partnership.

Therefore, I offered Gus and Frank either to buy us out, or I would buy them out at the price of $31,000 which was set by me. Both Frank and Gus couldn't imagine paying that much for it, so I forked over the cash and we had our own house. We before long added a wing for $30.000 and we now had a great place with another bed room and a great front veranda for lounging. At about the same time we added an improved utility shed. We were denied a building permit for it because it would have intruded into the alley. With the wisdom of George Tempest we constructed the building on "skids" without a permanent foundation thereby skirting the need for a building permit. I might say that in 2010 that building still exists even though the house itself was scraped after I sold it. We continued to enjoy the house until 1984, when I was forced to sell it(at $425,000) because of my financial difficulties. The house was sold to a Texas doll whose husband was a big developer in Texas. By 2010 without question the real estate (NE Corner of 3rd and Francis) was worth a couple million without a house upon it! With the real estate problems in Aspen, it would probably be hard to find a buyer at that price.

We spent many days of the summers there. Anne would stay there continually and several of our family would be there on and off. I would usually fly in Thursday or Friday for dinner and leave at 6 A. M. on the following Monday. Peter and Andy both went to Bob Johnson's ice hockey camp so they would stay from ten days (Andy) to 16 days (Peter). Peter was so exhausted physically when he took the second session in a row that he stayed in his sack for 24 hours.

Traveling Foursome
Pete Douglas, David Wilhelm,
Steve Owen, Bob Knickrehn

I would fly in and out in my airplane even though the summer weather was rather dicey with thunderstorms and erratic unpredictable weather. But it was usually passable. The airplane meant I could conduct my business and at the same time enjoy the summer in Aspen.

We enjoyed wonderful weather, great music, lots of tennis, good sociability, even a couple of summers of stick and ball polo with two horses that I brought up. Peter Vought owned a house overlooking Castle Creek that had a horse barn and corrals. He was kind enough to let me keep my horses with his, as we shared expenses and some upkeep of the facilities.

Anne would stay in Aspen for weeks at a time. She had a group of girls to play tennis with and of course she and all of us took in the concerts as often as possible. She and I played mixed doubles with the McBride's, Marquises and others.

In the fall when the leaves had changed, we often spent Thanksgiving there enjoying the sun on our south-facing patio. Christmas was usually ski time. We skied daily. Andy, Jeannie and Peter loved to ski and were very good, if not racing material. Jeannie's' boy friend, Willie Draper, was a first class skier who would lead Jeannie tearing around Ajax. She never skied again as well after Willie left the scene. Young love I guess. David was a sissy like his old man, and just tolerated his time on the slopes. Peter and Andy were good bold skiers. My use of the ski slopes diminished as soon as our children got so they could ski faster and better than I and when they had pals to cavort with. By the early eighties I had given up downhill skiing because I just never particularly enjoyed it. I did not like freezing and because of my questionable ability, I did not ski with ease. As my children would say to me "Relax, Dad, just Relax". Since I was always close to tumbling, how could I relax? In those skiing days we would roll out of bed at 6 A. M. to catch Lift #1 at 7 A. M. Then I would be frozen like an ice cube by the time I reached the warming house. No not for me, I'll leave it to other nuts.

Life in Aspen involved almost twenty years of our lives so the involvement had a big impact on us. Jean and Daggett Harvey (sister and brother-in-law) rented a house one summer next to ours, and that was fun with much camaraderie. We had many of the family visit with us including Daggett and Jane (wife two), Melissa Polmarkarkis, (daughter-in-law niece), Aunt Edie Jackson (Anne's aunt), Flossie Spalding, (my aunt) Helen Niblack, (my aunt) mother, and others. The Cudahy sisters had a hard time adjusting because of the lack of oxygen (8,200 feet) and usually departed gasping for air within a short time. Melissa notable visit was highlighted by the time she was skinny dipping in the Lincoln Creek pools when the law pounced upon the unclad. She scrambled home with only an Aspen branch to protect her nudity. Since Melissa had just had a scrape with the law in Chicago and was released on the condition of good behavior, her swimming violation scared the life out of her. She escaped their grasp and ran home under the cover of the woods bare-tailed. We all thought it more amusing than she!

Everyone lamented the necessity of the sale, but no one complained. Actually Jeannie and David were going in other directions and I began getting more involved with our ranch in Rand, so the transition worked happily and well for all. I am sure that Anne missed the music and life of Aspen. I think everyone in the family shared in my financial distress so they just pitched in and tried to help. Anne led the way and just thought "on we go to wherever-who knows". So we packed up our wares, scrunched furniture and fixtures, and moved much of it to our little cabin in Rand , Colorado.

Norway 1999

36

THE INTERNATIONAL
EXECUTIVE SERVICE CORP

With my relationship with Amfac finished, I was ready for some new adventure. David was running the operations in an efficient manner and the customers for the feedlots were signed up, so I felt I could take off (1978-1979).

I felt that I was free to expand my horizons. I have always been intrigued with the idea of projects in foreign countries both for the benefit of some recipient and for my own personal pleasure. I heard of the opportunity to join the I.E.S.C. (the International Executive Service Corps, also known as the "Paunch Corps") which provided technical assistance to needy foreign countries or to their citizens, as a volunteer for Foreign Service in some field related to agriculture or banking. I applied and was accepted.

The I.E.S.C. was an organization that conscripted volunteers to give technical assistance for businesses, agricultural enterprises, governmental operations or public institutions in foreign countries. The I.E.S.C. would sign a contract with a client (a foreign country agency or bank) to deliver to them an expert to try to aid in modernizing or correcting their particular problem. The I.E.S.C. then chose a volunteer from their bank of volunteers to fill that request. The I.E.S.C. and the client then share the expense equally. Because of the client's financial commitment and request for technical help, the client usually has keen interest in the project. The volunteer provides the expertise in the designated project. All food, lodging, transportation, or other applicable expenses incurred by the volunteer are paid for by the I.E.S.C.

The client for my work was the Kenya National Bank, owned by the Kenya government, which was responsible for monitoring, overseeing and managing the ranches that the bank had financed. The seven ranches that I was assigned to included about 1,000,000 acres of drought prone grazing land located near the town of Voi in Tsavo National Park halfway between Nairobi and Mombassa. The land was similar to much of Eastern Colorado or New Mexico. John Ugi, a very black 38 year old family man, was the Manager of the four ranches. The Kenya government wished to put the ranches on a sound financial footing and my instructions were to analyzes the shortcomings of the ranches and provide a plan to correct the problems.

My base of operations was located near the town of Voi. The town of 500 was a road junction where traders, smugglers, poachers, shoppers all came together. It was a dusty little village with one story nondescript buildings. The main events of each day were the arrival of buses.

My office was in Voi. It had ONE overhead 40-Watt bulb to illuminate four tiny offices. There were two secretaries that could not type who sat in their chairs and did nothing all day- not even talk. There were no phones, business adding machines, only one antique typewriter. The temperature was usually well over 100 degrees inside with not a fan to move the air. My assignment was to prepare budgets and plans, which was demanding since I had only a handheld adding machine. At the end of my three month tour, I presented my written recommendations after battling difficult working facilities.

The payroll on one ranch included close to 100 men to care for about 100 languid cows. One man could have handled the job. The ranch wanted jobs, not financial success of the ranch. Usually the cows would wander close to where they were corralled at night in their "Bama" and with their caretaker they would "graze" in a barren piece of land that required the least effort to get to. There was ample grass if they moved the cattle a half mile away. The ranch's management miscalculated the carrying capacity of their lands and therefore under stocked their ranches. I covered most of the 1,000,000 acres and totally revised their calculations of the carrying capacity. Water had to be relocated to entice the cattle to the best grazing ground. Many simple logical ideas were apparent but they seemed not to them. The ranch manager, John Ugi, after a slow suspicious start with me, finally agreed with my recommendations. So the written report endorsed by him was submitted. The result? I am quite sure the officials in charge agreed with my suggestions, but the long term practices would not be overturned because too many customs and incomes if implemented would be affected.

My home was Taita Hills a lovely old Rockefeller hunting lodge turned into a Hilton safari reception hotel. My office in Voi was 15 miles away. I had a second floor room with a spectacular vista and view of their private 2000-acre game park within Tsavo National Park. I looked out from my bedroom window to watch antelopes, waterbucks, lions, and other enchanting animals. Always something to see. There was a swimming pool below my window into which a waterbuck fell and there was great excitement as he was roped and pulled out for his survival. The hotel was the reception hotel for the tourists to register before they went to a nearby hotel where they stayed while visiting Tsavo National Park.

The Taita Hills hotel was the home for all the professional people who were working on various projects such as a veterinarian from Sweden, who was constructing cattle dipping vats to combat tick fever or British anti poaching helicopter forces or other professionals. As a result of this mixed bag of nationalities and skills, I did meet and participate in conversations with many different types in the evening when I returned home. My particular friend was a Swedish Vet who was installing cattle dipping vats to try to eliminate tick fever in cattle. Towards the end of the day I would be so tired trying to understand John Ugi's difficult to understand Kenyan English that I was open to any social conversation or cocktail.

So a little conversation and a drink was most welcomed by me back at the hotel. I became very aggressive in seeking out conversation the end of the day. I felt pretty isolated from any friends so I would talk to anyone. I would literally walk up to one's table at dinnertime and ask them if I could join them. It was trying and difficult to understand their Kenya English. A little vodka and tonic with a tourist was relief from the day's activities.

Since I was at the hotel as the sole I.E.S.C. representative, I occupied my time in many different ways. I would drive with camera in hand my Land Rover out from the Hotel onto the firebreak roads through the Tsavo National Park. Those drives were often 50 miles out into the wilderness. I would photograph birds, try to sneak up on elephants, and get pictures of any other animals. Some of the animals were calm, but most were wild, since my travels were not where tourists went. At Masa Mara where most of the tourists are taken, the lions sleep on the roads, the elephants block one's way, and basically wildlife ignores the tourist. On my drives in Tsavo the elephants were not docile especially the time I tried to take a picture of a baby elephant with his Mom. She chased me so I just made it back to my Land Rover. But the truly wild animals in an untouristy environment were a joy to watch even though they often were hard to get close to.

My radio was my pal. I received news from the Armed Forces Radio station or Voice of America so I had touch with the world. I did jog each morning on a little dirt airplane runway, but strolling around the environs was not advisable towards dark because there were plenty of unfriendly animals around. In fact, when I would jog in the morning, there usually were an abundance of pheasant sized birds and different kinds of antelopes grazing along the runway. However, quite often there were no signs of any animals, which was a warning to me that lions were in our vicinity. My jogs in those cases were a little shorter, faster and closer to home.

I drove early each morning in my issued Land Rover (that got three miles to the gallon) to Voi to my office along with a load of natives that I would pick up along the road. (I was told not to do that for my safety). I continued giving the rides, for I got a kick in their appreciation and my interest in them. The main trouble with that trip was that the Kenya native rarely washed, so by the time I arrived in Voi, the smell inside the cab was close to unbearable. But think of the good will and Good Samaritan work that I achieved being an American ambassador!

Kenya Friends

John Ugi had attended the University of New Mexico for two years so he had some knowledge of cattle ranching operations. However, he had some real obstacles in correcting the operations. Foremost was the tribal ownership of the ranches. Each tribe's main interest was to retain their jobs at each ranch. The interest was not to run an efficient financial ranching operation, but keep as many employed as possible. For example, on one ranch that ran some 200 cows and calves employed about 100 loyal tribesmen. By any standards two persons could have handled the operation. John could not fire the excess workers because the particular tribesmen would not agree. So, on this point I could not affect change.

Another obstacle to efficient operations was the fraud and under-the-table payments that were custom and difficult to stop. For example, the Tsavo ranches were supplied young and old growing cattle and cows from northern Kenya on an annual basis. The area that I covered received these cattle and at the end of the grazing season sold the grown calves and the cull cows. Such an operation required that the cattle bought by Tsavo be priced on a fair market price at the sale by Tsavo at the end of the season could be profitable. However, with many shenanigans at the buying end, payoffs and fraud meant that the cattle were being transferred at too high a price. I sensed unfairness so I requested that I go with John to northern Kenya and become involved with the purchasing of the cattle. I was told there was not enough room in their cars to include me. I said I would drive my own Land Rover there. Also John said we have no accommodations except to sleep in tents and probably in the mud. I said that's OK with me. Finally in desperation, John announced that the Secretary of Agriculture was coming to Voi to talk to me about the recommendations. That would be the same day as their trip started. It was clear that I had to meet the Secretary. I complied. But no Secretary. It was just a ruse to keep me away. I am sure that weights were falsified and payoffs were made so that the cattle were overpriced and those negotiating the deal became well healed.

Probably my attempt was beyond the scope of my assignment. I was told that I too had better layoff or I might get a slug in my back. A local white ranch manager had just been killed by tribesmen for actions that did not please them.

My relations and rapport with John were rocky at first. To begin, he resented a "Whitey" coming in there to spoil his little game. After a month I believe he understood that I knew the ranching business, that I was not an officious government type with no knowledge, and that I might help him. As a result we soon got along well, had a few laughs, and exchanged ideas. I think we both got to be friends and got to like each other.

After my many days of contact with him as we drove around the ranches and met with tribe leaders, I had thought I understood John and we had mutual respect. However that confidence deteriorated at the conclusion of my tour of duty because of an incident. I told him I was going to take a quick trip to the United States at Christmas. He asked me if I would buy him a camera. He said he could save some money that way. I did buy him a camera of his choice. He did not have the $85.00 to pay me when I gave him the camera, but would pay me later. He was most appreciative. A month later when I was about to return home at the completion of my duty, he still had not paid. After many requests by me, we set up a meeting at the Nairobi Hilton and he would come and pay up. No show. He just welched on the whole deal, and I figure he just felt he could get away with it. I really believe that's their code of ethics. If they can get away with something, do it. Obviously I was just another sucker. My confidence in the man disappeared after this betrayal. After 3 months with John, I thought we were on the same wavelengths, but it proved we were not. I regretted this development, but I guess I was naive to expect anything different.

On our many drives to the various ranches I would often go to their Swahili (I studied the language in Denver before the job) meetings and they would not discuss anything pertinent to their ranches (expenses, purchases, how the cattle were doing), but rather they would want to know who would get a ride to see the sights in Voi the next time the truck went to town. John would interpret that which I could not understand which was a lot. We were usually served lunch which was a big pile of steamed corn piled in the center of the table and we all pawed handfuls of the corn into our mouths. I think the natives liked the meetings so they get food and can socialize.

I returned to Denver after a month and half in Kenya to tend to my personal year ending business and to hope to invite Anne to accompany me back for the final month and half. She did agree so we flew the day after Christmas to Florence and Rome for about four days of enjoyment. We stayed at the Villa Rondini outside of Florence. The area was so cold that we either escaped to the Excelsior Hotel front lobby to warm up or retreat to the Villa Rondini and climb under the comforters into our sack in our room to warm up before our next art venture. There were about five other couples at New Year's dinner at the Villa and it was so cold everyone wore their mink coats for the whole evening. We were dressed for Kenya, so we sat and shivered as we drank our champagne. 35 Degree temperature in Italy when it drizzles it sure doesn't sizzle!

My second half of my tour was a great improvement since Anne was my companion. She was very courageous coming over with me with no particular assignment for herself. For six weeks we spent fun times exploring the huge lands of Tsavo and our times together. Graham Bosworth, an influential and important Kenyan native whom I had gotten to know during my work and who had offered me extensive secretarial help at his office, identified Anne as a tennis player. One weekend the All Kenya Tennis Tourney took place at a beautiful estate over looking Nairobi and Anne was invited to play. (I was not). The home had two lovely grass courts where the native white Kenyans and some foreigners were invited to participate. With waiters serving drinks and hors d'oerves, she displayed her talents. It turned out that Graham's wife was a fine player also, so Anne was in her element. But I think Anne did enjoy her stay and I certainly enjoyed her company.

After I had finished my work for the I.E.S.C. , Anne and I ended our tour in Kenya with an escorted tour of the country by Graham Boswell. He was native Kenyan, trusted and supported by Dictator Kenyatta, and an influential man who aided in the transition to native rule from British control. He had offered me his office and secretary to relate back home to Betty Hemmingson (my longtime wonderful secretary) at my office. We became friends and he offered to take us around the country after my duties were ended. We had a great and informative trip with him.

The Broncos were in the Super Bowl, so I decided to drive to Nairobi, get a room on the top floor at the Hilton Hotel so I could get the Armed Forces radio station that was broadcasting the Super Bowl. At my 12th floor perch, my little radio was receiving all the prelims of the game very clearly. Kick off time and I am sitting on the edge of my bed when I lost all reception. I heard nothing thereafter!

The first day I arrive in Nairobi, I took a walk to the park, when I was approached by three young 30 year old men. They said they had escaped Uganda's coop by Idi Amen by jumping out of their windows at college to escape. They were trying to get to Tanzanilla, but were "afraid of the lions." Could they borrow $50.00 so they could ride the train to cross Kenya's border. (It did run). I pondered. It's easy to say no, but if they are in such fearful state, why don't I have the guts to take the risk. I gave them the money after long talks. Quite soon with great thanks they departed. Promptly, a single man approached me and said you have been scammed, but I will recoup you money if you give me ½ what I recoup. I will meet you tomorrow in the Nairobi Hilton lobby. He wanted an advance for his efforts. I declined and said I'd meet him tomorrow. Of course, he never showed. I felt a little stupid when I went home for my first night's dinner in Kenya!

Before coming home, Anne and I flew to Government Lodge down on the Masa Mara game park, a comfortable tent camp right amongst the animals. One morning when I arose about dawn to go out and view animals and Anne stayed in her cot to take a few winks. But before long she was awaken by an elephant's trunk intruding into her quarters. To say the least a quiet panic button went off as she escaped to our bathroom tent. The elephant peacefully departed leaving the tent upright and nothing damaged—-except Anne's confidence. After a while she laughed (quietly) about the whole affair. But the cattle ranching work and our tour with Graham Boswell made the entire trip a great experience! We both loved it.

The only other I.E.S.C. trip I took was to Guadalajara, Mexico. My mission was to set up a feedlot for a "wet back" (now called an "illegal") that had become quite prosperous when he returned to Mexico. Sr. Mendoza was a nice man and I really helped him in what he wanted. I supplied him with detailed written plans and specs of how and what was needed to set up a small feedlot operation on his farm. Betty Hemmingson mailed me blue prints on all the details necessary. He supplied me with an interpreter, so our communication was excellent.

Anne came down for a couple of weeks and we stayed at the Camino Real in Guadalajara which was attractive and comfortable, but very Mexican i. e. after two weeks we both started to feel so squeamish we did not want to eat another Mexican dish.

The Mendoza's took Anne and me one weekend to a neat little city called La Piedad. We had a big beach barbeque where our hosts and some of their friends all feasted on lobster and red snapper cooked over a mesquite grill. The food was great, but what was a surprise was that their idea of a beach picnic was to bring along besides the food a huge supply of hard liquor and beer. The Mendosas do not drink at their home or in town except when they go on a "picnic" and then they really go at it. Anne and I restrained our drinking (in the 103 degree heat) and when we returned to our air-conditioned motel, we said and now we can relax. But alas as soon as we got to our room we got a buzz on the phone "come on down and have a little brandy". We felt as guests we should oblige which we did with considerable reluctance. They were nice people, very hospitable, family loving, and ready for a good time.

So ended my experiences with the I.E.S.C. I resigned shortly after except for interviewing in Denver numerous potential volunteers for another five years. Both those experiences in Kenya and Mexico were very rewarding for me. I worked 6 days a week with all the energy I could muster and hoped that I might have helped improvement of their operations and possibly extend a good feeling by them of the United States

As for the effectiveness of my efforts, I have mixed feelings. In Kenya I think many ideas that I offered were discussed and explained and accepted. The question I have is whether many of them were implemented. It was easy to go back to the old ways and run the ranches inefficiently even though it was not correct. I suspect much returned to the old ways. They built a feedlot, acquired equipment, established accounting, hired personnel and set up a going concern. So that was an exciting experience and hopefully I did help some.

Orphans in Honduras, 2003

My trip and job to Kenya made me realize how lonely it can be when you have no friend or any one to talk to. Much of the time I was by myself and I found I was washing clothes and trying to listen to the radio or read from a vanishing library. I did miss the companionship, but after awhile I adjusted if not particularly happily. I think its amazing how dependent on a association with other people.

I took another trip to Honduras sponsored by St. Phillip's church of Tucson where I was supposed to give advice on the economic relations between an orphanage and a farm that they owned and operated. It was quite apparent that the orphanage was transferring product that the farm was raising at below market value. The result was the farm appeared to be operating at a loss and discussions were being proposed to sell the farm. In fact, if the farm products were priced fairly, the farm would show a favorable economic account. The overall manager, a Vicar from Canada, had no interest in the farm and barely listened to my advice. He was interested in the orphanage and not the total viability of the entire operation. He could easily have shown a total profit with better understanding and better accounting.

37

FAMILY TRIP
TO IRELAND

I had a bright idea. Take the whole Emery-Wilhelm families on a great trip that would bring this rather vast group of relatives (28 in all) together. It would be fun for Doze and me in addition to delighting all the family. Doze and I considered a barge trip in Holland, or a house in the Dordonnes. After some deliberation we chose Ireland because the northwest of that country was sparsely traveled by tourists, was economical compared to Europe, and because Doze and I knew the country, since we had traveled there before and loved it. I started inquiries early and we sealed the plans in late June for our visit in late July of 1997. Everyone was jubilant and enthusiastic about the venture.

I was the main tour leader and guide. The arrangements were not without frustrations to get the trip on the way. We planned to fly by Air Lingus, but because of a National football exhibition game in Dublin, the airline would not confirm our many reservations until two days before departure. Everyone was hanging on their decision. We had no feasible escape plan. All the pleading, prodding, and persistence to the Air Lingus was to no avail until finally we were confirmed. The airline schedule over-flew Shannon, landed in Dublin, and then doubled back to Shannon. That seemed a little strange but I guess the most passengers were mainly headed for Dublin or maybe it had to do with fueling the plane for the return flight to the U. S.

Upon arrival in Shannon we picked up seven rental autos one for each family. We experienced considerable confusion regarding obtaining car insurance, but after registering the cars in our younger member's names, things were straightened out. (How could they have thought I was too old to drive?) My thought was that we all should have independence from the whole group so everyone could do as they wished and would not be herded around in a bus. I had to disregard the accident risk with the confidence that all the auto drivers were excellent and they would avoid the perils of the windy narrow roadways of Ireland. The confidence I had was justified for when we returned in the cars in Dublin ten days later, we had nary a scratch on any of the cars. The independence of each family contributed to the success of the whole trip. John Russell could take off at dawn to do his photography work. Some of us could go to an Irish football game. Others could explore ancient historical monuments or churches. And I could take a car to go fishing.

Our first stop was in Ballyvaughn after a drive north along the cliffs of Mohe. This small town was delightful and the Hylands Hotel just fitted our ticket. It offered us a hearty breakfast before our day's journeys and the pub on the first floor, where many of the locals congregated, gave us the flavor of Ireland, beer drinkers and family groups having wholesome enjoyment. The rooms were comfortable if not fashionable. The town was small so one could stroll on the streets in peace. The various restaurants varied from fish and chips to an elegant restaurant right around the corner.

Before leaving for Ireland I had contacted a certain Christie Browne to conduct an informed tour for the history of the surrounding countryside. With a strong Irish brogue fitted in his knickers, he guided us through the country side enthralling adults and children with his humor and his historical knowledge of the area. He not only gave us a six hour walking tour, but also gave us valuable advice on activities of things to do.

He obtained tickets for a Gallic football game which John Russell, Andy and David Jr. and I thoroughly enjoyed. Since the stadium provided no seats, we spectators watched the match standing on a paved elevated area on the east side of the playing field. We crowded together with boisterous and enthusiastic Irish fans who were vocally totally into the game. Driving to the stadium, we were forced to endure the biggest traffic jam I have ever seen. Every one of the 10,000 fans made their entrance using the one lane road.

After three days at the Hylands Hotel, we loaded up our automobile caravan and headed separately and on different routes north to the Belle Isle Estate near Lisbellaw, Enniskillen, and North Ireland. The estate belonged to an absentee Duke who employed a Charles Plunket ("One T", he emphasized) as his manager. The estate comprised a couple of thousand acres located on a tiny island that provided grazing land for a dairy herd. We were housed in a very large colonial red stone ivy covered baronial mansion that comfortably took care of all of us. The home was surrounded by rolling meadows that supplied their dairy herd with lush green grazing.

Our arrangement for our meals was spectacular. Two attractive British girls cooked the meals. All our children were attracted to these lively Brit girls as they helped them serve food and in the cleanup of the table. I am sure the attractiveness of the girls persuaded our young men to be so willing help. All 28 of us would eat at the same time for both, breakfast and dinner from a thirty foot long dining room table in this great high ceilinged baronial dining hall. Lunch time everyone spirited off with their sandwiches in various directions to explore the enchanting island. We enjoyed lots of laughs and togetherness as we convened for the evening hearty meals. The food was excellent and fun and joy reigned.

We took boat rides with Charles, I went fishing off the end of the Island, many participated in the Yoga classes conducted by Linda Wilhelm, Frisbee games, exploring old churches, trips to a theatrical performance (their dialect made it impossible to understand) just north of Belle Isle and trips to Belfast. After four days we loaded up again and headed for the big city of Dublin.

This move was a change from the quiet environment of Belle Island. The hustle and bustle of the city was a real enjoyment for the teen age group. Some of us preferred the uniqueness of Belle Isle rather than the busy city. After the pastoral life of the island, the big city allowed the youth to show their true independence. They enjoyed roaming in separate groups the streets, eating and drinking in the pubs. I think their bedtime was closer to 3AM than their recent early hours. There was ACTION! We stayed at the Georgian House Hotel on 18 Lower Baggett Street. It was attractive and functional since it was close to the center of Dublin. It gave us all a chance to enjoy Dublin.

Even though most everyone loved their three-day stay in Dublin, I found that after breakfast the group split up with eating at separate locations, venturing about to various interests, and participating in all different hours of day and night. The kids loved their time in Dublin. As a result the "family" split up into various interest groups and the togetherness disappeared. However, the younger probably had had enough of the oldsters, so this was an excellent balance for the trip.

We all returned home with everyone having had a superb time. Years later most have said that that trip was one they would remember as one the great times of their life. I agree with them and that certainly made Doze and me happy.

38

REFLECTIONS

My life of ninety-one years has covered a tumultous period of American history. I have been graced with a loving upbringing by an affluent family that has given me love, support, and comfort. Anne and Jean (Doze) and our children have given me joy in life. My activities have been varied and exciting. My business has been challenging and successful even with some bumps. And I have been granted wonderful good health (and a good head of brown hair). I have always felt that tomorrow will be an even better day. I have been an individual doer rather than a group doer. I have been my own "pilot" rather than associating myself with other commands.

I can't help but having thoughts of the present and the future which briefly are as follows:

HOW DO WE PAY OUR DEBT AND ARRIVE AT BALANCED BUDGET?

I do believe the financial deficits that the United States are becoming dangerously high. (90% of G.T.P). There is no indication the government has the solution to correct the situation. What are the ramifications if this is not rectified? Scary!

HOW DO WE PAY FOR THE GROWING NUMBER OF OLDSTERS?

In 2050, Europe is expected to lose 24% of its prime working–age population and it's 60—and older population is expected to increase by 47%. In the United States because of more immigration, the working-age population will grow by 15% by 2050, but 60 and older population is expected to double by 2050. How do we pay for this burden?

CAN INDIVIDUAL CAPITALISM SURVIVE IN THIS WORLD?

I fear that the economy of the United States is becoming so complicated and large that individual free enterprise is incapable of managing the economy effectively? The federal government is initiating regulations to control such excesses, but will our legislators be able to pass effective measures without destroying the individual initiative that the United States has embraced?

IS OUR CONSTITUTION RESTRICTING GOVERMENTAL PROGRESS?

A large obstacle is the stalemate of our Congress. The influence by lobby groups are so strong that new legislation is stymied by opposing voices. Our legislative procedures are so tedious that nothing is concluded. In China, with a click of the finger, a new program is initiated. In the United States after months nothing but bickering leads to a water downed compromised ineffective bill. The log jam must be broken for government to be effective. Can we make those changes?

WHERE DOES THIS GOVERNMENT CONTROL LEAD US?

It seems that we are slowly developing into a government controlled state. Our Congress is determined to initiate controls to manage the conduct of industry and business. With more government control, will creativity be diminished to the detriment of American progress.

ADJUSTMENT WILL BE SLOW AS WE DRIFT TO THE LEFT

Neither I nor my children should see the adverse effects of the present handling of affaires but I do believe that my grandchildren will see the evolution of the United Sates from being THE power of the world to being a lesser influential member of the world scenery. When the change comes about, it's highly possible that the diminishment of freedom will be accepted without the realization that have lost so much freedom.

AMERICA WILL
OVERCOME ITS PROBLEMS

I recognize that the United States has overcome seemingly impossible obstacles in the past and has always found a favorable solution. The War of Independence, the Civil War, Slavery, the Great Depression, The Missile Crisis, Viet Nam, 1960 Turmoil, World War I II Korea, Viet Nam, Iraq, 9-11, all seemed to be hopeless situations, but the United States has found a way to solve the problems and survived stronger. We wrung our hands and looked at the world with a hopeless future. But we overcame. I think we will rise to the challenge once again.